PRAISE FOR PETER DAVIDSON'S ...

"A first-rate true crime book necessarily requires two elements—a powerful and intriguing story, and a writer who can capture its soul. *Homicide Miami* has both. I highly recommend this story of murder and greed at their worst."

—Vincent Bugliosi, #1 *New York Times* bestselling author of
Helter Skelter and *Divinity of Doubt*

"Torture murder for sex has, unfortunately, become yesterday's news. It is what serial killers are all about. Torture murder for money is rare. This is what gives Peter Davidson's new book its punch. The two main characters in this sordid drama of predatory psychopaths are the embodiment of what we mean by 'evil.' Lugo and especially Dorbal are poster children for the death penalty. But they are as fantastical for stupidity as they are for depravity. First a bungled murder, then a bungled theft and a bungled dismemberment, foiled when a woman's hair jams the killers' electric saw . . . Davidson said his book is not for the squeamish. True. But once you start it you can't put it down."

—Dr. Michael H. Stone, professor of clinical psychiatry,
Columbia College of Physicians and Surgeons,
and host of *Most Evil* on Investigation Discovery

DEATH

BY

CANNIBAL

MINDS WITH AN APPETITE FOR MURDER

PETER DAVIDSON

BERKLEY BOOKS, NEW YORK

THE BERKLEY PUBLISHING GROUP
Published by the Penguin Group
Penguin Group (USA) LLC
375 Hudson Street, New York, New York 10014

USA • Canada • UK • Ireland • Australia • New Zealand • India • South Africa • China

penguin.com

A Penguin Random House Company

DEATH BY CANNIBAL

Berkley trade paperback ISBN: 978-0-425-27686-0

PUBLISHING HISTORY
Berkley mass-market edition / January 2006
Berkley trade paperback edition / February 2015

PRINTED IN THE UNITED STATES OF AMERICA

10   9   8   7   6   5   4   3

Cover design by Rachel Dixon; Thinkstock.
Interior text design by Kelly Lipovich.

To Paul Masters, Carla Lenz, Sandra Lindsay,
Deborah Dudley, Terry Green, Michael Weaver,
Alton "Freddie" Brown, and Zachary Ramsay.

They didn't deserve what fate had in store for them.

CONTENTS

PROLOGUE

Jeffrey Dahmer never sent an e-mail. He never tweeted or shared his plans with anyone via the Internet. Neither did the fictional Hannibal Lecter. And neither did Russian cannibal killer Andrei Chikatilo, who killed fifty-three, mostly schoolgirls and young men, during a twelve-year spree of rape, murder, and cannibalism that lasted from 1978 until his capture in 1990. No one had an inkling, not even his wife. Chikatilo, a schoolteacher, seemed like an average Russian—educated, married with two children, and a lifelong member of the Communist Party.

The five men whose stories are told in the first edition of this book, Albert Fentress, Nathan Bar-Jonah, Gary Heidnik, John Weber, and Marc Sappington, didn't communicate their diabolical plans in chat rooms or anywhere else. What they did was driven by their compulsions and came out of their own twisted minds. But today's cannibal killers have websites to guide and validate them. They can swap recipes and techniques in chat rooms, and they can conspire with other like-minded fiends, which is what federal prosecutors said Gil Valle, a young New York City police officer, did.

"The Internet is like atomic energy—it can blow up the world or light up the world depending on different circumstances," said Fred Berlin, a sexual deviance researcher at Johns Hopkins who works as a forensic analyst for several law enforcement agencies.

Former FBI profiler Mary Ellen O'Toole agrees. "Before the Internet, someone like Dahmer had no way to feed fantasies outside of [his] own imagination. If you are chatting and talking with someone who is on a site like you, and who validates your deviancy, you start to think, maybe I'm not so bad."

Without the Internet, Armin Meinwes would never have met Bernd Juergen Brandes. Armin, a computer technician from Rotenburg in Germany, desperately wanted to eat a human being, while Bernd, an electrical engineer from Berlin, desperately wanted to be eaten. In *Cannibal*, author Lois Jones explores their darkest desires, and she details how and why the two men found each other on the Internet. Both men realized their fantasies in March 2001. That's when Meinwes murdered Brandes. He chopped him into pieces and placed him inside his freezer, next to a pizza. Over the next few weeks, he defrosted and cooked parts of Brandes in olive oil and garlic, eventually consuming forty-four pounds of his flesh. Meinwes told detectives that he dined by candlelight, his dinner table was set with his best silverware and dinnerware, and he drank a fine red wine. Brandes's flesh, he said, tasted like pork.

And without the Internet no one would have heard of Gil Valle, a young New York City policeman dubbed "the Cannibal Cop." His Internet communications led to his undoing when his newlywed wife read about his chats and e-mails on the computer they shared.

Valle never murdered or kidnapped anyone. He never even

attempted an abduction. Nevertheless he was arrested. Lawmen believed they stopped him in the nick of time, while his lawyers claimed he was merely engaged in harmless fantasy. His story made headlines around the world, and has been added to this book—*Death by Cannibal: Criminals with an Appetite for Murder*—because he clearly had an appetite for murder. He was charged with conspiracy to kidnap and accessing a restricted law enforcement database to gather information about potential targets.

In *Cannibal Killers: The History of Impossible Murders*, author Moira Martingale wrote, "Cannibalism runs like a blood-red thread through the tapestry of mankind's history." If she is correct, then I fear we are in for more Dahmers and Chikatilos, thanks to the Internet. And thanks to a popular song by rapper Kesha, a singer songwriter who has sold more than thirty-five million recordings worldwide.

In a song titled "Cannibal," she sings these disturbing lyrics:

I eat boys up, breakfast and lunch
Then when I'm thirsty, I drink their blood
Carnivore, animal, I am a Cannibal

In the first edition of this book, I recalled attending a conference in Sarasota, Florida, at which the renowned true-crime writer Ann Rule talked about working at a crisis hotline in Seattle, manning the phones in the wee hours of the morning to counsel men and women in distress. She wasn't alone in the office. A handsome young man was with her, offering her comforting words and suggestions to ease the despair of callers, too. They became friends.

When their shift ended at 5 a.m., the young man, concerned about Ann's safety, would walk her to her car and wait until she drove away. When Ann revealed his name, everyone gasped: it was serial killer Ted Bundy and the experience led her to write *The Stranger Beside Me*.

Bundy was not a cannibal killer. The point is there are strangers beside each and every one of us. No one suspected Jeffrey Dahmer, Andrei Chikatilo, or Armin Meinwes until it was too late. And no suspected Gil Valle, whose arrest, indictment, and trial for bizarre and sordid fantasies indicate that we may be in a *Minority Report* world where authorities can arrest anyone for their thoughts.

1

GILBERTO VALLE III
The Cannibal Cop

Killer cops. Shakedown cops. Robber cops. Dope-dealer cops. Even "Mafia cops."* New Yorkers are no strangers to crime fighters gone bad. But nothing could have prepared them for yet another stain on the NYPD badge—the trial of a veteran policeman whose fetishes seemed darker and more bizarre than even the twisted sexual cravings of the infamous Marquis de Sade.

New York City
February 25, 2013
DAY ONE

---

* In 2009, former NYPD detectives Louis Eppolito and Steven Caracappa were convicted of using their badges to assist in eight mob-ordered executions and passing along confidential information to Lucchese crime family mobsters. Their mob pals paid "the Mafia Cops" four thousand dollars a month from 1986 to 1990.

What turns Gil Valle on is the idea of a woman oiled, bound, laid out on a platter with an apple in her mouth.

Defense Attorney Julia Gatto

The Thurgood Marshall United States Courthouse at Foley Square is a veritable fortress of law and justice. The courthouse, named for a former justice of the U.S. Supreme Court, with its ten Corinthian columns and one-hundred-foot wide portico, creates the unmistakable impression that matters of the utmost importance are decided within its gray granite walls.

And they are.

Since the building opened in 1936, justice has been meted out to notorious gangsters, drug kingpins, stock-market fraudsters, and spies.

Julius and Ethel Rosenberg were tried there in 1951, amid a national and international media frenzy. Convicted and sentenced to death for passing atomic secrets to Soviet agents, the Rosenbergs were executed in 1953.

In 1985, three simultaneous mob trials involving forty-three notorious gangsters drew extensive media attention. There was "the Pizza Connection Trial": twenty-one of twenty-two defendants were convicted of conspiracy to smuggle heroin into the United States . . . And "the Gambino Trial": ten defendants including Gambino godfather Paul Castellano faced charges of operating a stolen-car ring and conspiracy to commit murder. Six were convicted of smuggling stolen cars from Brooklyn to Kuwait, two were convicted of conspiracy to murder. Jurors were unable to reach a verdict for two others . . . And "the Colombo Trial": crime boss Carmine Persico Jr. and ten other defendants were tried on racketeering charges. Nine were convicted.

One year later, "the Mafia Commission Trial" saw eight mob bosses and underbosses convicted on racketeering charges.

Journalists from near and far packed the neoclassical courthouse when Martha Stewart stood trial for insider trading in January 2004. When, after a six-week jury trial, the good living guru was convicted of obstruction of justice and lying to investigators, reporters returned in droves to report on her sentence—five months in a federal lockup followed by two years' probation.

In 2005, the trial of rapper Lil' Kim—real name Kimberly Jones—triggered a media frenzy, too. Jurors convicted the diminutive hip-hop diva of lying to a federal grand jury to protect friends who had been involved in a blazing gun battle outside a New York City radio station. A federal judge sent her to jail, too. Although the Grammy winner was sentenced to a year and a day, her incarceration ended in eight months.

As in those trials, reporters, photographers, and sketch artists were out in full force, along with curious citizens and legal professionals who braved the winter cold for opening day of the "the Cannibal Cop Trial," the *United States v. Gilberto Valle III.*

Valle, a veteran New York City policeman, stood accused of conspiracy to kidnap. It had all the earmarks of a precedent-setting landmark case. No one was kidnapped, and the defendant never attempted to abduct anyone, which prompted legal scholars and pundits to speculate that Valle was on trial for his dark thoughts.

It also promised to be the most grotesque trial ever to take place in a Manhattan courtroom. The testimony would be emotional and dramatic, the exhibits gruesome and macabre. The trial was set to get underway inside Courtroom 110 with United States district court Judge Paul Gardephe presiding. There are a hundred and fifty spectator seats in the courtroom, and each one was occupied when Judge Gardephe bounded onto the bench at 12:50 p.m. He directed court officers to escort the jury of six men, six women, and two alternates to the jury box. Following opening statements from federal prosecutor Randall Jackson and defense attorney Julia Gatto, Assistant U.S. Attorney Hadassa Waxman called the government's star witness to the witness stand.

"I was going to be tied up by my feet and my throat slit, and they were going to have fun watching the blood rush from my body," a tearful Kathleen Mangan-Valle told the packed Manhattan courtroom.

The twenty-seven-year-old mother and schoolteacher had recently returned to New York from Nevada to testify against her estranged husband Gilberto (Gil) Valle III, the young police officer the media dubbed "the Cannibal Cop." The six-year veteran of the NYPD was on trial for conspiracy to kidnap women, his wife among them, so they could be raped, killed, cooked, and eaten.

It is a long-held principle of American common law that spouses cannot be compelled to testify against each other. It's called the marital privilege, and it meant that Kathleen could choose to testify against her husband. The government could not compel her to take the witness stand, nor could the defense prevent her from testifying. The choice was hers alone.

But her testimony would be limited to what she saw and what she did. That's because defendant Gil Valle had privileges, too. Kathleen could not testify about any conversations, text messages, letters, chats, or e-mails she received from or sent to her husband. Prosecutors were limited, too, barred from introducing anything the young couple wrote or said to each other. Unless the evidence was introduced by the defense, the jury would never hear about the extensive e-mails they exchanged prior to Gil Valle's arrest. In them Kathleen expressed her feelings of betrayal and implored her husband to reveal the extent of his Internet activities. Nor would jurors hear about his regret and sorrow over what he had done and how it had impacted her.

To the lawmen who investigated Gil Valle and the attorneys assigned to prosecute him, the baby-faced cop was a Hannibal Lecter wannabe, a depraved, flesh-hungry predator armed with a gun, carrying handcuffs, and wearing the badge of authority—his NYPD shield. He was, they decided, about to become a serial cannibal killer.

A federal grand jury charged Valle with two criminal counts: Count One, conspiracy to kidnap, and Count Two, accessing a restricted law enforcement database. His victims would not be randomly snatched off the street. Instead, Valle's alleged targets were, like his wife, women personally known to him. And they were remarkably similar—young, petite, and athletic with long hair.

To convict, prosecutors would have to persuade the jury that Valle and at least one other person agreed to kidnap at least one of the women, that he knowingly and willingly joined with them in the conspiracy, and that at least one of the conspirators committed an overt act in furtherance of the diabolical plot. A guilty verdict could send the twenty-eight-year-old NYPD veteran to prison for life. The second charge, illegally accessing federal and state law enforcement databases, could send him away for five years.

In their opening statements federal prosecutor Randall Jackson and defense attorney Julia Gatto laid out their views of the gruesome case.

Jackson, a Harvard Law School graduate and the son of a cop, promised jurors that the government would present evidence and testimony to prove that Gil Valle was on the verge of carrying out a "heinous plot to kidnap, rape, murder and cannibalize a number of very real women in order to satisfy a deeply held desire to cannibalize human flesh."

They would hear, the prosecutor said, that the veteran cop "chose to desecrate the trust that his community placed in him." And they would learn that Valle repeatedly searched the Internet for information about the tools he would need to carry out his diabolical plans: the best rope to bind someone with, a formula for homemade chloroform, a recipe for cooking human flesh, and more.

They would also learn about the grotesque websites Valle visited, his extensive collection of ghastly autopsy photos, his cache of computer files on dozens of women, his surveillance of his alleged targets, and his research of kidnapping cases.

"Make no mistake," prosecutor Jackson told the jury. "Gilberto Valle was very serious about these plans."

Julia Gatto went next. Not surprisingly the veteran defense attorney offered a different point of view.

The government's case is "pure fiction," she said, arguing passionately, as she had during months of pretrial wrangling, that Gil Valle never conspired with anyone to kidnap anybody. There is no evidence, not even an allegation, that he had ever acted on his fantasies by kidnapping anyone. It was all "role play," just a game, a fantasy, like a horror movie or a novel by Stephen King. Gil Valle, she said, did nothing more than engage in dark fantasies on fetish websites.

Her client's sexual fantasies are deviant and sadistic, the defense lawyer conceded. And she admitted that the young cop is aroused by "unusual things." She even revealed "his dirty little secret"—he is turned on "by the idea of a woman oiled, bound, laid out on a platter with an apple in her mouth, about to be cooked," which explains why he "foolishly" engaged in online chats about "suffocating women, cooking and eating them."

The charges against Valle, Julia Gatto declared, are an overreach by prudish lawmen who just don't get S&M. They're prosecuting Valle for his thoughts, she said. The online chats were horrific but they were nothing more than "preposterous, infantile chatter" fueled by a sexual fetish that never posed a threat to anyone. Valle, she said, never revealed his alleged targets' last names, never attempted to kidnap anyone, never threatened to kidnap anyone, and never gathered any equipment to kidnap anyone. No one was raped, murdered, or eaten.

And Gatto, who studied law at Georgetown University before going joining Federal Defenders of New York, a nonprofit public defender organization that represents federal defendants who cannot afford to hire a private attorney, framed the case in constitutional terms. "This is a really, really important case," she told the jurors. "You are not coming in here every day doing the hard work just for Gil Valle. You are really doing it for all of us. It is cases like this that [test] bedrock principles—the freedom to think, freedom to say, the freedom to write even the darkest thoughts from our human imagination."

When Gatto finished, Judge Paul Gardephe directed prosecutors to call their first witness.

"The government calls Kathleen Mangan-Valle," Hadassa Waxman announced.

The packed courtroom went silent as Kathleen cautiously made her way to the witness stand. She passed a scowling Elizabeth Valle, her mother-in-law, who looked on from the second row of the spectator's section. And she passed the defense table, where her husband of less than one year sat with Gatto and co-counsels Robert Baum and Edward Zas.

Five months had passed since the estranged couple last laid eyes on each other. They had not had any contact or communication since Valle's arrest. And this morning they avoided eye contact as Kathleen made her way to the front of the courtroom, raised her right hand, and swore to tell the truth.

For two grueling, tear-filled hours, the young mother, in a pink top, her face framed by her long dark hair, testified about how she discovered her husband's bizarre secrets—the shocking websites he'd spent hours looking at and the grotesque plans he had for her and other women.

It all came to light one afternoon the previous September, when Kathleen opened the Macintosh laptop the couple shared. She read dozens of her husband's twisted online chats with a cohort who called himself meatmarketman. Her husband, calling himself girlmeathunter, planned "to stuff me into a suitcase," she said. He would hog-tie her, then slit her throat, and "watch the blood pour out of me for fun." And if she cried or begged for her life, "Don't listen to her. Don't show her mercy," meatmarketman advised. Her husband's cold-blooded reply shocked her: "Gil just said, 'It's OK. We'll gag her,'" she recalled before bursting into tears.

There was more.

Gil, she said, wrote that a college friend "was going to be burned alive." He also discussed "devising an apparatus so the girls could be on the spit for thirty-minute shifts and be taken down so they would live longer." Another woman, Kathleen said, "would be roasted alive." They would suffer "for his enjoyment, and he wanted to make it last as long as possible."

In yet another shocking online chat Valle discussed raping two women "in front of each other to heighten their fear." He also talked about kidnapping a young teacher, a former colleague of Kathleen's. He planned "to get her in her apartment and put her in a suitcase and wheel her out and deliver her for rape and murder." Kathleen recalled cleaning out a closet in their apartment. She told jurors she threw out a very large suitcase that she found inside. It sparked an angry outburst from her husband. Kathleen did not think anything of it at the time—until she read her husband's chilling chats with meatmarketman.

During her two hours on the witness stand, Kathleen was repeatedly overcome by emotion, and Judge Gardephe declared several brief recesses to allow her time to regain her composure.

Valle, in a dark suit and tie, his hair closely cropped, sobbed, too. He frequently dabbed his eyes. He did not look at his wife, preferring instead to listen to her testimony with his head down and his face buried in his hands. He became distraught when a photo of him in his police uniform appeared on courtroom video monitors. In the photo, a beaming Valle carried their baby daughter, Josephine, in his arms. The adorable tot wore a pink bunny outfit. "It's before church, before a Holy Name Society* breakfast," Kathleen explained as she and her estranged husband both broke into sobs.

The NYPD cop appeared to be a proud dad, but his wife of less than one year told a different story.

They met in the fall of 2009, through OKCupid.com, a dating website. In his online profile Valle listed food as among the things

---

* The Holy Name Society is an organization of Catholic NYPD officers.

he could never do without, with "Italian, Mexican, Chinese, Japanese" as his favorites. He indicated, however, that he was willing to try other cuisines: "I'll eat anything and am not picky at all."

He also described himself as a "very calm individual" with "an endless supply of hilarious short stories from work that can't be made up." And he revealed his favorite book—*Green Eggs and Ham*, a children's story by Dr. Seuss, the moral of which is you have to try something to know if you will like it.

Kathleen was smitten. "He opened doors and pulled out chairs," she said. They lived together in a tiny apartment on East Eighty-eighth Street. When Kathleen became pregnant they moved to a two-bedroom apartment in Forest Hills, where they set up housekeeping along with Dudley, an English bulldog, in a six-story apartment building not far from where the NYPD officer grew up.

Valle, Kathleen said, seemed indifferent to her pregnancy. When she had doctor's appointments, he'd complain. And when she went into labor, she remembered, he made her wait for him to take a shower before driving her to the hospital. Valle was reluctant to tie the knot, but he eventually relented and agreed to do the right thing. They married on June 19, 2012, in a Catholic church, ten months after the birth of their daughter, Josephine.

Kathleen hoped that her husband would become more attentive after she gave birth, but she was disappointed. He showed no interest in sex with her after the delivery. Instead he became even less affectionate and more distant.

Attempts at intimacy were futile because her husband "couldn't finish," she said tearfully. He also started spending an inordinate amount of time online, sometimes staying awake into the wee hours of the morning.

In June, shortly after the wedding, she opened the Mac laptop they shared. Gil was still logged in. She saw an icon for a website called darkfetishnet. "It was porn, and it was disturbing," Kathleen said. "I know S&M is popular, with *Fifty Shades of Grey*, but this seemed different. The girl on the front page was dead." Kathleen confronted her husband about his extreme sexual fantasies. That's when "things got bad," she said.

She took up jogging "because I thought it would help if I was thinner or prettier." Her husband, she said, encouraged her to run at night. She became suspicious when he "seemed very interested in my route," asking if the streets she jogged on were dark or well lit and if there many people around. Kathleen suspected that her husband might be sexting or exchanging instant messages with a real-life lover. To find out she installed spyware on the laptop they shared. What she discovered on September 10, 2012, was worse than anything she had imagined.

"A lot of websites that I'd never seen before, and pictures of feet that weren't attached to bodies, and pictures of me. I'd never seen anything like this," she said through tears.

"On one of the websites there was a woman on the front page. She was dangling. She was naked with blood all over her."

Kathleen also came across a trove of violent and hateful chats, and detailed plans to commit atrocities against women including herself and two others she knew: a college friend of Gil's whom she met in July, and a former colleague of hers, a schoolteacher she had not seen in more than a year. She also viewed individual electronic files that her husband had created on dozens of other women, many of whom were listed by their first and last names with at least one photo of each as well as their height, weight, and other distinguishing characteristics like their bra cup sizes.

Horrified and fearing that the man she married, the father of her infant daughter, was a madman, Kathleen fled the apartment with Josephine, the Mac laptop, and little else. She spent the night across the street, at a neighbor's apartment. The next day mother and daughter boarded a flight to Reno, Kathleen's hometown, where they found a safe haven with her parents.

A few days later she looked at the computer again, and then she called the FBI.

Calling itself "the Biggest Little City in the World," Reno is four hundred and fifty miles northwest of Las Vegas. Because the city sits more than four thousand feet above sea level on the leeward side of the Sierra Nevada Mountains, winter snowfalls are light, and unlike the less-elevated Las Vegas, summer highs rarely hit a hundred degrees.

The city of two hundred and thirty thousand is the seat of Washoe County. Reno began in the mid-1800s as a jumping-off point for pioneers who planned to make their way through the mountains to Central and Northern California. By the 1930s it had become famous as the divorce capital of America. Unlike anywhere else in the United States at the time, Reno divorces were quick and simple. Socialites, celebrities, and average men and women flocked there for what became known as the "Reno cure" for an unhappy marriage.

But Kathleen did not file for divorce. Instead, after a few days with her family, she took the Mac laptop to the FBI's field office on Sandhill Road. She told agents there what she'd found on it, and that she feared that her police-officer husband planned to kidnap, kill, torture, and cannibalize women.

After viewing some of the chats and images, the agents copied the computer's hard drive. Kathleen signed a detailed statement.

She gave the lawmen keys to the Forest Hills apartment and consent to copy the contents of an older HP laptop she'd left there. The Reno agents sent everything to the bureau's New York office, where the case was assigned to Squad C-19, the Reactive Violent Crimes Squad, which investigates armed bank robberies, bank burglaries, armored-car robberies, kidnappings, murder for hire, cyber threats, extortion, and crimes on the high seas. It wouldn't be long before lawmen would uncover what prosecutor Randall Jackson called the "heinous plot to kidnap, rape, murder and cannibalize a number of very real women."

On September 20, agents and computer technicians began sifting through the contents of the copied hard drive. They obtained a warrant and entered the Valles' Forest Hills apartment while he was at work. They copied the other laptop's hard drive and brought it back to their Manhattan office at 26 Federal Plaza. Using a forensic computer analysis program, FBI computer technicians were able to restore deleted files and track online searches. What they found confirmed Kathleen's worst fears:

- Thousands of visits to fetish websites featuring kidnapping and death.

- Dozens of file folders, each containing photographs of women complete with their names and other personal information.

- Numerous grisly still images and videos including a clip of a stark-naked woman chained hand and foot, crying out as flames burned her crotch.

- Alarming Google searches: "how to tie someone up," "how to kidnap a girl," "how to abduct a girl," "how to knock someone unconscious," and more.

- Online conversations and e-mails in which the NYPD cop seemed to be plotting with like-minded fiends to kidnap, kill, and cannibalize women.

FBI agents discovered that the NYPD cop had been communicating extensively with three like-minded individuals via the Internet. They connected on darkfetishnet.com, where Gil Valle stated in his profile, "I like to press the envelope, but no matter what I say, it is all fantasy."

With each one he discussed the logistics of carrying out kidnappings and ways to torture and commit murder. He also described specific women who apparently were in his crosshairs.

Investigators learned their identities: Valle's former college classmates Kimberly Sauer, a radio-station executive, and Andria Noble, an Ohio prosecutor; Alisa Friscia, a special-education teacher at the Manhattan elementary school where Kathleen once worked; and Kristen Ponticelli, an eighteen-year-old high school student from Queens.

They also identified another likely target: Maureen Hartigan, a young woman who had rebuffed Valle's romantic overtures years before. Although she had never been specifically mentioned in any of his online conversations, investigators theorized that Valle would target her, too, in order to get even with her for spurning him years before.

Convinced that a dreadful crime was imminent, and that the young NYPD cop was its mastermind, agents interviewed and warned the women as well as others whose names were found on the computers. And they brought the case to federal prosecutors in Manhattan.

FBI special agent Anthony Foto, the case agent, signed off on a criminal complaint charging Valle with conspiracy to "kidnap, kill, cook and eat body parts of women." The complaint alleged that the conspiracy began in January 2012. Valle was also charged with illegally accessing the National Crime Center Information database to locate potential victims.

To establish probable cause to arrest the NYPD cop, the criminal complaint cited excerpts from electronic communications between Valle and a suspected co-conspirator—CC-1—in which they targeted a woman identified as Victim-1:

July 9, 2012

CC-1: *How big is your oven?*

VALLE: *Big enough to fit one of these girls if I folded their legs . . . The abduction will have to be flawless . . . I know all of them . . . [Victim-1], I can just show up at her home unannounced, it will not alert her, and I can knock her out, wait until dark and kidnap her right out of her home.*

CC-1: *You really would be better to grab a stranger. The first thing the police force will do is check out a friend.*

VALLE: *Her family is out of state.*

CC-1: *I have anesthetic gasses.*

VALLE: *I can make chloroform here.*

CC-1: *It's really hard to dislocate a jaw. Also, how would we put her over the fire, spitting kills the girl. Have to put her into a kind of cage. What is your favorite cut of meat?*

VALLE: *I was thinking of tying her body onto some kind of apparatus . . . cook her over low heat, keep her alive as long as possible.*

VALLE: *I love that she is asleep right now not having the slightest clue of what we have planned. Her days are numbered. I'm glad you're on board. She does look tasty doesn't she?*

CC-1: *You do know if we don't waste any of her there is nearly 75 lbs of food there.*

In another online chat excerpted in the criminal complaint, this time with a different co-conspirator (CC-2), Valle and his cohort discussed a price to kidnap and deliver a woman (Victim-2):

February 28, 2012

CC-2: *And also, about the price . . . would you do a payment plan or full up front?*

VALLE: *Full payment at delivery. Just so that you know, she may be knocked out when I get her to you. I don't know how long the solvent I am using will last but I have to knock her out to get her out of her apartment safely.*

CC-2: *I definitely want her and how much again?*

VALLE: *$5,000 and she's all yours.*

CC-2: *Could we do 4?*

VALLE: *I am putting my neck on the line here. If something goes wrong somehow, I am in deep s—. $5,000 and you need to make sure that she is not found. She will definitely make the news . . . It is going to be hard to restrain myself when I knock her out but I am aspiring to be a professional kidnapper and that's business. But I will really get off on knocking her out, tying up her hands and bare feet and gagging her. Then she will be stuffed into a large piece of luggage and wheeled out to my van.*

CC-2: *Just make sure she doesn't die before I get her.*

VALLE: *No need to worry. She will be alive. It's a short drive to you. I think I would rather not get involved in the rape.*

*You paid for her. She is all yours and I don't want to be
tempted the next time I abduct a girl.*

CC-2: *I understand. Also is there anything I can trade you
that might knock down the price a bit?*

VALLE: *No nothing at all. Like I said this is very risky and
will ruin my life if I am caught. I really need the money
and I can't take under $5,000.*

Also detailed in the criminal complaint:

March 1, 2012

*A cellular phone assigned [to] a telephone number belonging
to GILBERTO VALLE, the defendant, made and/or received
cellular communications [while he was] on the block in Manhattan on which Victim-2's apartment building is located.*

May 31, 2012

*GILBERTO VALLE, the defendant, accessed the National
Crime Information Center (NCIC) and obtained information
about a woman whose name matched the name of one of the
individual files created by VALLE ("Victim-3"), and stored
on the Computer. VALLE did not have authorization to perform that search or to access any information about Victim-3.*

The complaint stated that lawmen had recovered reams of
e-mails and chats in which Valle conspired with another individual
to kidnap, cook, and eat a woman. They also found a sinister
"operation plan," apparently authored by Valle, entitled "Abducting and Cooking [Victim-1]: a Blueprint."

On October 24, 2012, FBI agents arrested Valle. Knowing that he was armed and concerned that he would resist, the lawmen lured him into the hallway outside his apartment by buzzing him on the building's intercom. They told him his car, which had been parked on the street, had been damaged. When Valley stepped into the hallway unarmed, FBI special agent Anthony Foto was waiting. With him were NYPD Internal Affairs detectives who took custody of Valle's firearm, NYPD shield, and police ID.

The next day, just six weeks after Kathleen fled to Reno, United States attorney for the Southern District of New York Preet Bharara made a stunning announcement: Gilberto Valle III, a veteran New York City police officer, had been arrested on federal charges of conspiracy to kidnap and illegally accessing the federal National Crime Information Center (NCIC) database.

Valle's "alleged plans to kidnap women so they could be raped, tortured, killed, cooked, and cannibalized shock the conscience," the U.S. attorney declared, adding, "This case is all the more disturbing when you consider Valle's position as a New York City police officer and his sworn duty to serve and protect."

The case would be prosecuted by the U.S. attorney's Violent Crimes Unit with veteran prosecutor Hadassa Waxman as lead prosecutor.

"Our investigation is ongoing," Bharara said, signaling there would be more arrests.

At Valle's arraignment later that day, Waxman insisted that a kidnap attempt was imminent.

"If he was not arrested, he would have carried out this plan," the auburn-haired assistant U.S. attorney declared, adding that the NYPD cop, now shackled and wearing a brown jailhouse jumpsuit, spied on some of the women he targeted while in his police uniform and on duty.

Federal magistrate judge Henry Pittman ordered Valle held without bail pending trial. The jurist described the allegations as "very, very serious, unspeakable conduct." He remanded the young cop to the federal lockup in Manhattan, the Metropolitan Correctional Center (MCC), where he was placed in isolation for his own protection.

The jaw-dropping charges set off a media feeding frenzy. Story-hungry reporters fanned out across the city to dig up whatever they could about the sordid case. They searched for the identities of the alleged victims and the suspected co-conspirators. And they wanted to know more about Gil Valle.

They learned that he'd grown up in Forest Hills, in a middle-class family. He never got into fights or trouble, never gave his parents, Gilberto and Elizabeth, any problems. After graduating from Archbishop Molloy High School in 2001, he enrolled at the University of Maryland, where he majored in psychology and criminal justice. He graduated in 2005. He joined the NYPD the following year.

Reporters scoured the Forest Hills neighborhood where Gil and Kathleen lived, and they besieged the Twenty-sixth Precinct in West Harlem, where the now-suspended Valle worked. The cops there were mostly tight-lipped, but the few who did speak said they did not believe the charges. Valle was generally low-key. He partnered with a sergeant, driving the marked cruiser they shared to crime scenes and assisting with supervisory activities. There was nothing about him that indicated a penchant for violence. He did his job protecting and serving the public without fanfare, machismo, or bravado. That he was secretly planning to serve women on a platter seemed inconceivable to his fellow officers.

To his neighbors in Forest Hills, Valle was a pleasant young man with a pretty wife, an adorable baby, and a well-trained dog. No one had ever considered him dangerous, at least not until now.

Several neighborhood women admitted they were frightened—"freaked out," one neighbor said. They wondered if they had been main dishes on Valle's depraved menu, and if they were small enough to fit into his oven. Another neighbor thought that Valle might have eaten his dog—he didn't—explaining that the canine had not been seen in a while.

Reporters also reached out to Gil Valle's teachers, friends, and former classmates.

His fellow students from Archbishop Molloy High School remembered him as a bright and friendly student who starred at third base for the coed Catholic school's baseball team. Classmates at the University of Maryland in College Park recalled that he wore a New York Yankees baseball cap around campus and seemed like a typical New Yorker, brash and sometimes angry. One college classmate, a woman, told a reporter that his arrest did not come as a complete surprise. "I can't say I'm shocked," she said, explaining she recalled hearing Valle making misogynistic jokes.

Reporters checked the young cop's Facebook page. He'd posted nothing about his schemes to kidnap, cook, and eat women. Instead, he ranted about the court system and dissed New York City. "Fifteen years until I can move the hell out of this rotten scumbag-filled city," he wrote.

Referring to an ex-convict charged with killing a Nassau County cop eight years after gunning down a citizen, Valle wrote: "Four and a half years for attempted murder, then released and kills a police officer. This state's court system is an absolute joke. Absolutely outraged."

Referring to another officer shot in the line of duty, he wrote, "Thug who shot a Queens cop last night was only locked up for numerous armed robberies and attempted murder. Thank you very much liberal court system for letting this guy out."

The Cannibal Cop case went viral. News of the allegedly flesh-hungry NYPD cop made headlines around the world. But on the day the sensational story broke, it did not make the front pages of New York's tabloids.

Those banner headlines went to an even more horrific New York story—the heartbreaking murders of three-year-old Leo and six-year-old Lulu Krim, the son and daughter of Marina and Kevin Krim, a CNBC executive. They were found by their mother in the bathtub of the family's West Seventy-fifth Street apartment, dead from stab wounds. Police charged their fifty-year-old nanny with the killings. The nanny would plead not guilty. As of this writing, she is awaiting trial.

Despite relegating the Cannibal Cop case to inside pages, the tabloids covered the story with relish. The headlines and lead paragraphs from the New York *Daily News*:

COOK 'EM, DANNO*

COP BUSTED IN PLOT TO KILL & EAT 100 WOMEN

TALKED ON INTERNET OF SLOW-ROASTING "TASTY" VICTIMS

A city cop with a taste for human flesh was charged Thursday with plotting to kidnap, torture, "slow cook" and eat women he tracked down through law enforcement databases.

---

* From the long-running CBS-TV show *Hawaii Five-O*, a police drama in which many episodes would end with Lieutenant Steve McGarrett (Jack Lord) instructing his subordinate, Danny Williams (James Macarthur), to "Book 'em, Danno," usually for murder.

Accused cannibal cop Gilberto Valle, 28, was living a double life—a married dad and civil servant who moonlighted as a secret psycho straight out of a James Patterson crime thriller, federal authorities revealed.

HUNT CANNIBAL COP'S SICK PALS

A full-court press is on for two co-conspirators who exchanged instant messages with alleged cannibal cop Gilberto Valle about kidnapping and slow-cooking women.

And from the *New York Post*:

NYPD STEW AS CANNIBAL COP PLOTS TO COOK AND EAT WOMEN:

He wanted to protect and serve women—on a dinner plate!
A newlywed NYPD cop was accused yesterday of moonlighting as an aspiring cannibal—plotting to "kidnap, rape, torture, cook and cannibalize" up to 100 women in a twisted plot discovered by his wife.

NYPD COP IN PLOT TO COOK, EAT WOMEN

Newlywed NYPD Officer Gilberto Valle III, here on his wedding day, conspired to cook and cannibalize women, and even haggled over price, the feds said yesterday.

COP CHICKS' FREAKASSEE SPOOKED BY "CANNIBAL"

They're the ladies who might have been his lunch. "Freaked-out" female acquaintances of would-be cannibal cop Gilberto "Gil"

*Valle yesterday wondered whether they were on his alleged list
of 100 ladies to kidnap, rape, torture, cook—and eat.*

Within days, however, the gruesome Cannibal Cop case and
the heartbreaking Krim murders disappeared from the headlines,
washed away by a more compelling story. It would dominate the
news for weeks to come, driving news of the impending presiden-
tial election to the inside pages, too.

On the morning of October 22, 2012, two days before FBI agents
arrested Gil Valle, Tropical Storm Eighteen was born in the western
Caribbean near Jamaica. Six hours later it was upgraded to Tropical Storm Sandy. The next day, Valle's last as a free man, the fast-
moving storm became a Category-1 hurricane.

On October 24, Valle appeared in a federal courtroom in
shackles to hear the charges against him. Meanwhile, Sandy, now
a Category 3, was hammering eastern Cuba. It moved through
the Bahamas the next day, weakened a bit, then turned north-
northeast. On 8 P.M. on October 29, under a full moon and during high tide, Sandy, now dubbed Superstorm Sandy, made
landfall on the Jersey Shore near Atlantic City. The result was a
record-setting fourteen-foot storm surge that battered New Jersey
and New York through three cycles of high and low tides.

Sandy became the second-costliest hurricane in American history, its damage surpassed only by Hurricane Katrina. Fifteen
million people in the Northeast lost power. Lower Manhattan
was flooded and most of the area was without power. The New
York Stock Exchange suspended operations and city schools
remained closed until November 5.

More than one hundred houses burned to the ground in the Breezy Point section of Valle's home borough of Queens, a neighborhood bordered by Jamaica Bay and the Atlantic Ocean. Flooding and high winds in the nearby neighborhoods of Belle Harbor and Neponsit destroyed homes and took lives. More than thirty thousand New Yorkers were left homeless. Forty-five died, including a resident of the Coney Island section of Brooklyn who was swept away by the Atlantic Ocean as he headed to a hardware store.

Valle and the other prisoners in the MCC were locked down for an entire week. The facility lost power, water, and heat. Toilets didn't flush. TVs and radios didn't work. Prisoners panicked. Cut off from the world beyond their cells, they screamed, banged on cell doors, and threw things.

The Cannibal Cop case was all but forgotten until November 8, when Valle and his attorney, Julia Gatto, appeared in federal court before federal district court judge Lewis A. Kaplan to ask for bail. Also in court that day were Assistant U.S. Attorney Hadassa Waxman and Michelle Mechanic, a lawyer representing Alisa Friscia, the woman identified in the criminal complaint as Victim-2.

Valle, prosecutors claimed, would have earned five thousand dollars to kidnap and deliver Friscia to his co-conspirator, a New Jersey man known as CC-2. Her lawyer was in court to object to bail. Her client, she said, had been living in fear since she learned about the alleged kidnap plot from the FBI.

"She's terrified for her life and safety if he should be released," the attorney told the judge. "She's not sleeping. She's frightened and has confined herself to her home with her mother."

Judge Lewis reserved decision until the next day when he ruled in favor of Magistrate Pittman's denial of bail. Valle would remain locked up.

A federal grand jury indicted the NYPD officer in November on two counts. Count One, conspiracy to kidnap, and Count Two, illegally accessing a restricted federal database. Valle was back in court the following Monday, this time before Judge Gardephe, the jurist who would preside over his trial.

Appointed in 2008 by President George W. Bush, Judge Gardephe brought an eclectic legal résumé to the bench. It included a ten-year stint as a prosecutor with the U.S. Attorney's Office in New York City, as well as extensive private-practice experience in criminal defense, civil litigation, and corporate law.

With his attorney beside him, Valle pled not guilty, and with Thanksgiving just three days away, Gatto made yet another passionate bid for bail.

"You have a tough road [sic] to hoe," the fifty-five-year-old jurist told the defense attorney, referring to her two previous unsuccessful attempts to spring Valle from the federal lockup.

"Pretrial services now recommends release as long as appropriate conditions are set," the defense attorney told the judge. She had a plan: Valle would be released to his mother's home. He'd wear a GPS ankle monitor. Besides, Gatto said, a psychiatrist who examined Valle is convinced that he is not a danger.

Arguing against bail, Hadassa Waxman revealed that an FBI expert had also reviewed the case and had reached a different conclusion. That expert, she said, warned that Valle would pursue his plans if released. To bolster her argument against bail, Waxman read aloud an excerpt from a February Internet chat during which Valle discussed his plans for Thanksgiving with a co-conspirator known as Moody Blues.*

"I'm planning on getting some girl meat," Valle said.

"Really? Tell me more," Moody Blues responded.

"It's this November, for Thanksgiving. It's a long way off, but I'm getting the plan in motion now. She's not a volunteer. She has to be abducted. I know where she lives. I will grab her from her house."

The harrowing chats were only "sick, twisted sexual fantasies," an exasperated Gatto declared in rebuttal. "All over the Web it says no matter how real this sounds, this is all fantasy." Despite everything Valle had discussed on the Internet, "there's nothing the government can point to outside the computer."

But Judge Gardephe was not about to issue a Get Out of Jail card. The NYPD cop would remain in custody, confined to a cell twenty-three hours a day in the facility's Special Housing Unit. "There has been nothing rational about this case," the jurist explained. "It is depraved, bizarre, aberrational and, as of now, entirely unexplained, particularly for someone who is a law-enforcement officer."

But Julia Gatto did not take no for an answer. She appealed to a higher authority, the United States Second Circuit Court of Appeals in Manhattan. A three-judge panel quickly rejected that bid for bail, too.

Meanwhile, with the city and the region cleaning up the debris left by Superstorm Sandy, the media spotlight once again fell on the Cannibal Cop case. And no one outside the courtroom

---

* Called CC-1 in the criminal complaint, also known online as "meatmarketman" and "Chris Collins."

was more passionate in defense of the NYPD officer than his mother.

Elizabeth Valle joyfully announced the impending birth of Gil and Kathleen's baby on her Facebook page: "I'M GOING TO BE A GRANDMA IN OCT!!!!! MY LIFE IS COMPLETE. THANK YOU GOD."

That was in April 2011. Kathleen gave birth at the end of September. Elizabeth had another announcement a year and a half later, only this time she did not post it on Facebook.

"He hasn't eaten a human being!" she declared. Enraged at her son's portrayal by prosecutors and the media, she lashed out. She wanted everyone to know that her son is not a cannibal.

"Look it up in the dictionary, the true meaning of cannibal is that he ate human meat [but] he hasn't eaten a human being," the angry mother told a reporter for the New York *Daily News*.

"This horrible story comes out and then the media runs with it," she said. "The whole world thinks my son eats people!"

She pointed out that the charges against her son had yet to be proven, and she called his online writings nothing more than "Internet chatter." She complained that she had not been able to talk to him since his arrest.

She also spoke about her son's gentler side, how he cared for and loved his infant daughter and his dog, Dudley. And she recalled that before her son's arrest she'd offer to watch the canine so he could look after baby Josephine. "He'd say 'Ma, he's still sleeping, I don't want to wake him up.' Does that sound like a freaking person who would harm anybody? He wouldn't even wake up the dog!"

The young cop's mother wasn't the only one rallying to the

young lawman's side. Park Dietz, one of the country's leading forensic psychiatrists, a recognized expert on sadism and paraphilia—a condition that causes some men to become sexually aroused from violent fantasies—would weigh in, too.

Dietz had examined, studied, and testified as an expert witness—mostly for the prosecution—in some of the most sexually sadistic criminal trials in recent American history, among them cannibal killer and necrophiliac Jeffrey Dahmer and sexual serial killers Arthur Shawcross, Joel Rifkin, and Charles Ng. Going face-to-face with them, he probed the darkest corners of their twisted minds and sick souls.

Other high-profile criminal cases in which he testified include the trials of Unabomber Theodore Kaczynski, Washington, D.C., area snipers John Allen Muhammad and John Lee Malvo, and John Hinckley, who attempted to assassinate President Reagan in 1981.

Dr. Dietz helped develop the protocols regarding sexual sadism for the American Psychiatric Association's *Diagnostic and Statistical Manual of Mental Disorders* (DSM), which provides standard classification of mental disorders according to symptoms. And he is the author of dozens of books and articles on sexual sadism, sexual bondage, pornography, criminality, and paraphilia.

Brought into the case by the defense, the psychiatrist spent eighteen hours over three days interviewing Gil Valle. He administered the Personality Assessment Inventory, a diagnostic tool. He reviewed documents related to the case: Valle's Internet conversations and writings, the sexually explicit images the FBI recovered from his computer, and FBI reports of interviews with Valle and the women he had allegedly targeted. Dietz also interviewed the accused cop's parents, Elizabeth and Gilberto (Bill) Jr., and his brother, Daniel.

Dr. Dietz had access to Valle's NYPD file, which included the results of the Minnesota Multiphasic Personality Inventory, a test meant to detect psychopathology. The test, which the NYPD uses to weed out undesirable recruits, showed no clinical psychopathology, Dietz said.

He found no indication that Valle "ever suffered from a psychotic or other mental illness." He pronounced the NYPD cop "free from psychopathy, antisocial personality, or any other personality disorder associated with violence."

In his written report to the court, Dietz noted that "Mr. Valle has been sexually stimulated by images and thoughts of other men abducting and binding females since he was a teenager, without ever attempting to abduct or bind a female in any manner whatsoever."

During their sessions, Valle told the psychiatrist that he experienced erotic arousal in early adolescence by imagining naked women. He became aware that bondage aroused him sexually while viewing a scene in *The Mask*, the 1994 movie starring Jim Carrey and Cameron Diaz in which the character played by Diaz was tied to a tree and terrorized by the film's villain. He discovered Internet pornography while in high school, and he became particularly interested in bondage websites as a college student. He was too ashamed to reveal his fetish to anyone or to ask anyone to participate in it with him.

It was in college, too, that Valle discovered pornographic DVDs. They belonged to one of his roommates. This discovery led him to other fetish websites, including Muki's Kitchen, a BDSM* website that displayed naked women in poses that

---

* The acronym for bondage, domination, sadism, and masochism, or bondage, sadism, master, and slave.

indicated they were about to be cooked and eaten, and dark-fetishnet.com.

The explicit photos excited him and inspired him to contribute a series of pornographic short stories to one website. Positive feedback from readers prompted him to continue writing. As a result of these writings, Valle connected to others with similar interests with whom he communicated through e-mails and chats.

According to Dr. Dietz, just as there are men who are "aroused by images of women wearing underwear or stockings or pantyhose or tight jeans or heels," others "are particularly aroused by images of women wearing latex or leather or gas masks or gags." No one knows why. "It's just a matter of chance that determines what images become particularly arousing to an individual."

BDSM is widespread, Dietz wrote, "so high in every study that the inference that millions of American males experience sexual arousal from thoughts, images, and stories of violence against women is inescapable," but "the overwhelming majority of men with these kinds of recurring, sexually sadistic thoughts never act on their fantasies in a criminal manner."

They cope, the doctor said, "in non-criminal and non-violent ways, as did Mr. Valle," by suppressing their thoughts, by masturbating, or by using their imaginations "while engaging in conventional sexual behavior with their partners."

Or they find partners who will participate with them in "mutually acceptable sexual activities," which Valle said he was too ashamed to do.

They also, like Gil Valle, visit "chat rooms where they can share their fantasies with others." Or "they may amass collections of pornography that address their fetish."

Valle revealed that while his earliest sexual fantasies concerned celebrities and an attractive teacher, thoughts of these women were eventually replaced by thoughts of women he met in school or in daily life. According to Dr. Dietz, there is nothing unusual about that:

> *Normal men incorporate images of women they've noticed into their erotic fantasies during sex, masturbation, and passing thoughts, and they freely mix, match, and embellish body parts, clothing, poses, actions, personalities, and anything else they please, turning these bits and pieces of real women into imaginings of lustful bisexuals, nymphomaniacs, and freely accessible sex goddesses in any way they please, whenever they please.*
>
> *It's no different for the millions of men who prefer their fantasy women bound, enslaved or tortured . . . only for them the woman's imagined submission, resistance, distress, struggle, suffering, protest, crying, pain, screaming, fear and terror take the place of what for more conventional men is the woman's imagined lustfulness, willing access, and ecstatic pleasure.*

More indicative that Valle's e-mails and chats were fantasy were "the absence of any follow up or complaint when plans went unfulfilled or conversations were interrupted; the absence of any of the gear or facilities needed to carry out such a plan, and the absence of any meeting or identification of his collaborators."

Moreover, Dietz declared, there was "no evidence that Mr. Valle assembled a kidnap or rape kit, accessed a suitable vehicle, or accessed an isolated or soundproof location panel truck or a secured soundproof location, committed or even contemplated an attempted abduction, and no evidence that Mr. Valle ever committed any abortive attempts to commit an abduction, rape, torture, or homicide."

In his professional opinion, Gil Valle's Internet communications were "fully consistent with non-criminal activities designed to stimulate and entertain himself, his readers, and his collaborators with erotic fantasies, pornography, erotic stories, and erotic role play."

In other words they were, as defense attorney Julia Gatto had claimed, nothing more than fantasy. Even though they were sordid and gruesome, Dietz opined that nothing he found suggested that the NYPD cop's "erotic conversations could be reasonably construed as conspiratorial plans."

To keep the jury from considering a contrary diagnosis from a prosecution expert, Valle's defense team decided not to call Dr. Dietz to testify. But jurors would hear from the women the NYPD cop allegedly targeted, and from the lawmen who investigated him.

DAY TWO

*I'll be eying her from head to toe and licking my
lips, longing for the day I cram a chloroform-soaked
rag in her face.*

Gilberto Valle III

The second day of the Cannibal Cop trial began at 9:35 a.m. After some legal skirmishing between prosecutors and defense lawyers, Judge Gardephe had the jurors brought into the courtroom. They would hear testimony from three women allegedly targeted by Valle. As soon as the jurors were seated, Randall Jackson called the first witness.

Kimberly Sauer, the woman identified as Victim-1 in the criminal complaint, made her way through the crowded courtroom.

She had been friends with Valle since 2002. They met while students at the University of Maryland. They were never a couple, she said, but they traveled in the same social circle and lived in the same dorm. They remained in touch after graduating, "mostly via some text messages over the years."

JACKSON: How often in a typical year do you think you communicated with Mr. Valle?

SAUER: Via text message maybe ten or fifteen times in a year.

JACKSON: What was the general nature of those text messages?

SAUER: Mostly just, Hey, how is work? He would send a picture of the baby. Once he had had his baby, I would say, How adorable.

Gil Valle had been a police officer for more than five years when, on January 18, 2012, he sent her a text message, asking if she would like a PBA card.*

"I have me some extra cards," he wrote. "They can be handy if you get pulled over. Want me to send you one?"

"Sure," she replied.

"Text me your address, I will mail it tomorrow," he promised.

Two days later he sent another text message, asking her not to tell anyone about the card. "Just keep it hush-hush because I can't give one to everyone," he said. "No guarantees but very likely a free pass for a minor traffic violation." It seemed a reasonable request at the time, so Sauer thought nothing of it.

And she thought nothing of it when her college pal announced

---

* Patrolman's Benevolent Association of the City of New York, the organization representing rank-and-file members of the New York City Police Department.

he would be traveling to Maryland in July. He inquired if they could meet. They had not seen each other since 2005, and Valle wanted to introduce her to Kathleen and baby Josephine.

They arranged to meet for brunch on Sunday, July 21, the day after Gil, Kathleen, and baby Josephine attended a barbecue with two other friends from the University of Maryland. While in Maryland, Valle sent Sauer a message: "We drove by your pink building today." She did not think anything of that at the time either, but it set off alarm bells for lawmen when they learned that he was referring to the building in which Sauer worked. Valle had never visited her there, she said, nor had she ever sent him photos of the building.

They met for brunch at Café Deluxe in Gaithersburg, a Washington suburb. "It was fun," Sauer said. They cooed over the baby, talked about their lives, and gossiped about college classmates. Sauer revealed she did not live alone, telling the Valles that she shared her residence with two roommates.

The first hint that something was amiss came one month later, in an early-morning message via Facebook from a frightened and frazzled Kathleen after she discovered her husband's depraved plans.

It was so bizarre Sauer feared Kathleen's Facebook account had been hacked. Sauer took a screen shot of the message, which talked about killing and selling her and others into slavery. She sent it to Gil to warn him.

JACKSON: Why did you think it had been hacked?

SAUER: Because the content was so crazy.

JACKSON: What did you say to Mr. Valle after you sent him the screen shot?

SAUER: I relayed the content of the message.

JACKSON: In essence, what were you communicating to Mr.
   Valle? What were you asking him?
SAUER: If his wife's Facebook account was hacked, and I
   made a joke about the content of the message, and I said
   "or is this true, ha, ha."
JACKSON: What was the joke that you made?
SAUER: I said are you trying to sell me into white slavery.
JACKSON: What did Mr. Valle respond?
SAUER: He said, "Not that I am aware of."
JACKSON: During that conversation, at any point did he
   explain to you anything that he was doing that gave you
   an explanation for what had happened?
SAUER: No.
JACKSON: Did he tell you anything about any online fantasy
   role play or anything that he was doing?
SAUER: No.

Sauer remained in the dark about her college friend's twisted appetites until the FBI contacted her. That Gil Valle thought of her as someone who was "going to be delicious," whose head he would use "as a centerpiece, frozen with her final expression of fear," which is what he told Moody Blues during an online chat, sent her reeling.

It was all a ruse, investigators concluded. The PBA card, which Valle mailed to her in January, was nothing more than a ploy to learn where she lived. And the trip to Maryland for brunch with her—Gil Valle really had another kind of meal in mind.

Sauer, investigators feared, was in grave danger. Her college pal, someone she considered "a nice guy," was on the verge of carrying out his sordid plan for her. They arrived at their conclusion based on what they found on Valle's computers:

- A computer file titled *Kimberly Sauer*. Inside were a number of photographs of her, and two images of a woman roasting on a spit.

- On July 9, 2012, Moody Blues told Valle that he'd previously kidnapped and cannibalized two individuals. Moody Blues explained that he "tended to work alone" because he had not found anyone who was serious and willing to assist him. During that same conversation, Moody Blues sent Valle photos of individuals he claimed he had cannibalized. He asked Valle if he was shocked. Valle responded, "Not really. You seem legit."

- While discussing plans to kidnap Sauer, Valle sent Moody Blues a link to a video of Sauer on vacation with her family. Valle commented that Sauer "will be a terrific victim." Moody Blues replied, "I would love to have her arm on a barbecue." Said Valle, "She is going to be delicious."

- Moody Blues asked Valle, "You WILL go through with this? I've been let down before. That's why I work alone." Valle answered, "Yes." Later he declared, "Kidnapping her and getting away with it is an absolute truth."

- On July 10, Valle authored a two-page plan of action, "Abducting and Cooking Kimberly: A Blueprint." It contained an itemized list of "materials needed"—a car, chloroform, rope, duct tape, plastic bags, cheap sneakers, and a tarp. Valle e-mailed the "blueprint" to Moody Blues. He wrote, "I'll be eying her from head to toe and licking my lips, longing for the day I cram a chloroform-soaked rag in her face."

That same night Valle conducted Internet research—preparation, investigators believed, for kidnapping Sauer:

- 4:27 A.M. "how to kidnap someone."

- 4:30 A.M. "how to abduct a girl."

- 4:38 A.M. "how to chloroform a girl."

- 4:39 A.M. "can you use chloroform to have sex with your girlfriend."

- 4:40 A.M. "how to chloroform a girl."

- 4:52 A.M. "kidnapped girl."

- Valle set Sauer's kidnap date. He told Moody Blues, "I'll go to her place on September 2, kidnap her from there and we'll get her cooking Monday afternoon."

- On July 17, Valle told Moody Blues that he planned to meet Kimberly Sauer on Sunday, July 21. Moody Blues asked Valle if he had found a recipe for chloroform. Valle sent him a link to a recipe for the anesthetic.

- "I think Kim is a great choice," Moody Blues opined. "Keep the others as spares and let's see how Sunday goes. If you decide against it after Sunday, then we can look at one of the others or at a stranger if you'd then prefer. Maybe a Mall Rat."

- "Be aware you will be a possible suspect when she goes missing. Get your alibi in early," Moody Blues advised, adding that he'd been "giving thought to your ideas about cooking her alive. You need to understand your motivation for torturing the girl. Also I'm interested why you want her to realize in such a way what is going to happen to her." Valle replied, "I just enjoy the thought of making her suffer, that's all."

- On July 22, the day after brunch with Kimberly Sauer, Valle sent Moody Blues a chilling message: "She looked absolutely mouthwatering. I could hardly contain myself."

Under cross-examination, Gatto established that Sauer had never known Valle to be anything but nonviolent.

GATTO: In the ten years that you have known him, whether in college or after, was he ever physically abusive to you?
SAUER: No.
GATTO: He never hurt you, correct?
SAUER: No.
GATTO: He was never aggressive to you?
SAUER: No.
GATTO: Did you see him being abusive to any other woman in the last 10 years?
SAUER: No.
GATTO: Did you hear him make any serious threats against any women in the last 10 years?
SAUER: No.
GATTO: Before hearing the allegations that are at issue here, would you describe him—you would describe him as a nonviolent person, is that fair to say?
SAUER: Yes.

Gatto's cross-examination ended when she asked if anything unusual occurred during the brunch. She expected a definitive no. Instead, Sauer said Valle wanted to make plans to see her in November.

The jury heard from Andria Noble, another petite University of Maryland classmate. She was shocked when an FBI agent told her the NYPD cop had offered her to Moody Blues, telling him, "She is the girl I would most want to eat." "She is number one by far." "The second I met her I knew I had to have her." "If Andria lived near me she'd be gone now." And, "going to law school saved her life."

The agent also informed her that Valle e-mailed images of her and details about her—her occupation, location, ethnicity, height, weight, and other identifying details—to Moody Blues. Testifying for the prosecution, Noble confirmed that the details identified her.

Under cross-examination, the twenty-seven-year-old married prosecutor's testimony was similar to Kimberly Sauer's—she had never known her classmate to be violent; had never seen him abuse or threaten anyone; and had never had any inkling of his sadistic fantasies.

She recalled visiting Valle in New York not long after they graduated. Prior to her visit, she made Valle promise she would have her own bedroom during the visit. He kept his promise, Noble recalled. "I made sure he knew it was just strictly as friends."

The jury also heard from Maureen Hartigan, a friend of Valle's from Archbishop Molloy High School. While Valle had never specifically mentioned her in any of the chats or e-mails, NYPD records showed that he sought information about her through the NCIC database. He also created a computer file with her name on it and photos of her inside. Lawmen concluded that Gil Valle considered her a potential target. He had a score to settle with her, they theorized, because more than ten years before, while they were both still in high school, she rebuffed his romantic advances.

During questioning, Hartigan told the jury that she and Valle had been "fairly good friends" in high school. They shared an interest in sports—she played on the women's basketball and soccer teams while Valle played on the men's baseball team, and they frequently attended sporting events together.

They had remained in contact through the years via text messages and Facebook, exchanging birthday wishes and other details about their lives. Valle boasted about his daughter and revealed that he was hoping for a promotion to sergeant. He suggested that he and Kathleen and the baby visit her at her new apartment.

"Did you ever date?" Randall Jackson wanted to know.

"No," she answered.

"Ms Hartigan, at any point in high school did you perceive that Mr. Valle wanted to date you?"

Before she could respond, Julia Gatto jumped up. "Objection!" she shouted.

Judge Gardephe ordered the lawyers to a sidebar, where the defense attorney, her voice in a near whisper so jurors could not hear, explained that she objected to the form of the question and to the relevance of Hartigan's state of mind when she and Gil Valle were in high school. What's more, she argued, there were no online chats with any of the alleged co-conspirators in which Hartigan was specifically named or described.

But "there are multiple indicators that she is one of the people that he is obsessed with and a target for the conspiracy," Jackson said. Then he told the judge what the FBI found on one of the computers Gil Valle used:

- A file with Hartigan's name on it with photographic images of her that had been copied and pasted from her Facebook account.

- Inside the Hartigan file, a cartoon of a woman inside a boiling pot. Hartigan's face had been superimposed over the original face.

- A computer folder that held files the NYPD cop created for Sauer, Noble, and one other woman he had targeted as well as a file for Hartigan.

Jackson also told the judge that NYPD records would show that Valle had used the NCIC database to gather information about Hartigan.

Deeming Maureen Hartigan a "potential victim," and Valle's database search a "preparatory step towards possibly kidnapping her," Judge Gardephe overruled Gatto's objection. The sidebar over, the prosecutor repeated the question that prompted the defense attorney's objection.

JACKSON: Ms. Hartigan, at any point in high school did you perceive that Mr. Valle wanted to date you?
HARTIGAN: Yes.
JACKSON: Why do you say that?
HARTIGAN: Because he had indicated that he was interested in me in that way.
JACKSON: What was your response to him?
HARTIGAN: That I just wanted to be friends.

She also testified that in June 2012, as she prepared to move to a new residence, Valle sent her text messages inquiring about her new address. Like Kimberly Sauer, Hartigan thought nothing of it at the time, until agents from the FBI paid her a visit. And until contacted by the FBI, she thought there was nothing unusual about a message she received from Gil Valle suggesting that they meet at her workplace, even though they had not seen each other in several years.

She recalled that they met for about ten minutes at the end of her workday. Valle, she recalled, was in uniform when he drove up in a marked NYPD police car, and he was not alone. Another cop sat in the front passenger seat.

Before ending his direct examination of Hartigan, Jackson brought his line of questioning back to Gil Valle's dark thoughts.

JACKSON: At any point did you indicate to Mr. Valle that you consented to be the focus of any discussion or characterization involving sexual violence or any other kind of violence?

HARTIGAN: No.

During cross-examination, Julia Gatto again turned attention to her client's gentle nature.

GATTO: You have known Gil for how many years, Ms. Hartigan?

HARTIGAN: Since high school, which I started in 2000.

GATTO: So about thirteen, twelve-and-a-half years, correct?

HARTIGAN: Yes.

GATTO: In those twelve-and-a-half years has he ever been physically abusive to you?

HARTIGAN: No.

GATTO: He has never hit you?

HARTIGAN: No.

GATTO: He has never been aggressive to you?

HARTIGAN: No.

GATTO: He has never hurt you?

HARTIGAN: No.

GATTO: In those twelve-and-a-half years have you ever seen him be physically abusive to any other women?

HARTIGAN: No.

On redirect, prosecutor Randall Jackson elicited testimony to remind jurors that there was another side to Gil Valle, a side that Hartigan knew nothing about until the FBI contacted her.

JACKSON: At the time that you were receiving those messages, did you have any access to Mr. Valle's e-mails or computer?

HARTIGAN: Did I have access? No.

JACKSON: Did you know anything about what Mr. Valle was communicating with other people?

HARTIGAN: I had no clue, no.

JACKSON: Did you have any knowledge of any documents that Mr. Valle had created that involved you?

HARTIGAN: No.

Following the lunch recess, Jackson called eighteen-year-old Kristen Ponticelli, who, like Maureen Hartigan, was a star athlete at Archbishop Molloy High School. Valle became fixated on her during visits to his alma mater to watch her team, the women's varsity softball team, play.

"She is the most desirable piece of meat I ever met," he told Moody Blues. Valle mentioned that she played softball, adding that he was "trying to figure out a way to keep her unconscious the whole day." Moody Blues advised him to "knock her out with a baseball bat."

Ponticelli would be on the witness stand less than ten minutes during which she would answer eighteen questions posed to her by the prosecutor and two from defense attorney Gatto.

Pretty and petite with long dark hair, the teen testified in a trembling voice about her stint on the Archbishop Molloy High School women's softball team. Jackson asked Ponticelli about her relationship with the NYPD cop.

According to Ponticelli, however, they had never met.

JACKSON: Do you know a man named Gilberto Valle?
PONTICELLI: I do now.
JACKSON: Have you ever met him before?
PONTICELLI: No.
JACKSON: Do you ever actually remember meeting him before?
PONTICELLI: No.
JACKSON: Have you ever had any conversations with Mr. Valle?
PONTICELLI: No.
JACKSON: Have you ever told Mr. Valle that you consented to be a part of any plans or conversations he was making?
PONTICELLI: No.
JACKSON: No further questions.

Julia Gatto had two seemingly innocuous questions for the nervous teen: "Did you have a Facebook account?" and "Did you have Facebook friends who were from Archbishop Molloy?"

After replying yes to both, Ponticelli was excused and left the courtroom visibly relieved that her ordeal was over.

Alisa Friscia was scheduled to testify next, but prosecutors called FBI special agent Corey Walsh to the stand. A former army captain who served as a combat platoon leader in Iraq, Walsh had been a member of the FBI team that sifted through the copied computer hard drives used by Valle—the Macintosh laptop Kathleen Mangan-Valle brought to the bureau's Reno office and the HP laptop lawmen copied in his Forest Hills apartment. He would be on the witness stand for a grueling day and a half, answering questions first from prosecutor Hadassa Waxman, then from defense attorney Robert Baum.

The Macintosh laptop, Walsh said, contained two user profiles, one for Gil Valle and the other for his wife. Under the Gil Valle profile were eighty-nine file folders that contained the first and last names of eighty-nine women.

Responding to a question from prosecutor Hadassa Waxman, Walsh explained, "There were screen shots taken using a spyware program that Ms. Mangan installed on the computer. Those images were of chats between an individual known as mhal52@yahoo.com [Gil Valle] and various other individuals where they discussed kidnapping, raping, killing, torturing women . . . There were approximately two dozen."

Walsh said he separated the chats into two piles—fantasy and real.

"Why did you make that separation?" Waxman asked.

"In the ones that I believed were fantasy, the individuals said they were fantasy. In the ones that I thought were real, the two people were sharing details of real women—names, what appeared to be photographs of the women, and they also said that they were for real."

The fantasy communications were dark and violent, the lawman said, but they contained explicit assurances they were make-believe, which was not the case with the online conversations Walsh deemed to be for real. Those chats were between Gil Valle and Michael Van Hise, Valle and Moody Blues (screen names meatmarketman and Christopher Collins), and Valle and Ali Khan (screen name Alisherkhan79).

Walsh read reams of chats and Internet messages to and from Valle and his alleged co-conspirators. Some were recovered from the computers Valle used, while others were recovered from Internet service providers like AOL and Yahoo. As he read aloud from transcripts, jurors followed along on a large video monitor. Valle appeared dazed when the transcripts first appeared on the screens.

The lawman read a chat dated January 27, 2012:

Mike Van Hise to mhal52: "What's up? So are you interested in trading if I can get a girl for you?" Officer Valle responds, "Honestly I am more in it for the cash. I have a few women who I plan on grabbing for myself." Mike Van Hise responds, "Okay. So I have two questions. One is: Do you do payments. And two, do you have pics of the ones we're talking about that are cheaper?" Officer Valle responds, "Cash only upon delivery and, yes, these are Alisa and she is 28."

Hadassa Waxman interrupted him. "During the investigation did you come across an individual named Alisa?"

"Yes, ma'am," Walsh replied. "Alisa Friscia. She is the one they are talking about in these e-mails."

Walsh continued:

Mike Van Hise responds, "I still like Alisa." Officer Valle responds, "Then it sounds like Alisa is doomed." Officer Valle responds, "Very, very nice. She is a sweet girl. Not sure how soon before she would submit. I will abduct her out right of her apartment, stuff her in a large piece of luggage, have

*her tied up her hands and feet and off we go. Do you want
her clothed and what she is wearing or stripped naked?" Mike
Van Hise responds, "Whatever is better for you. When we
get her, we'll meet somewhere so we can rape her together
before I leave with her." Officer Valle responds, "Excellent.
I will leave her on. I will give you the pleasure of unwrapping
the gift." Mike Van Hise responds, "Sounds great to me.
Also, do you want to hang her with me just for laughs before
we leave?" Officer Valle responds, "It is up to you. She is all
yours. I really don't mind if she experiences pain and suffering. I will sleep like a baby."*

In an online communication on February 28, Valle offered
Van Hise what he thought would be an appetizing alternative:

*If you are interested, I know a few girls who are cops. A
couple of them I sent you. How about a cop instead? Mike
Van Hise says no, I want a reg girl.*

"What do you understand 'reg' to mean?" Waxman asked.
"Regular, not a cop," Walsh told the prosecutor.
He continued reading:

*Valle responds, "The second girl at the top, Evelyn, is 33 years
old." Mike Van Hise says, "Damn. I will just stay with Alisa
then." Officer Valle responds, "Okay. She is Cuban anyways.
She would suit your needs just fine." Mike Van Hise says,
"Can you send me more pics of her please?" Mike Van Hise
sends another e-mail. "That is the teacher, right?" Valle
responds, "Yes. Fifth grade teacher, single, 28 years old."
Mike Van Hise, "Good. I have a lot of uses and fun with her."*

Officer Valle responds, "That is the most recent picture of her taken this past Friday."

Mike Van Hise responds, "I definitely want her and how much again? I am sorry to ask, but I don't remember." Officer Valle responds, "five thousand dollars she is all yours." Mike Van Hise says, "Could we do four?" Officer Valle responds, "I am putting my neck on the line here. If something goes wrong somehow, I am in deep shit. Five thousand. You need to make sure that she is not bound. She will definitely make the news." Mike Van Hise responds, "No problem. She is never leaving the house." Also, "okay, up the price can we go on a payment plan or full up front?"

Officer Valle responds, "Full payment due at delivery just so you know she may be knocked out when I get her to you. I don't know how long the solvent will last, but I have to knock her out to get her out of the apartment safely." Officer Valle, "Would there be anything that you want me to grab out of her apartment, souvenirs?" Mike Van Hise, "No. Just her and maybe a sexy spare outfit and pajamas for her."

Mhal52 says, "Sounds easy enough. Other than putting her in a hog tie and getting here, she won't be touched. She will be nice and fresh." Mike Van Hise responds, "Great. I love it. Can you have her tied barefoot? I don't want her kicking me when I untie her at home."

Valle responds, "Still with me there?" Mike Van Hise responds, "Yes, sir. Why what's up? Did you get my 'barefoot' message?"

Valle responds, "Yeah. Did you get my reply?" Mike Van Hise responds, "No." Valle, "Oh, okay. No wonder. I had said the plan was to definitely remove her shoes for the reason you cited. When in her apartment, I doubt she will be wear-

ing shoes, but barefooted is for sure. Do you have any other questions about her?"

Mike Van Hise asks, "Yes, do you know anything about her sexually?" Officer Valle responds, "Actually she had a boyfriend as recently as around eight months ago and I heard from a friend when talking about her say that it's been a while since she's gotten laid and it is frustrating her. She is straight for sure. No lesbian tendencies."

Mike Van Hise responds, "Awesome. Even better, which means she will be tight and also even if she had les tendencies, she won't be leaving the house anyways. Also, do you want to know what I am going to do with her if the cops get close or she gets too much to handle?" Officer Valle responds, "Yeah. Fill me in a bit on her . . . I think she will be tough to break. She is kind of feisty. No nonsense." Mike Van Hise responds, "That is fine. I can beat her and break her in more ways than one. Also, her ordeal is after she fills her purpose and the cops get close, she will be raped until she passes out from suffocation, tied up, [driven] to somewhere secluded, raped again, she passes out again by strangling and when she comes to hung and raped up the ass while hanging before being buried while I take pics or tape it."

Officer Valle responds, "That is fucking great. Whenever you come here to meet me, it will be absolutely amazing to watch her come out of her school, follow her without her knowing all the while we both know that her days of freedom are limited. I think you'll be happy with what you see. Pictures don't do her justice."

Mike Van Hise responds, "I like that and believe. I will be so fucking happy I will probably fuck her right then and then once we get her in my car." Officer Valle responds, "It is going to be so hard to restrain myself when I knock her out, but I am inspiring [sic] to be a professional kidnapper and that is business. I will really get off on knocking her out, tying up her hands and bare feet and gagging her. Then she will be stuffed into a large piece of luggage and wheeled out to my van." Mike Van Hise responds, "Make sure she doesn't die before I get her." Officer Valle responds, "no need to worry. She will be alive. It is a short drive to you. I think I would rather not get involved in the rape. You paid for her. She is all yours."

Mike Van Hise, "Talk later this week." Officer Valle, "Okay. Just a point of reference, a good custom made half hour video on a fetish site could go for around $1200 to $1500. With Alisa you are getting your own, very own, living breathing girl who is a real victim and not acting. You get to do whatever you want to her and get her terrified reactions in real-time. You even get to kill her. $5,000 I think is very fair."

Next, Walsh read aloud chats between Valle and Moody Blues. They were transmitted, the lawman said, via Yahoo Messenger:

Officer Valle, "So you want a petite victim, yes?" Meatmarketman, "Well petite isn't so important, just meaty, not fatty. LOL." Officer Valle, "That is victim number three, Kathleen." Meatmarketman, "Very nice. That is more like it. How old and what does she do?" Officer Valle, "Kathleen 26 and she's a teacher. But she is also a mother. So I don't know if that will affect things." Meatmarketman, "how old is the kid and what sex?" Officer Valle, "Infant, girl. Kimberly will be easy to get. She is a little more petite."

Meatmarketman, "The one I have got up now is Kimberly, red polka dot top, tell me about her. Why is she so easy to take?" Officer Valle, "Kimberly is 27, single very very sweet. I can also send you my Thanksgiving victim. Maybe you can make it here and help me out with her. Since you have experience and it would be free. I definitely need an assistant." Meatmarketman, "Tell me about her. I live in England but easy to get to the Big Apple. [I'll] teach you a proper way to prepare a girl . . . So tell me about her. Also, is Kathleen married?" Officer Valle, "Yes, Kathleen is married as is Andria, which is why they will be tougher to get. Kimberly is by far the easiest."

Meatmarketman, "How would you like to prepare one of them. BTW, is Andria Italian?" Officer Valle, "No. She is Portuguese. Andria is also a prosecutor, though." Meatmarketman, "Can anyone prosecute from inside an oven? No one." Officer Valle, "They will be looking for her right away. The abduction will have to be flawless." Meatmarketman, "So she isn't really that easy. Do you know her?" Officer Valle, "Yes. I know all of them. Kimberly I can show up at her home unannounced. It will not alert her, knock her out and kidnap her right out of her home."

Meatmarketman: "Have you considered eating her alive? I think of it as eating her to death. Then you try to sweet tender living Kimberly and she gets to really suffer." Officer Valle: "I am pretty set on having her cooked alive, not into raw meat." Meatmarketman: "You need to find out the dimensions of your oven. I'm still not sure she will fit even as small as she is." Officer Valle: "Well, then may maybe we'll tie her to the rotisserie and cook her outside." Meatmarketman: "You need to be very secluded." Officer Valle:

"I am, believe me. I have a place up in the mountains. No one around for three-quarters of a mile."

Next, Walsh read transcripts of chats between Valle and Ali Khan, who claimed he was a butcher living in India. Lawmen, however, traced his IP address to a location in Pakistan.

Ali Khan also claimed that he was experienced in kidnapping and committing violent acts against women. He was yearning to do it again, and he wanted to work with Valle. He even offered to guide the young cop through the process and teach him how not to get caught.

And he sent Valle a gruesome video of a goat being slaughtered, commenting that "the most easier thing in life is slaughtering. When I killed my first goat, my workers said it's easy . . . So it was. But the most important thing, 'never get caught.'"

The depraved butcher complained to Valle about being unable to find a suitable victim, and that as a result he was going "crazy."

"I'm trying to pick out a girl who I can send over," Valle told the butcher. In the course of their discussions, they decided on a victim—Kathleen Mangan, Valle's future bride. He then described her—age twenty-five, height five feet seven and weight one hundred forty pounds. The description matched Kathleen.

The butcher responded, "If you bring her here, I promise I will make a good meal for you," but "how can you send her to me if she will know what I will do with her?"

"I can talk my girlfriend into going to India for a trip and then we will meet up," Valle said.

When Ali Khan promised to "kill her" as humanely as possible, Valle said, "It's alright, you don't have to worry about humane."

"Will you participate in the slaughtering process with me?" Ali Khan wanted to know.

"Absolutely," Valle wrote back. "I have longed to butcher and cook female meat."

The two also shared twisted plans to torture and debase Kathleen by tying "her down spread eagle" and taking turns raping her.

"It would humiliate her. Do you have something to keep her mouth open?" Ali Khan asked.

"Hell yes," Valle replied. "She is a sweet girl. I like her a lot. But I will move on."

During a subsequent chat, Ali Khan accused Valle of not really being serious about slaughtering women. "You are wasting time, buddy, I am for real not fantasy," he said.

Valle explained that he was "just afraid of getting caught . . . if I were guaranteed to get away with it, I would do it."

Later in the same conversation, Ali Khan asked Valle, "Are you really, really into it. Are you ready to slaughter one?"

"Yes," the young cop replied.

Ali Khan then asked, "Are you sure?"

The answer, "Definitely."

Later on, Valle told Ali Khan he had another woman in mind: Archbishop Molloy High School senior Kristen Ponticelli. He said he wanted to tie her "to a metal frame and slowly roast her alive until she dies,"

"Are you sure?" Ali Khan asked.

"Definitely," Valle replied.

Valle and Ali Khan also chatted about Andria Noble. "For eight years I've thought about cooking her," he wrote.

As with Van Hise and Moody Blues, and based on their online communications, investigators concluded that Valle and the depraved butcher were plotting to kidnap one of the women and subject her to several kinds of violence, including rape, torture, and murder.

After a day and a half of reading the twisted chats and e-mail transcripts, the rookie agent was about to face off against a tough-as-nails cross-examiner, veteran public defender Robert Baum.

DAY THREE

I predict Valle will soon be free.
                New York Post columnist Andrea Peyser

He had been a public defender for more than thirty years. Prior to joining the Federal Defenders in 1996, Baum, a graduate of Brooklyn College and Syracuse University College of Law, had been the attorney-in-charge of the Criminal Defense Division of the Legal Aid Society. In 2010, he represented Anna Chapman, the beautiful femme fatale who became the poster girl for a ten-member Russian spy ring that had been operating in the United States. After pleading guilty to conspiracy to act as an agent of a foreign government, the red-haired Mata Hari was deported to Russia.

A tough advocate with a booming voice and a strong courtroom presence, the gray-haired defense attorney wasted no time punching holes in Walsh's testimony.

To show that Valle's alleged plans were nothing more than make-believe, Baum zeroed in on the lawman's testimony during direct examination when the G-man said investigators categorized thousands of Valle's e-mails and chats as either "fantasy" or "real."

They were real, the lawman said, if actual names of identifiable people were used; otherwise they were considered fantasy.

Of the two dozen people Valle corresponded with, only three were considered to be engaged in "real" discussions with him—Ali Khan, Moody Blues, and Michael Van Hise.

"Around eighty percent were fantasy role-playing involving Mr. Valle?" Baum asked.

"They could have been," Walsh answered.

"No, you concluded that they were," Baum shouted over an objection from the prosecution.

"Yes," Walsh replied.

"Was Sally Kane ever kidnapped, knocked out and tied up in any basement?" Baum asked.

"No, sir," Walsh answered.

Sally Kane was a real person, Agent Walsh admitted. And there were other e-mails and chats that named real women, he conceded. Nevertheless, chats about kidnapping them were deemed fantasy.

For more than two hours, Baum reviewed the transcripts of online chats Valle had with nine of the fantasy correspondents, noting the many similarities between those chats and the ones Agent Walsh deemed real.

Asked if he still believed Valle's plans were for real, Agent Walsh responded emphatically, "I do, sir."

Walsh admitted that investigators never found the must-have items Valle included in his "blueprint" for kidnapping Kimberly Sauer—no chloroform, rope, duct tape, tarp, or any other tools that could be used to abduct someone were discovered in Valle's apartment, vehicle, or precinct locker.

And there were the lies Valle told his alleged co-conspirators: he said he owned an oversized oven to stuff women into. Was that true? Baum asked.

"No," Walsh replied.

He claimed he owned a secluded mountain house with no one around for half a mile. Was that true?

"No."

He claimed he owned a van. Was that true?

"No."

He said he was building a rope-and-pulley apparatus in his basement. Was he?

"No."

The FBI believed Gil Valle was on the verge of abducting someone; was he under surveillance at any time during their month-long probe? He was not, Walsh admitted.

Finally, Baum asked Walsh if any of the women Valle discussed with his alleged co-conspirators had been kidnapped, raped, or cooked.

"Thankfully, no," the lawman said.

To courtroom observers, it seemed that Robert Baum's withering cross-examination of Agent Walsh was a home run for the defense. And the tabloids agreed.

CANNIBAL COP LAWYER HAS A FEAST—MAKES MINCEMEAT OF EMAILS, the next day's *Daily News* trumpeted. "The lawyer for the 'cannibal cop' ate an FBI agent alive on Wednesday."

CANNIBAL COP CASE A SICKO FANTASY, YES, BUT GOV'T CASE IS COOKED, the rival *Post* blared. "The government has proved that Valle is morally demented and mentally twisted," Post columnist Andrea Peyser opined, predicting an acquittal. "He fantasized during sweaty nights and ravenous days about making women, even the one he married, cry out in agony as he preheats his Viking and readies his fork. But these are fantasies, people."

But the government's case was far from finished, and predictions of a not-guilty verdict were premature. There were more prosecution witnesses waiting to testify. In the days ahead, jurors would hear from the last of the women Valle allegedly targeted, two other FBI agents, an instructor from the NYPD's police academy, a retired NYPD cop who had been a police union delegate, as well as the founder of darkfetishnet.

And, possibly, from Gil Valle himself.

DAY FOUR

*I will really get off on knocking her out, tying up
her hands and bare feet and gagging her.*

Gilberto Valle III

Spring was in the air on Thursday, February 28, the fourth day of the Cannibal Cop trial. The weatherman promised temperatures would climb into the fifties. The balmy weather put smiles on New Yorkers' faces. But it was not springlike in England, where authorities announced the arrest of Valle's online pal Moody Blues, real name Dale Bolinger, but also known online as meatmarketman and Christopher Collins.

In a surprise predawn raid that included cadaver dogs, a forensic team, and shovels, British police in Canterbury, a city of forty-three thousand fifty-five miles southeast of London, took the fifty-seven-year-old married father of three into custody after spending fifteen hours digging up his garden and backyard. They also searched his home and seized his computers.

American lawmen provided their British counterparts with transcripts of Bolinger's online communications with Valle in which he claimed to have eaten two women and a five-year-old boy. Bolinger also said he had many recipes for cooking human flesh. His favorite was for haggis, a Scottish pudding made from a sheep's heart, lungs, and liver. Bolinger, a nurse at a local hospital, would use human organs instead.

Presenting himself as an accomplished cannibal, Bolinger offered Valle advice on how to avoid getting caught: "Don't follow the same pattern. Pattern is what they look for." He opined that the foot is the best body part to eat, and he advised Valle to "cut off their tits and slow roast. That way you'll get lots of girl fat. Great for roasting potatoes and Yorkshire pudding."

When the British press got wind of Bolinger's arrest and his connection to New York City's Cannibal Cop, they tagged the portly nurse with his own unique moniker—"the Canterbury Cannibal." But British cops found no evidence of cannibalism, and Bolinger vehemently claimed the online chats were fantasy.

They did, however, charge him with possession of child pornography and grooming,* the latter based on a chat with Valle in which Bolinger said, "Her name is Lian. Very cute Chinese accent . . . will get a pic of her this weekend if she meets me for coffee sometime this weekend. I've got so many plans for her! Once she comes to my house I'll just snap her neck. It's worked before."

Detectives in Canterbury figured out that Lian was a pretty twenty-seven-year-old worker at a Chinese takeout Bolinger frequented. He had developed a cordial but strictly business relationship with her. He was released on bail.

Back in New York, the court day began with defense attorney Robert Baum finishing his recross of Agent Walsh during which the G-man admitted he visited darkfetishnet.com as part of the investigation. When recross ended, the government called Alisa

---

* *Grooming* refers to the process whereby a sexual predator attempts to gain the trust of a potential victim in order to a commit sexual assault.

Friscia, Victim-2 in the criminal complaint, the last of the alleged kidnap targets to testify.

Like the others, she was petite and pretty with shoulder-length hair. And, like the others, the twenty-nine-year-old teacher did not look happy about testifying. She spoke quickly and appeared rattled and on the verge of tears throughout her time on the witness stand.

Friscia had learned about Valle's plans from the FBI. The news terrified her. It left her unable to sleep and in fear of her life. The alleged Cannibal Cop planned to kidnap her for five thousand dollars payable on delivery to co-conspirator Michael Van Hise. She would become the New Jersey man's sex slave, and then she would be murdered.

Chatting with Van Hise, Valle said, "I will really get off on knocking her out, tying up her hands and bare feet and gagging her. Then she will be stuffed into a large piece of luggage and wheeled out to my van."

Questioned by Hadassa Waxman, Friscia, the young woman Valle said he would bind and stuff into a suitcase, recalled that she met Gil Valle through Kathleen, her former coworker at PS 375, an elementary school in East Harlem. The women, who were colleagues for only one school year, weren't close. Friscia said they had socialized "a handful of times" along with other school staffers, but they had not seen each other since 2011. When asked if she recalled where she was on March 1, 2013, Friscia replied that she was in her classroom during the day and had dinner with a friend in the evening.

"Did you meet Ms. Mangan that day?" Waxman asked.

"No," replied Friscia.

And she testified that she had exchanged hellos with Valle a couple of times, but other than that, they had "no relationship at all." But the NYPD cop was very much taken with the petite brunette. Valle copied photos from her Facebook account. He posted them on darkfetishnet.com, placing them inside a folder he labeled *Tasty Girls.*

When asked if she knew how Valle earned his living, Friscia said she did. "He's a police officer." And she recalled that he wanted her to have a PBA card. In her testimony, Kathleen said her husband insisted he give it to her, which she did. Friscia testified that she did not drive and had no need for a PBA card.

Court watchers were taken aback when defense attorneys declined to cross-examine the Manhattan schoolteacher. Friscia was excused and quickly exited the courtroom.

The next witness was Robin Martinez of the NYPD's Computer Training Unit. She testified that every NYPD police officer receives training on database access. They are explicitly instructed not to use the database for personal reasons. All database searches, they are told, must relate to official police business. And they are warned that accessing the database for any reason other than police business can result in fines, termination of employment, and even criminal prosecution.

Police department personnel records indicated that Gil Valle underwent database training twice, in 2006 and again in 2010. Martinez explained the kinds of useful information about potential victims Valle could gather from the databases: their addresses, height, weight, eye color, whether they had been involved in any law enforcement activity, and if they had ever been arrested or had ever asked for an order of protection.

It was five o'clock when Hadassa Waxman ended her direct examination. Judge Gardephe called a halt to the proceedings. Before adjourning the court, the jurist ordered the NYPD computer trainer to return the next day, Friday, to answer questions from Valle's lawyers.

DAY FIVE

I would not have gone through with it.

Gil Valle

Officer Robin Martinez returned to the witness stand at half-past nine. During cross-examination, Julia Gatto asked her if police officers are allowed to check law enforcement databases as a favor for a friend or a citizen, and if they are permitted to submit someone's name through the system as a test "to make sure that the system is working." The NYPD's computer training expert answered no to both questions.

NYPD sergeant Edwige Anatsui followed her to the stand. She testified that Valle became her patrol partner in October 2011. She testified that he had access to a Taser—it was kept in the trunk of their police cruiser. In a number of chats Valle told co-conspirators that he possessed one, while in another chat he said he could easily acquire one.

The sergeant recalled that in the spring or early summer of 2012, she and Valle were patrolling the Times Square area as part of an antiterror detail. It was late afternoon and Valle, who was behind the wheel of their cruiser, stopped to visit with a female friend for a few minutes. Her recollection supported Maureen Hartigan's account of meeting Valle.

Before stepping down, Anatsui recalled that in September 2012, around the time that Kathleen left her husband, Valle was out of work for a week. When he returned he looked gaunt. She asked him about his weight loss. "He said something to the effect [of] 'the good thing about being sick is losing ten pounds.'"

After a brief recess, the sergeant faced cross-examination from Julia Gatto. The defense attorney wanted to know if she remembered stopping by an Upper East Side hospital on March 1, 2012, where Kathleen was visiting a friend who had just given birth.

Anatsui said she recalled the visit but could not confirm that it occurred on March 1, the day prosecutors say Valle was near the apartment building where Alisa Friscia lived.

Next to take the witness stand was FBI special agent Anthony Foto, the case agent. He testified about interrogating Gil Valle, and he recalled Valle's reaction when he was confronted by the lawmen in the hallway outside his apartment. The NYPD cop, the lawman said, thought he had been arrested for conspiracy to commit murder or attempted murder. Informed that the most serious charge against him was conspiracy to kidnap, Valle told Foto, "I would not have gone through with it."

The interrogation lasted almost four hours. Valle was, the agent said, mostly cooperative. He even offered to help investigators hunt down dangerous fiends lurking on darkfetishnet.com. Valle, Foto said, admitted to the lawman that he was obsessed with the website darkfetishnet.com.

He was a "premium" member, which meant he paid a fee to download gory videos depicting torture, murder, and cannibalism. He told Agent Foto about spending hours every night viewing photos and videos of women being tortured and beaten. He also told the lawman about countless chats with other darkfetishnet members regarding slaughtering and cannibalizing women.

"He said he didn't enjoy the site and he didn't know why he was using it," Agent Foto said. Valle revealed that his fascination with cannibalism began in college. It had become an obsession in recent years, so much so, Foto recalled, that "he began to pull away from his wife, and he ultimately stopped having sex with her."

Valle confessed his obsession interfered with his police work—he'd log on to the sordid website from his iPhone while cruising the streets of upper Manhattan in his NYPD police car. He'd engage in sordid chats while on duty. And he claimed his online conversations with Moody Blues and Ali Khan seemed to be more "serious" than those with other darkfetishnet members. His chats with them, Valle told Foto, were "bleeding into his personal life."

Foto said Valle admitted he was outside Alisa Friscia's Manhattan apartment building on March 1, 2012, just two days after agreeing to abduct her for five thousand dollars. He went there, Valle claimed, to drop his wife off for a lunch date with Friscia.

Valle lied, if his wife and her former coworker were to be believed. Kathleen testified that she did not have a lunch date with Friscia on March 1, telling jurors she had not seen Alisa Friscia for more than a year before then. During her testimony the day before, Friscia told jurors she had not seen Kathleen since sometime in 2011.

Robert Baum cross-examined Agent Foto. The defense attorney zeroed in on the length of the interrogation: "You took no notes over a four hour period and now, four months later, you are recounting for the jury what Mr. Valle said?"

The lawmen replied tersely: "Yes."

It was late in the afternoon when Judge Gardephe interrupted Baum's cross-examination of Agent Foto. The judge sent the jury home for the weekend, explaining that he and the lawyers needed to spend the rest of the court day wrangling over evidentiary issues. With the jury out of the courtroom, they discussed the proposed testimony of Stephen Flatley, a forensic examiner with the FBI's

Computer Analysis and Response Team. He reviewed Valle's computer files and his browser history. Prosecutors planned to call him on Monday, to show and tell the jury about dozens of gory images and horrific videos he'd recovered from Valle's computers.

Defense lawyers fought hard to prevent the most horrific of them—women undergoing torture, dead bodies, and body parts—from being shown. They argued that the images would be highly inflammatory and there was no proof that Valle had ever seen them because it appeared they had been automatically downloaded from websites.

After viewing the gruesome images, including a picture of severed feet inside a refrigerator, an image Kathleen testified she saw on the computer she shared with her husband, Judge Gardephe postponed his decision until Monday morning. He wanted the weekend to decide.

DAY SIX

*If it was only fantasy, why did Valle search for a
huge cooking tray?*

New York Post

The first day of the second week of the Cannibal Cop trial began with a return to winter temperatures. New York's morning papers carried news of a massive winter snowstorm in the Midwest that was bearing down on the Northeast, and news of another NYPD scandal—a lieutenant from the Twenty-fifth Precinct in East Harlem allegedly coerced a policewoman into performing oral sex. The officer, a single mom, filed a complaint with the NYPD's Internal Affairs Bureau and started a lawsuit in state court. The lieutenant denied the allegations. Nevertheless, he was disciplined for sexual harassment, transferred out of the precinct, and ordered to attend a seminar called "Professionalism in the Workplace." The policewoman remained with the precinct. As of this writing, her lawsuit, which was filed in Bronx County, is pending.

With the jury waiting to enter the courtroom, Judge Gardephe took the bench and began reading his ruling. It was long. It was detailed, and he cited cases to support his decisions. Gil Valle, in a black suit and yellow tie, paid close attention as the jurist ruled that thirty-four of the goriest images would not be seen by jurors because prosecutors were unable to show that Valle himself had viewed them. He described the barred images as "murdered and mutilated women in scenes related to cannibalism." But prosecutors could show jurors screenshots of Valle's Internet searches as well as evidence of the NYPD cop looking for articles about rape, murder, and kidnapping on the Internet.

Before Flatley would take the stand, Baum resumed his cross-examination of Anthony Foto:

BAUM: Did he make any claim to you as to whether his discussions about kidnapping, raping, murdering and eating the women were real? Do you recall being asked that question?

AGENT FOTO: Yes, I believe so.

BAUM: Do you recall that the answer you gave was, "He claimed that he would not have gone through with it." Do you recall that answer?

AGENT FOTO: That's correct.

BAUM: In fact, Mr. Valle made other statements concerning whether or not his discussions were real, is that accurate?

AGENT FOTO: Yes, that's correct.

BAUM: In fact, Mr. Valle had told you that he would never hurt anyone, correct?

AGENT FOTO: That's correct.

BAUM: Did Mr. Valle also tell you that he tried to make people think it was real by saying it was not fantasy and that he would go along with it if he could get away with it he would, but that was a lie to those people. Do you recall Mr. Valle telling you that?

AGENT FOTO: Yes. He did explain that point.

Foto's testimony reinforced the defense contention that Valle was, in his own mind, fantasizing. It was a major victory for the defense team, but the jury had not yet heard from the FBI's computer expert. Randall Jackson called Stephen Flatley to the witness stand. The computer whiz, a 1986 Boston College graduate with a degree in computer science, joined the FBI in 2005 after working as a programmer. He testified that in October he accompanied lawmen to Valle's Forest Hills apartment, where he personally copied the HP computer's hard drive.

He explained the copying procedure, the steps he took to analyze the HP hard drive's content, and the contents of the Mac hard drive sent to New York from Reno. Jurors were shown a PowerPoint presentation.

There were screenshots of Valle's browsing history: "what to look for in human meat"; "how to cook a woman alive"; "human meat recipes"; "how to kidnap a girl"; "how to knock someone unconscious"; "how to chloroform a girl"; "huge cooking tray"; and "eat her for dinner." They also viewed "how to kidnap someone," which, Flatley said, Valle searched for only three days prior to his visit to Kimberly Sauer in Maryland.

Flatley said the NYPD cop logged onto darkfetishnet.com "over one thousand times." And there were "tens of thousands of hits" relating to violence against women. On Valle's hard drive, the computer whiz found dozens of images of dead women, many of whom were disfigured and disemboweled. The images were put up on video monitors for jurors to see.

Until then, the jury of six men, six women, and two alternates had remained impassive and unflappable through days of mind-numbing testimony from the FBI's Corey Walsh as he read aloud Valle's chats with his alleged co-conspirators. And they were poker-faced during emotional and heartbreaking testimony from Valle's alleged targets, even as both Kathleen and Gil Valle wept.

But they could not hide their feelings when sordid images began appearing on the courtroom video monitors. They squirmed, gasped, covered their mouths, and winced as they viewed dozens of gory images. It was a peek into the dark corners of the Internet and the sordid fantasies of Gil Valle. Among the images were:

- A woman with her throat slit, and another being barbecued on a spit.

- Two naked women roasting on a giant spit. Flatley said they were recovered from a file Valle kept on Kimberly Sauer.

- Maureen Hartigan's face cut out and superimposed onto a cartoon of a woman boiling inside a pot.

- Women with their mouths forced open with vaginal speculums, a medical device used by physicians.

- A group of men gang-raping a woman.

They also viewed the contents of files Valle created for Kimberly Sauer, Alisa Friscia, and Andria Noble, and the screenshot of a Google search seeking Kristen Ponticelli's address.

The most shocking item culled from the computers was a video of a young woman, naked and chained, standing with her legs spread as a flaming torch burned her genitals. Her screams could be heard throughout the silent courtroom. There was no doubt that Valle had seen the video, Flatley said—it had been recovered from his computer's recycle bin. The video, he said, was titled "Girl Being Burned." The computer whiz said he thought it had been staged.

Cross-examination was brief. Julia Gatto elicited testimony that the NYPD cop also viewed fantasy baseball sites and Weight Watchers, and Flatley acknowledged that two of the fetish sites Valle frequented billed themselves as "fantasy" sites.

On redirect, prosecutor Randall Jackson asked Flatley if he knew of any website that declared, "We are strictly for actual murderers and rapists."

"No, I've never come across that," he answered.

After more than three hours on the witness stand, the FBI computer examiner was excused, and Randall Jackson announced that the prosecution rested. Judge Gardephe sent the jury home. The defense team would begin presenting their case in the morning, he said.

But before adjourning court for the day, the jurist wanted to know if Gil Valle would testify. Julia Gatto told him that decision had not yet been made.

DAY SEVEN

*The only thing scarier than a wanna-be cannibal is a
social media site where he can meet others of like mind.*
                                        New York Daily News

On the last day of testimony, Courtroom 110 was abuzz with anticipation, waiting to find out if Gil Valle would testify. It was standing room only despite the threat that a massive late-winter snowstorm was headed toward the city. The storm had already blanketed the Midwest and forced the cancellation of hundreds of flights into and out of the Northeast.

Through six days of chilling and grotesque testimony, prosecutors bombarded the jury with evidence that the NYPD cop had an appetite for murder and had taken steps to carry out a diabolical conspiracy to kidnap, kill, and cannibalize women. Defense attorneys fought back by conceding that that their client's fetishes are grotesque, but the NYPD cop is a nice guy who engaged in harmless role play over the Internet and never intended to harm anyone. Only one person could testify to his true intentions, Gil Valle himself, and the day had come for him to reveal whether or not he would take the witness stand.

First, however, the jury would hear from three witnesses for the defense:

- Sergiy Merenkov, Webmaster and co-owner of darkfetish net.com. Jurors viewed his videotaped deposition, which was recorded from his home in Moscow on February 19 via Skype. Merenkov said he built the site in 2010 for people who are into sexual asphyxiation, bondage, and cannibalism in order to "fill a niche"; he wanted to create a meeting place online for people with similar interests. He said the thirty-eight-thousand-member website is for "fantasies only," and girlmeathunter—Gil Valle's screen name—was a premium member. He likened darkfetishnet.com to Facebook with one difference: darkfestishnet.com "is oriented to people with fetishes that are not considered standard."

- Alexandra Katz, defense-team paralegal. She gave jurors a tour of darkfetishnet.com via a video she made. She even joined the fetish website, posted a profile, and received nineteen responses from people who invited her to chat. She said she did not respond to any of them.

- Michael McDermott, retired NYPD cop. The twenty-four-year veteran cop and former police union delegate testified that police officers were allotted twelve PBA cards annually. He said it was common practice to give cards to family and friends, doctors, dentists—"a lot of people like to have them," and they do not have to be drivers. "People can be stopped for numerous reasons by a police officer—smoking in the subway, unfortunately, urinating in public—there are all sorts of different reasons why police officers stop people." During cross-examination, the retired lawman said he never gave a PBA card to someone he had not seen in years, and he never asked his wife to give a card to anyone who was not his friend.

With the end of McDermott's testimony, the defense rested. Judge Gardephe sent the jury out of the courtroom. Looking down from the bench, he asked Valle, "Presumably, it is your desire not to testify in this case?"

"It is my desire not to testify, that's correct," Valle replied. It was his first public statement since November when the NYPD cop had pled not guilty.

DAY EIGHT

*The scariest thing we saw during this whole trial
was that staged video of that woman pretending to
be tortured. This is disgusting. That's Gil's porn.
But it simply is not proof of a conspiracy.*

Julia Gatto

It was standing room only inside the Cannibal Cop case courtroom the morning of Wednesday, March 7. Final arguments were
set to begin at nine o'clock. Court watchers anticipated a no-
holds-barred legal battle. They would not be disappointed.

At ten minutes past nine, Judge Gardephe took the bench.
After some legal wrangling, court officers brought the jury into
the courtroom. When they were seated, lead prosecutor Hadassa
Waxman rose to deliver the opening summation.

She began by repeating what Gil Valle said in one of his chats:

"His words: 'Five thousand dollars and she's all yours. I am
putting my neck on the line here. If I were guaranteed to get away
with it, I would.' His searches: How to tie someone up. How to
kidnap someone. How to abduct a girl. How to knock someone
unconscious."

Speaking without anger or indignation, she explained why the
government of the United States had charged Valle with conspiracy to kidnap:

*Where a person like New York City Police Officer Gilberto
Valle plots to kidnap young women, where he researches
methods to knock women out and tie up his victims, where
he surveils potential targets and collects photographs of them,*

where he uses confidential and restricted law enforcement databases to gather personal information about them, where he agrees to accept money in return for abducting and delivering a woman to be raped, the law does not require that we wait until he carries out his plan. The law permits us to stop him before he acts. The law permits us to charge him with the crime of conspiracy, and the law requires that he be convicted.

The facts of the case, she said, were undisputed.

- Gil Valle communicated with Michael Van Hise, Moody Blues, and Ali Khan via the Internet.

- His chats and e-mails were about kidnapping, rape, torture, murder, and cannibalizing young women.

- He carried a gun and handcuffs and wore a police shield.

- He had access to confidential law enforcement databases.

She told the jurors that just one issue needed to be resolved: Was the NYPD cop engaged in nothing more than harmless fantasy role play, or was he serious, deadly serious?

"The evidence proves he was serious. The evidence proves he was ready to act," Waxman said. The jury would decide. To convince them, Waxman reviewed Valle's February 28 chat with Michael Van Hise, when the accused cop agreed to abduct Alisa Friscia and deliver her to Van Hise to be raped and murdered.

Valle, she reminded the jurors, told Van Hise he would kidnap and deliver Friscia to him for five thousand dollars. Van Hise asked for a payment plan. Valle demanded five thousand dollars on delivery. He explained he risked getting caught. "I am putting my neck on the line here. If something goes wrong I am in deep shit," he told Van Hise, who then tried to bargain the price down to four thousand dollars. But Valle remained firm, and Van Hise agreed to pay the NYPD cop's price and the haggling ended.

It was not a fantasy, Waxman said. They were not involved in role play. They were serious.

"A fantasy conversation would be different," Waxman told the jury. "In a fantasy he could pay any amount of money for any woman he wants." And "In a fantasy, no one really worries about getting caught, because in a fantasy, no one ever gets caught."

Next, she read from a chat during which Valle and Moody Blues targeted Kimberly Sauer. "I'm glad you're on board," Valle said. "I love that she is asleep right now, not having the slightest clue of what we have planned."

"'On board'; these words are critically important," Waxman told the jurors. "They signify working together. They signify an agreement.

"Valle had an agreement with Ali Khan, too: He says, 'Get some courage. I am not happy with you. I think you are not for real, otherwise they wouldn't be living. You are not really interested in slaughtering them. You are wasting my time, buddy. I am for real, not fantasy.'

"What does Valle say in response? He says, 'If I were guaranteed to get away with it, I would. I'm just afraid of getting caught.' Ali Khan then says, 'Are you really, really into it?'

"Valle answered immediately and affirmatively: 'Yes.' But Ali Khan wants to make sure. 'Are you sure?' he asks. Valle responds, 'Definitely.' And through these words, an agreement is formed— an agreement between Ali Khan and Officer Valle to kidnap, torture, kill and cannibalize young women."

Next, Waxman turned her attention to the overt acts Valle undertook to further the conspiracy.

- He conducted extensive research: "how to prepare and preserve human meat"; "how to make chloroform from household products"; "how to tie up a girl"; "how to knock someone unconscious"; "how to cook a human." Valle's research, Waxman said, "offers a road map to a plan for kidnapping and violence."

- He searched online for unique products: "largest cooking tray" and "smoker grills."

- He authored a detailed plan, "Abduction and Cooking of Kimberly: A Blueprint," and he e-mailed it to Moody Blues.

- He accessed confidential law enforcement databases for information about Andria Noble, Kimberly Sauer, and Maureen Hartigan.

- He conducted Internet searches for Kimberly Sauer, Andria Noble, Alisa Friscia, Maureen Hartigan, and Kristen Ponticelli, not just once but "again and again and again."

- He surveilled Alisa Friscia just two days after he and Van Hise agreed to abduct her.

- He traveled to Maryland: "The purpose of this trip was surveillance and planning in furtherance of the kidnapping conspiracy," Waxman said.

He also took "incredible risks." He did so, the prosecutor said, "because he is serious." He declared time and again "that he is for real and is afraid of getting caught." And "Nowhere, absolutely nowhere in the chats with Ali Khan, with Moody Blues, with Van Hise, does Officer Valle say it is just fantasizing—absolutely nowhere."

She reminded the jurors of FBI agent Anthony Foto's testimony regarding his postarrest interrogation of the NYPD cop when "Valle admitted to being on Alisa's block on March 1, 2012, just two days after Valle and Van Hise agreed to kidnap her," even though he "had no legitimate reason to be on Alisa's block."

Valle, the prosecutor said, "was there for one simple and one awful purpose: to conduct surveillance and planning in further-ance of Alisa's kidnapping."

And Waxman reminded jurors that FBI agent Foto testified that Valle thought he had been arrested for conspiracy to commit murder. He thought that "because this is real and this is not just a fantasy . . . [It is] what he wants to do."

Anticipating her adversary's argument, Waxman said she expected defense attorney Julia Gatto "to say nothing happened, this was all in Valle's mind." But that was not the case. "Some-thing did happen. Real women were put in grave danger by *that* man, Gilberto Valle," Waxman said angrily, pointing her index finger at the defendant.

"*He* discussed these women with men he believed were serious. *He* sent photographs of these women. *He* sent a video of Kimberly on vacation. *He* sent accurate information about their height, their weight, about their professions, And in so doing, *he* made it pos-sible for these women to be identified and harmed in very horrific ways." That no one was kidnapped "is incredibly fortunate," Wax-man said.

She implored the jurors to "connect the dots, to look at the big picture," and "to use your common sense." If they did that, Waxman said, "You will conclude that Valle intended to kidnap Kimberly and other young women he knew."

Following a short recess, Julia Gallo began her summation. Her job was to plant seeds of doubt into the minds of the jurors. And, as Waxman had done, she began by quoting from one of Gil Valle's chats.

"I just have a world in my mind and in that world I am kid-napping women and selling them to people interested in buy-ing them." Those are Gil Valle's words, words he wrote in February 2012, long before he could ever imagine that he would be sitting in that chair having to defend himself; long before he could ever fathom that the United States Attorney's office would think his fantasy role play was reality.

Those words, Gatto said, make the entire case clear. "There really was just a world in his mind. It wasn't reality." She recalled a conversation she had with her father the night before. He told her the case sounded like *War of the Worlds.*

She went online. She learned that *The War of the Worlds* was a novel written by H. G. Wells and published in Great Britain in 1898. Forty years later it was adapted as a radio play for the Mercury Theatre on the Air, a radio drama that was broadcast nationwide in 1938, on Halloween. The program sparked a panic.

That was because much of the drama was presented as "news bulletins" that were read by actor Orson Welles. There were also "live" on-the-scene reports from nervous "correspondents" and frightened "eyewitnesses" who described the destruction wrought by Martians. They landed in Grover's Mills, a community north of Trenton, New Jersey. The army seemed powerless to stop them.

"It appeared to be real," Gatto said. "People fled their homes.

They thought it was an alien invasion, but it wasn't—it was make-believe."

She asked the jurors to imagine another situation:

> A *twenty-eight-year-old man goes online and he creates a pretend character. He called it Girlmeat Hunter, an aspiring professional kidnapper. He tells stories and he sprinkles them with details to make them sound scary. And then someone stumbles upon portions of that broadcast, his wife and then the FBI. Panic ensues because they think it is real, but it is make-believe.*

She was talking about her client, whose "stories are no more real than the alien invasion.

"There is no chloroform. There is no rope. There is no oven. There is no spit. There is no kidnapped woman. Just like *The War of the Worlds*, Gil's stories are scary but they are truly make-believe."

About Valle's online conversations, Gatto called them "fantasy chitchats through cyberspace." There were no agreements, and there were no overt acts. The chats were "disgusting—there is no denying that, but they are also preposterous. They are fantasy role play, something thousands of people are engaging in on the Internet, exploring their fantasies through pretend role-play scenarios" which Gatto likened to "dark improv theater" with "each participant building on the last participant's script line."

The chats were also akin to tennis volleys, she said.

"They pick a woman to fantasize about and then they riff off each other, like a game of volley, tennis volley. One participant hits the ball and says, 'This is what I would do with her.' Then they go back and forth, and the next member says, 'Cool. This is that I would do with her.' Then they go back and forth and back and forth."

That's what happened in Valle's chat with Ali Khan, Gatto said.

"That conversation, [where Ali Khan asks] are you really serious? That is part of the volley I was talking about. If in response to that question Gil said no, the volley ends."

If the plans were real, as prosecutors claimed, why is it that no attempt was ever made to abduct anyone? Gatto asked rhetorically. And "where are the human sized ovens and the life-sized spits, and the basic torture devices and mountain house in the country?" The chats, Gatto said, are not the plans of real men planning real crimes. Instead, "they are crude, stupid, infantile masticatory storytelling." Which explains why they are "riddled with exaggerations."

Gil Valle may talk about a house in the mountains, she said, but it doesn't exist. He doesn't own a van. It's not true that he lives in the country, or that he works nine-to-five, or that he is building an apparatus in his basement. These details were merely "fantasy enhancers" to make his stories "sound real, to make them sound scary."

Gatto reminded jurors that FBI agent Corey Walsh testified that he separated Gil Valle's chats into two "piles," fantasy and real. He deemed twenty-one of the twenty-four online conversations fantasy because either Valle or his chat partner explicitly stated they were only telling stories; they would not actually do what they were chatting about. Walsh decided that three, those with Van Hise, Moody Blues, and Ali Khan, were real—they were planning to do what they were discussing.

He was wrong, Gallo said. "They are all storytelling." But lawmen do not understand fantasy role play, she explained. "They never have." If Agent Walsh "had been educated on the subculture out there, if he had been educated on fantasy role play, he would have never made a real pile. And none of us would be here today."

The chats, she declared, "are reasonable doubt." There were no agreements between Valle and Van Hise, Moody Blues, and Ali Khan. Gatto accused prosecutors of distorting the chats "to make what is obviously not real sound real."

The defense attorney attacked the testimony of FBI special agent Anthony Foto.

First, its length: "He testified about a four hour post arrest interrogation, and the government had him on the stand for fifteen minutes, the shortest in length of all the witnesses the government put on."

Second: "He didn't take any notes."

And third: "He didn't record it in any way."

And Gatto attacked the premise that Valle's intent could be inferred because he told the lawman that he believed he was under arrest for conspiracy to commit murder. That was "not a confession," the defense lawyer declared. It was "an obvious observation."

Regarding Count Two, illegally accessing restricted law enforcement databases, Gatto said, "As an NYPD officer, Valle is authorized to use the system." But she implored the jury to carefully review the records of his database searches. If they did, she said, they would see that Valle put Maureen Hartigan's name into the system on May 31, 2012. And what they would also see was that "Mr. Valle inputs his own name into the system many times. He inputs [his brother] Daniel Valle. He inputs other names."

She reminded jurors that they heard testimony that the database system does not always work flawlessly, but for officer safety it is vital that it does. "Isn't it possible," she asked rhetorically, that "Gil inputs these names to check the system, to make sure it is working? Isn't that reasonable doubt as to Count Two."

Among other points Gatto made:

- Valle's public profile on darkfetishnet announced to the world, including to his alleged co-conspirators, that he was an "aspiring professional kidnapper" in "fantasy only."

- The alleged co-conspirators never met, or spoke by telephone, or took any real-world steps to kidnap anyone.

- The alleged kidnapping dates came and went with no action, no explanation, and no follow-up conversations about why nothing happened. Valle never complained that an abduction had not occurred.

- Valle frequently gave imaginary and untrue information about his location, potential victims, properties, about a woman being tied up in his basement, about equipment, and other parts of the pretend scenarios.

- He never revealed detailed personal information about any woman that would permit another person to identify and locate them.

- He never requested or received information regarding the address or phone number of any of his alleged co-conspirators or other online correspondents.

- The government provided no reliable evidence that these acknowledged fantasy chats were materially different from the alleged "real" chats.

Before concluding, she told the jurors, "This is a prosecution based on fantasy chats." Lawmen "worked their way backwards, looking for evidence of a crime that didn't exist." She conceded that

Gil Valle has a disturbing fetish that he explored online. But his searches never were research to abduct and cook women. Instead, "they are searches for masturbatory material." Gatto implored the jurors to not let Gil Valle's repulsive fetish influence their verdict:

> The government's case has paraded in front of you bizarre Google searches and disturbing porn. The scariest thing we saw during this whole trial was that staged video of that woman pretending to be tortured. This is disgusting. That's Gil's porn. But it simply is not proof of a conspiracy. It is only proof of ugly thoughts. We don't convict human beings because [of ugly thoughts] even if they are police officers.

Valle has lost his "pretty wife, and an adorable baby, and an NYPD badge," she said. "His foolishness on the Internet, his insensitive, ugly thoughts have cost him everything. But what it cannot cost, what his thoughts cannot cost him if you follow the law[,] is his liberty."

Before sitting down, Gatto asked the jury to "take great care in deliberating, not because Gil Valle's conduct is exemplary, but because the presumption of innocence and the law are, and we ask that you return a not guilty verdict."

Following a recess, Randall Jackson delivered the rebuttal summation. He pulled no punches. His tone was indignant and contemptuous as he ripped into the defense.

What jurors heard from Julia Gatto was "remarkable," he declared. The defense is "trying to sell you on two broad concepts that are in total conflict with each other."

First, that it is okay for a New York City police officer, armed with a loaded weapon, to make detailed plans on a daily basis about the execution of actual women. Second, "that a police officer, [who is] walking around New York City every single day with a loaded weapon, has a primary sexual fantasy of seeing women mutilated in horrific ways."

He reminded jurors of what Julia Gatto said on day one of the trial: "What turns Gil Valle on is the idea of a woman oiled, bound, laid out on a platter with an apple in her mouth, about to be offed."

The prosecutor attacked the defense notion that Valle was merely engaging in fantasy chats. Fantasies, Jackson said, "are the stories you told to your children—fairies, pixie dust, unicorns." But Valle's fantasy is "about seeing women executed, sexually assaulted, executed and left for dead."

And he claimed that the NYPD cop's fantasy was a reflection of his intent, telling jurors it "gives you deep insight into what this man's motivations are." That, Jackson told the jurors, is "the lens through which you have to look at the evidence."

The fact that no woman was ever kidnapped has no bearing whatever on Valle's guilt because "the illegal agreement itself is the crime." There are laws on the books to prevent crimes before they happen. He cited DUI arrests as an example. "The purpose of the law is to get at people before the tragedy."

And he blasted Gatto's argument that all the conversations were fantasy, even those between his three alleged co-conspirators. Valle, he said, was involved in both fantasy and actual plotting to kidnap, kill, and cannibalize women. The two were not mutually exclusive.

The prosecutor also attacked Gatto's claim that the online conversations were fantasy role play because Valle communicated details to his cohorts that were untrue.

Said Jackson, "Criminals all the time communicate details to one another that are not true . . . There is a reason that one of the oldest clichés in world is there is no honor among thieves."

As evidence of Valle's intent, Jackson reminded jurors that the accused cop repeatedly said he was concerned about getting caught, and he "would actually do it if I thought I could get away with it."

And he countered the defense contention that Valle's conversations were "preposterous," too "over the top," to be believed.

"What is it that is so over the top?" Jackson asked. "Mr. Valle is a sadistic person. He is a person that wants to engage in activity that would degrade and harm women . . . He is stimulated by the idea of abducting a woman. He is attracted to the idea of a woman being sexually violated in front of him, a woman being roasted alive, screaming for her life.

"Mr. Valle is watching women screaming for their lives . . . Women being roasted over flames. That is the photo that was in the file that he had under the name Kimberly Sauer. This is not a masticatory sexual fantasy. This is a man who has a deep-seated desire to see harm coming to women and the evidence reflects that he was taking actual steps to advance that."

Next, Jackson went after Gatto's argument that Valle was not conducting surveillance:

"Common sense tells you people take advantage of the opportunities they have to observe the places and the people they want to look at in a way that will appear normal." They do not disguise themselves as ninjas wearing night-vision goggles, he said. Valle's brunch with Kimberly Sauer was for the purpose of learning about her life—where she worked as well as where and with whom she lived.

The PBA card was the first step in the surveillance. Valle and Sauer had not seen each other in years, Jackson said, when "out of the blue he decides to [offer her a PBA card] at the same time that he is engaging in discussions about kidnapping her and subjecting her to violence, at the same time that he is placing photographs of a woman on a spit into files with her name on it." And he reminded jurors of the text message about Sauer's office building.

With a photo of the building on the video monitors, Jackson said:

He says, "We drove by your pink building." This is where the building is. This is Rockville Pike. It is as you can see a wide[,] almost highway[-]like street in the middle of a busy metropolis. This is the building. It is a nondescript standard low-rise build-ing. Ask yourself from your own common sense, have you ever taken note of the office building of one of your friends? Most people don't even know what their spouse's office building looks like if they have never been there. Most people are not driving down a busy street like this with a baby in the car, their wife in the car and taking particular note of a random office building in the middle of the day while they are on a trip. [Sauer] said that he had never visited her at that location so why is Mr. Valle making note of the fact that he went by the pink building?

The answer: He was surveilling her. And this supported the prosecution's contention that the real purpose of the Maryland trip, the only purpose, was the surveillance of Kimberly Sauer.

Next, Jackson fired a broadside at Julia Gatto's *War of the Worlds* analogy, castigating the defense attorney for comparing the Cannibal Cop case to the 1938 radio drama.

"Every single thing that Mr. Valle says that he wants to do to a woman is something that can actually be done." And he reminded the jurors yet again of what Valle said he wants to do: "see the look of pain on their faces as they are roasted over flames, and he wants to inflict pain on them."

Jackson told the jury that Gatto's explanation for Valle's illegal database searches—she said Valle was "checking the system"—made no sense. "That is pure speculation." There was no evidence whatsoever that he was "trying to test the system."

Besides, Jackson said, Gatto offered "no reasonable explanation" why Valle would jeopardize "his job, his freedom and his livelihood by conducting blatantly illegal searches of the very women he is talking about."

Jackson talked about reasonable doubt: "Proof beyond a reasonable doubt does not mean proof beyond all doubt. If jurors have any doubts about Valle's guilt, they should ask themselves: Is it possible that a man who actually engages in specific detailed conversations about victimizing real women, who engages in surveillance of the women, who shows up on their block two days after discussing victimizing [one of] these women, who violates the law and NYPD regulations by running their names through sensitive law enforcement databases, who is conducting Google searches on the various ways to execute the type of plan he is putting together? Is it possible that the man who is doing all that is somehow not guilty of actually engaging in a conspiracy?"

Said Jackson, "These are the things you would expect to see if you were dealing with a person engaged in an actual plot to victimize these women. And that is what you saw in this case."

But there was more. If they still harbored doubts, they should think about Kristen Ponticelli, the eighteen-year-old high school student. Valle fantasized about killing her. He searched for her address on Google. "You don't need Kristen Ponticelli's address just to fantasize about her in your mind," Jackson said. "And that is proof beyond a reasonable doubt that he is taking steps far beyond thinking about this in his mind. That is a man who is trying to move a plan into action."

The evidence "is overwhelming," Jackson declared. "Mr. Valle is guilty. That is a verdict the evidence requires you to return."

DAY NINE
The Verdict

Jurors deliberated for sixteen hours over four days to decide if Gil Valle was an evil sadist on the verge of becoming a cannibal killer, or a just a man with an ugly fetish who never harmed anyone and never would harm anyone. They reached their decision on Tuesday, March 12. It was announced at 11 A.M. They found the NYPD cop guilty on both counts.

Valle bowed his head and wept. His mother, who had been at the trial every day, was in a state of disbelief. "What trial were they watching?" Elizabeth Valle snarled, referring to the jurors.

"This was a thought prosecution," Julia Gatto said. "These are thoughts, very ugly thoughts, but we don't prosecute people for their thoughts. The jury couldn't get past the thoughts."

Kristen Ponticelli told a reporter she was relieved, while cops at the Twenty-sixth Precinct, where Vale worked before his arrest, were stunned. "We still don't know what he did wrong," one cop said. "It was just a fantasy in his mind."

Juror Victor Pineiro explained what went on in the jury room. The jurors created a time line and concluded that Valle was indeed on the verge of carrying out an evil plan. "I think like an addict needs a larger and larger dose, he was needing things that were more and more real, and he was progressing. The majority of what we were looking at we felt was fantasy," but "he was speaking to . . . serious people and he didn't back away from them. He willingly continued the conversations and sometimes was the provocateur."

And, the Cannibal Cop juror said, he carried out "overt acts, bringing it into real life," using the law enforcement databases "to go through with it."

EPILOGUE . . .

Sentencing was set for June 19, which would have been Gil Valle's first wedding anniversary. But defense attorneys filed a motion to vacate the verdict, and June 19 came and went. On June 30, 2014, more than one year later, Judge Gardephe issued a stunning one-hundred-and-eighteen-page ruling in which he overturned the jury's guilty verdict on Count One, conspiracy to kidnap, declaring that "no reasonable juror could have found that Valle actually intended to kidnap a woman."*

"This," the judge said, "is a conspiracy that existed solely in cyberspace." He explained:

- "There is no evidence that the alleged conspirators ever exchanged telephone contact information or accurate information about the area[s] in which they lived."

- There is no evidence "that they ever sought to learn each other's true identities."

---

* Judge Gardephe, however, upheld Mr. Valle's conviction on Count Two, illegally accessing a law enforcement database.

- "No real-world, non-Internet-based steps were ever taken to kidnap anyone."

- The communications between the alleged conspirators were sporadic: "Months passed between chats, with the alleged conspirators forgetting what had previously been discussed."

The ex-cop's chats and e-mails, the judge said, while "deeply disturbing" and "misogynistic," and "written by an individual obsessed with imagining women he knows suffering horrific sex-related pain, terror and degradation . . . are not sufficient, standing alone, to make out the elements of [a] conspiracy to commit kidnapping."

Federal prosecutors vowed to appeal. They urged the judge to keep Valle behind bars. Nevertheless, the former NYPD officer left the federal lockup, where he had worked as a cook, the next day. "I want to take the opportunity to apologize to everyone who's been hurt, shocked and offended by my infantile actions," he told a horde of waiting reporters.

Released on a one-hundred-thousand-dollar bond, Valle was ordered to remain under house arrest at his mother's Queens home, prohibited from using a computer or accessing the Internet, and required to undergo a mental health assessment.

Kathleen Mangan lives in Reno, where she is raising their daughter and working as a special-education teacher.

On March 14, 2014, a federal jury convicted Michael Van Hise and another man, retired high school librarian Robert Christopher Asch, of conspiring to kidnap women and young girls in order to satisfy their macabre fetishes concerning rape and murder. The co-conspirators, who were tried before U.S. district court judge Paul Gardephe, were found guilty of planning to abduct and kill Van Hise's wife, sister-in-law, and young nieces.

Asch was also convicted of plotting to kidnap and murder another woman, who turned out to be an undercover FBI agent. Asch even brought a stun gun, whip, and gynecological instruments to a meeting with another undercover FBI agent where they plotted the abduction of the female crime fighter.

Defense attorneys argued that the men were engaged in fantasy role playing, but prosecutor Hadassa Waxman told the jurors, "None of this was fake. They were absolutely serious."

Van Hise, twenty-three, and Asch, sixty-one, whose appeals are pending, could spend the rest of their lives in prison. A third co-conspirator, a former police chief at the Bedford Veterans Administration Medical Center in Massachusetts, pled guilty in January. Richard Meltz, sixty-five, could be incarcerated for up to ten years. Like Gil Valle, the three men were registered members of darkfetish net.com.

British nurse Dale Bolinger faced more charges since his arrest in February 2013. In September of that year, authorities charged him with one count of administering poison to someone, two counts of possessing an indecent photograph of a child, one count of attempting to meet a girl under sixteen following sexual grooming, and seven counts of publishing an obscene article. Convicted on all counts, he was sentenced to nine years in prison.

Darkfetishnet.com is still up and running, as are other similar websites where wannabe cannibal killers can feed their fetishes.

2

ALBERT FENTRESS
Middle School Madman

Sunday, August 19, 1979, was to have been Paul Masters's last weekend at home in Poughkeepsie, New York. Instead it was his last night on Earth.

There wasn't too much left for the eighteen-year-old to do this steamy summer Sunday; some last-minute packing, tie up some odds and ends, then load the car in the morning for the ninety-mile drive to the campus of the State University of New York at Albany, where he planned to enroll as a freshman.

His parents—Burt, a physicist, and Barbara, a homemaker and substitute teacher—had mixed emotions about his leaving home. Paul was the youngest of their five children and the last to leave the nest. Mark, twenty-four, was working in Vermont; Anne, twenty-three, was married and living in California. Steve, twenty-two, a medical student, and Susie, twenty-one, a college coed, had been home for the summer, but they would be going back to school within days. Burt and Barbara consoled themselves with the fact that Albany was only ninety miles away, and that Paul would be coming home on weekends and holidays, but for the first time in more than twenty-four years, there would be no children at home.

The five Masters children were born in New Mexico, where Burt worked on top-secret projects at the Los Alamos National Laboratory. In 1963, IBM—which occupies a sprawling 423-acre complex six miles south of Poughkeepsie—hired him to help them develop new and improved materials for use in semiconductors. Paul was just a toddler when the family of seven moved into a spacious home on Timberline Drive. It was the only home he ever knew.

They were a close-knit, traditional Catholic family. On Sundays they attended church together, and they never ate meat on Fridays, not even after the Second Vatican Council said it was okay in 1965. As the baby of the family, Paul was doted on by his brothers and sisters. He had thick dark brown hair and bright blue eyes. He was affectionate, playful, and inquisitive, and it seemed he always had a smile on his face.

"Paul was the family clown," said Burt Masters. "He loved nothing better than playing practical jokes on his older brothers and sisters."

By all accounts, a child couldn't have had a more all-American upbringing. Paul learned to ski, played baseball and football, and enjoyed tinkering with anything mechanical or electrical—especially his brothers' and sisters' cars and his mini motorcycle, which he liked to ride through the woods and fields near his home. He had permission to drive the vehicles, but not beyond the Poughkeepsie area. Like most teens, Paul was a rock-and-roll fan—he especially liked British rockers Pink Floyd, Peter Frampton, and Jeff Beck.

By the beginning of his senior year in high school, Paul had blossomed into a strapping six-foot-tall, 165-pound young man. Popular and personable, he was also handsome, smart, and athletic. Everyone who knew him agreed that he had a great future ahead of him.

"Paul was an outstanding student," recalled Louis Mosconi, one of his teachers at Spackenkill High. "He was very bright, very articulate, had a great personality, and came from a great family." Paul, the teacher added, would have been successful in any career he chose.

Burt Masters thought his youngest son would follow in his footsteps and pursue a career in either science or mathematics, and with good reason. In June, Paul graduated from Spackenkill High School with honors, ranking near the top of his class. He was a New York State Regents Scholarship winner, and the recipient of the annual Citizenship Award from the local chapter of the Masons. He excelled in math.

He was also a star player on the school's football team, the only member of the team who started on both offense—at tight end—and defense—at defensive end. In his junior year Paul helped the Spackenkill Spartans win the Hudson Valley Conference football championship. The local daily paper, the *Poughkeepsie Journal*, frequently wrote about his exploits on the gridiron.

And he was a hard worker. During the school year he earned money working as a counterman at Friendly's Ice Cream and Sandwich Shop on Hooker Avenue, near the campus of Vassar College. The summer after graduation he drove a truck, working six days a week for a local home improvement company. He saved every penny he earned for college.

While he was excited about beginning the next phase of his life, this day Paul looked forward to one last chance to hang out with his friends before leaving for college.

Just three and a half miles from the Masters's home, Poughkeepsie Middle School teacher Al Fentress was resting after a morning on the tennis court. As he neared middle age, the thirty-eight-year-old bachelor prided himself on his athletic prowess and his trim six-foot physique. In just two weeks the long summer vacation would be over, and the eighth-grade history teacher hoped he'd be able to get some more time in on the tennis court before the new school year started right after Labor Day.

Albert Francis Fentress Jr. was born in Brooklyn, New York, on July 20, 1941. He would be the first of three children—two boys and a girl—born to Elizabeth and Albert Francis Sr. When he was four years old, the Fentress family moved to Venezuela, where Albert Sr., an engineer, went to work in the oil fields. The family stayed in South America for seven years before returning to the United States. Albert Jr. was eleven years old when his parents bought a small tomato farm in Melville, New York, on Long Island.

Fentress would say that the years he spent growing up were filled with lofty intellectual pursuits like music and drama, and that he had been an honor student and the valedictorian of his high school class. His weekends and holidays, however, were more down to earth: He had to help out around the farm. Albert Sr. insisted on it, and Albert Jr. wasn't about to defy his father, a firm believer that sparing the rod spoiled the child.

He entered college with plans of becoming an engineer like Albert Sr., but switched his major to history. He also enrolled in education courses in order to qualify for a teaching license in New York State. He graduated from the State University of New York at New Paltz in 1965 and was hired to teach history to middle schoolers in Poughkeepsie.

Founded in 1687, Poughkeepsie is a city of about thirty thousand. It sits on the east side of the Hudson River, seventy-five miles north of New York City. It takes its name from the area's original settlers, the Wappinger Indians, a tribe of the Algonquin Nation. The name means "the reed-covered lodge by the little-water place," but it refers not to the Hudson but to a tiny spring a few miles south of the city's downtown.

The first whites to settle the region were from Holland. They arrived in the wake of Henry Hudson, an English explorer who sailed under the flag of the Dutch East India Company. He stumbled on the majestic river in 1609 while searching for the elusive Northwest Passage from Europe to the Orient.

The Dutch called their colony New Netherlands, but their control of the region was short-lived; in 1664 British warships sailed into the Hudson and seized control of the colony, which they promptly renamed New York. They designated Poughkeepsie the county seat of Dutchess County.

Thanks to fertile land, gently rolling hills, and an abundance of beaver, deer, and moose, the early settlers prospered, first as fur traders and later as farmers, shippers, and merchants. Protected by highlands to the north and east, the county was spared major violence during the Revolutionary War.

From the early 1800s on, a steady stream of immigrants from England, Ireland, Wales, Scotland, and Germany provided workers for the region's farms, breweries, and mills. In the years leading up to the Civil War, Dutchess County was a stronghold of abolition and a major stop on the Underground Railroad. Then in 1892, the federal government opened Ellis Island to process the waves of immigrants that were pouring into America. Because it was located in New York Harbor less than a hundred miles away, a new wave of newcomers from Scandinavia, Italy, and Eastern Europe easily found their way to Poughkeepsie and its environs.

The rich and famous of the era moved there, too. Prominent families like the Roosevelts and Vanderbilts built mansions along the banks of the Hudson in nearby Hyde Park, while Samuel Morse, the inventor of the telegraph, built his estate, Locust Grove, in Poughkeepsie. But by the time Al Fentress arrived in 1965, the city was caught in a downward spiral, its downtown plagued by crime and urban decay and the steady loss of manufacturing jobs to other states.

Nevertheless the young schoolteacher decided to make his home in Poughkeepsie. It was only twenty miles from where he'd gone to college in New Paltz, and close to some of the best ski slopes in the Northeast, and Al Fentress loved to ski. Besides, it was a two-and-a-half-hour drive from his parents' home in Melville, just far enough away from Albert Sr., with whom he'd always had a contentious relationship.

He bought a wood-frame house at 216 South Grand Avenue, on the city's affluent upper south side, not far from the campus of Vassar College. It was one of the smallest homes in the neighborhood, but the schoolteacher liked the tall trees and well-tended homes that surrounded it. What's more, it was close to the middle school—within walking distance, in fact, but Fentress almost never walked the nine-tenths of a mile. Instead, he preferred to drive to school in his cream-colored Cadillac.

He was very proud of his car, which, like all his possessions, was always kept in pristine condition. He especially liked to park the big Caddy in the teachers' lot, where it stood out next to the more modest cars his colleagues drove to school.

The Cadillac wasn't Fentress's only prized possession. He owned valuable coin and stamp collections, expensive crystal, and a set of historical signatures that included a signed and framed photo of Richard Nixon that bore a personal message to him from the thirty-seventh president. It occupied a place of honor in the center of his living room, just above the sofa. He collected books about art and history, fancied himself a gourmet cook, and spent a lot of time caring for his lawn and flower garden.

By all accounts Al Fentress was an outstanding teacher. He was passionate about history, and he had a vivid imagination. He also had a flair for drama, which he managed to incorporate into his lessons.

"He literally made history come alive," recalled former student Wayne Witherwax, who was in one of his classes in 1972. "He became a character in his lessons."

For example, if his eighth graders were learning about Napoleon, Fentress would come to school in full Napoleonic regalia. To teach his students about the horrors of segregation and racism, he'd masquerade in a Ku Klux Klan costume to demonstrate just how scary the Klan was.

When he didn't come to school in costume, Fentress showed up elegantly dressed in a three-piece suit or a Brooks Brothers blazer, a Rolex on his wrist, looking more like a Fortune 500 executive than an underpaid schoolteacher. It was an image he liked to project.

While his lessons were interesting, to his students he was a tyrant—a stern disciplinarian who ran his classroom like a Marine Corps drill instructor. They were required to keep their feet flat on the floor and their eyes straight ahead at all times. Calling out and gum chewing were strictly forbidden. His classroom was always neat and tidy, and there would be hell to pay if anyone messed it up.

In addition to teaching classes, Fentress also supervised two after-school activities—the model-building club and the chess club—and he frequently took favored students on trips.

He didn't mingle much with his colleagues at Poughkeepsie Middle School. To them he was arrogant and self-righteous, a snobby loner who gave the impression that he thought he was better than everyone else.

But Al Fentress had found his calling, or so it seemed.

He was a dedicated teacher and, as far as anyone knew, a solid citizen. But by 1978 the life he had so painstakingly constructed had begun to unravel. He craved respect, but instead of getting it he had become the frequent target of a group of toughs. They taunted the flamboyant teacher. There were snide remarks about his sexuality, even among his colleagues, and persistent rumors that he was a pedophile with a penchant for young boys.

Neighborhood punks egged his house, and once they even broke in and trashed it. On one occasion his prized stamp collection was stolen. Another time chemicals were poured on his front lawn in a pattern that burned the grass to spell "FAIRY." His car was vandalized, and raunchy magazines that he never ordered began turning up in his mailbox.

Angry and frightened, Fentress applied for and was issued a license to carry a handgun. Then he went out and bought one—a .38-caliber revolver.

As the sun set over the Hudson, Paul Masters left his home on Timberline Drive for the last time.

"Don't worry, Mom," he called to Barbara on his way out the door. "I'm only going to Leonard's house."

He walked a quarter mile to the Scenic Drive home of his friend and classmate Leonard Greenberg. He might have stayed in this evening to watch the New York Giants, his favorite football team, play the San Diego Chargers in a televised preseason game, but Paul and Leonard had been friends since junior high school and Greenberg was hosting a Sunday evening get-together for the graduating class. It would be the last one before they all headed off to college.

Meanwhile, Al Fentress sat in his home alone, driven mad, he would later claim, by a gruesome fantasy inspired by *Deliverance*, a movie he claimed he'd watched the night before.

Starring Burt Reynolds, Jon Voight, Ned Beatty, and Ronny Cox, it's the story of four city slickers on a canoe trip through the backwoods of Georgia. Their adventure turns into a nightmare when they come face-to-face with a pair of mountain men who take turns raping one of the men at gunpoint while the others watch.

The film aroused a passion in Fentress, inspiring him to write and rewrite his own versions of the brutal rape scene which he called "scripts," adding castration and murder. Hours later he would bring his macabre fantasy to life with Paul Masters in a leading role. Before the sun would rise on another day, the teen would die a gruesome death, and Al Fentress would be transformed from a dedicated schoolteacher into a heinous cannibal killer, a man who would one day be dubbed "New York's Hannibal Lecter."

The horrific crime would send shock waves across New York State. It still haunts the people of Poughkeepsie, but it would be decades before the true face of Albert Fentress would be revealed.

There was bad blood between the players on the Poughkeepsie High School football team and their crosstown rivals from Spackenkill High. It was more than a gridiron rivalry. It was personal, and the feud had been simmering for a long time, ever since a Poughkeepsie player insulted the girlfriend of a Spackenkill player. The two were itching to settle the score.

In the culture that is high school, macho football players are gladiators, which means there was no way the slight would go unanswered. Despite the threat of rain, players from both teams who were in town this evening agreed to meet at midnight at Krieger Elementary School on Hooker and South Grand, where they would watch their feuding teammates duke it out. As Sunday turned into Monday, Paul left the get-together on Scenic Drive along with some of his teammates and headed for the field of battle. It was only two blocks from Al Fentress's home.

The football players had tried to do battle the week before, when they agreed to meet at Spratt Park, but police got wind of the impending rumble and were on hand to prevent it. Tipped off again by an anonymous phone call, they arrived on the scene just in time to head off the fight.

As cops converged on the school, the teens scattered in every direction. Running alone, Paul Masters crossed South Grand, then made a right turn into the alley that ran between the homes on the east side of South Grand and those on the west side of Mitchell Avenue. Residents used it to gain access to their garages. It was also where they left their trash for collection.

As he made his way through the dark alley, Paul Masters came face-to-face with Al Fentress.

Sometime after 3 A.M., a ringing telephone roused Detective Sergeant Roland T. Witherwax from a sound sleep. The call was from headquarters. "We have a homicide on the upper south side," the dispatcher told him. "It's at 216 South Grand."

Within minutes the forty-year-old detective was dressed and pulling up in front of the home of Albert Fentress, the middle school teacher who had brought history to life for the detective's son Wayne when he was an eighth grader.

Uniformed Poughkeepsie cops were already on the scene, having been sent there in response to a frantic call from Poughkeepsie resident Enid Schwartz, the mother of Wally Schwartz, Fentress's real estate attorney. She had been alerted to trouble at the Fentress house by a phone call from her son in Hartsdale, sixty miles south of Poughkeepsie. He had been called by Fentress, which prompted him to call his mother. Mrs. Schwartz then phoned the teacher, who told her, "I shot someone." Mrs. Schwartz called the police.

When Witherwax arrived at the house, the teacher was sitting quietly on a hassock in his living room. The detective had met Fentress before, when the teacher reported the theft of his prized coin and stamp collections. This time, however, Fentress's hands were cuffed behind his back and a uniformed cop stood next to him.

He'd been taken into custody just minutes earlier by three cops from the patrol division who'd approached the house with guns drawn. One took up a position at the screened living room window and peered in while the others entered the house through the front door, which was unlocked. They waited in the vestibule while the cop at the window spoke to Fentress.

"Mr. Fentress, do you have a gun?" he asked.

"I do."

"Where is it?"

"It's on my knee."

"Throw the gun down!" the cop commanded. But Fentress refused.

"No, you take it," he replied.

With his service revolver aimed directly at the teacher, the officer at the window repeated his command. Once again Fentress refused.

"It's on my knee. It's simple. Please, just take it," he said.

Reluctant to shoot and not wanting the situation to escalate into a standoff with an armed man, the quick-thinking cop tried another tactic.

"Mr. Fentress, put both your hands on your face," he barked.

This time Fentress complied. Immediately, the officers who were waiting in the vestibule charged him. One secured the gun while the other cuffed Fentress. After patting him down, they sat the schoolteacher on the hassock.

"I shot someone. He's in the basement," he told them. While one of the officers stayed with Fentress, the other two headed for the door that led to the basement.

"There's someone here," one of them shouted.

Sprawled on the steps, about halfway to the top of the stairs, was the lifeless body of Paul Masters. The cop checked for a pulse, then returned to the living room and immediately gave Fentress the Miranda warning—informed him that he had the right to remain silent and that anything he said could be used against him in court, and that he had the right to have an attorney present during questioning.

The warning, a staple of every TV police drama since the late 1960s, was named for Ernesto Miranda, an Arizona man who, after intense questioning by detectives, confessed to kidnapping and raping an eighteen-year-old woman. It's been a requirement of police procedure since 1966, when a landmark U.S. Supreme Court decision overturned Miranda's conviction because he had not been advised of his rights under the U.S. Constitution.

"Is there anything you want to say?" the cop asked.

"No. Not until my lawyer arrives. I've already called him."

But it wasn't his lawyer who walked into the house next. It was Detective Sergeant Witherwax. The uniformed officers briefed him. They showed him the .38 they had taken from Fentress. Then one of them said, "There's a body on the basement stairs."

Witherwax went to the doorway and peered in. The body was on its side with the head toward the top of the stairs. A trail of blood led from the steps into the basement.

Since the early 1970s, Poughkeepsie cops had been required to undergo training as crime scene technicians. By 1979 every member of the detective division and many patrol officers were thoroughly schooled in latent fingerprint identification, evidence handling, and how to properly process and secure a crime scene. As he investigated, Witherwax was careful not to contaminate the scene or disturb the body in any way.

Crouching down for a closer look, the detective noticed two bullet wounds to the right side of the teen's head. He noted that he was wearing a white T-shirt and jeans. The T-shirt covered his torso, but the jeans and underpants were down around his ankles. Marks around the teen's wrists indicated that he had been tied up. A look at the teen's groin area told the detective that something very grotesque and horrific had happened there.

Witherwax was born and bred in Poughkeepsie. His wife and two sons were born there, too. He'd lived there all his life except for a stint in the Navy, where he served as a gunner's mate aboard the U.S.S. *Canberra*, a guided missile cruiser. He joined the city's one-hundred-man police force in 1963, and during his years on the job had been to dozens of bloody crime scenes. He'd seen up close and firsthand the carnage that human beings are capable of inflicting on one another, but nothing he'd ever seen prepared him for what he was looking at now: Paul's penis was missing. In its place was a gaping wound that was oozing blood.

Witherwax took a moment to regain his composure, then he carefully made his way past the corpse and into the unfinished basement. The concrete floor was splattered with blood. The walls were, too. A sponge and a bucket filled with a reddish liquid sat near the middle of the room. Lengths of clothesline were looped around a post. Several plywood boards were stacked in a corner, while a single board was propped up against a wall nearby.

More cops arrived. Even the chief of police, Stuart Bowles, was on the scene. Investigators photographed the entire house, inside and out, front and back. They collected and bagged evidence, including the .38, the clothesline, and a bloody straight razor. From the garage they removed a tarpaulin that was lying on the floor next to the cream-colored Cadillac, which they found backed in with its trunk open. Officers were even detailed to dismantle the plumbing in a futile attempt to locate the missing penis.

By this time Fentress had been put into a police cruiser and driven away from the slaughterhouse on South Grand. The car, with Fentress in the backseat, headed north on South Grand, then turned left on Hooker. It passed Krieger Elementary School, where just three hours earlier the rival football players were to have done battle. In less than five minutes it was at police headquarters, where the teacher was fingerprinted, photographed, and put into a windowless interrogation room.

As Paul Masters's body was transported from the murder scene to the morgue at Vassar Brothers Medical Center, a uniformed patrolman walked up to the front door of the Masters home on Timberline Drive. Policemen are called upon to do many things. They protect, investigate, rescue, and enforce the law. They're often asked to mediate disputes between spouses and between neighbors, and sometimes they're called upon to be the bearers of bad news. Even the most hardened veterans will tell you it's the part of the job they dread the most.

The cop rang the bell several times, knocked on the door, and waited for a response. As he scrambled out of bed, Burt Masters's first thought was that Paul had lost or forgotten his keys and was locked out, but his wife knew otherwise. Barbara Masters was the worrier in the family, and whether it was women's intuition or a mother's premonition, she knew instinctively that a ringing bell at 3 A.M. could only mean trouble.

She held her breath while her husband answered the door, praying that she was wrong. Burt hoped he would see Paul when he opened it, but instead he saw a policeman. Then he heard the words every parent dreads: "Sir, I regret to inform you . . ."

When Burt returned to their bedroom, he gave his wife the dreadful news: "Paul's been shot. Paul's dead! Bobbie, Paul's dead!"

Later that morning Burt and his son Steve drove to Vassar Brothers Medical Center. They were directed to the morgue, where they viewed Paul's body and officially identified him.

Word of the gruesome slaying reached the citizens of the Mid-Hudson Valley later that day, when the *Poughkeepsie Journal*—then an afternoon newspaper—began making its way onto their lawns and into their homes. It was front-page news: TEACHER HELD IN TEENAGER'S SHOOTING DEATH, read the headline. It ran with a black-and-white photo of a smiling Paul—his yearbook photo—and it revealed that the eighteen-year-old had gunshot wounds to the head that "apparently came from a .38 caliber handgun that belonged to Fentress."

Most of Paul's friends didn't need to wait for the paper to hit the streets to learn of his death. Their phones were ringing before 7 A.M. as they dialed one another with the shocking news.

Later that morning Al Fentress was arraigned in Poughkeepsie City Court. Peter J. Maroulis, a local attorney, stood next to him. Looking haggard and bewildered, the teacher pleaded not guilty to murdering Paul Masters. He was remanded to the county jail without bail.

The task of prosecuting Fentress fell to thirty-five-year-old Tom Dolan, a six-year veteran of the Dutchess County District Attorney's Office. Dolan had studied law at St. John's University in the borough of Queens, New York. After graduating in 1965, he joined the U.S. Army's Judge Advocate General Corps. He spent eight years in the Army, where he attained the rank of captain before resigning to join the Dutchess County prosecutor's office.

Fearing that a barrage of pretrial publicity would taint the jury pool, making a fair trial impossible, Dolan immediately ordered investigators to remain tight-lipped about the gruesome crime. But word travels fast in a small town, and in no time the rumor mill was grinding out grotesque stories of torture, rape, and mutilation. There were even whispers that Paul had been a willing participant in a macabre homosexual bondage tryst that had gone awry, and that somehow he'd had a hand in his own death.

Those who knew both men were stunned. Paul "was one of the nicest guys you would ever want to know," said a tearful Tom Finley, a close friend. Lonnie Palmer, an assistant principal at Spackenkill, told the *Journal*: "He was the type of person that other kids listened to. He had a lot of fun and a lot of friends."

As for Fentress, people on South Grand couldn't believe that he had been arrested for a murder that took place on their quiet block. Next-door neighbor Jeff Scott described the history teacher as "a nice guy." He had spoken with him at 9 P.M. on Saturday, and Fentress, he said, had seemed just fine. Another neighbor described the teacher as "a very quiet person who lived alone, never bothering anyone."

Poughkeepsie Assistant Superintendent of Schools Ronald Valenti praised the teacher, telling the *Journal* that Fentress "had an outstanding record in the district and has received several letters of commendation on his performance and involvement." Dr. Valenti added that he was "completely shocked" by the arrest.

The wheels of justice usually turn very slowly, but for Albert Fentress, at least initially, they were spinning at full speed.

On Tuesday, August 21, Dolan went to the grand jury for an indictment against Fentress for murder in the second degree. In those days New York State reserved first-degree murder, which carried a possible death sentence, for the killing of a police officer or a prison guard, or for murder committed by an inmate already serving a life sentence. The grand jury gave the prosecutor what he asked for. If convicted, Fentress would face twenty-five years to life in prison.

On Wednesday the Masters family finalized funeral arrangements, and a bewildered-looking Fentress made his second court appearance, this time in Dutchess County Court, where he was arraigned on the grand jury charge. Observers were taken aback by the teacher's appearance. His brown hair hadn't been combed and he looked like he hadn't eaten or slept in days. Instead of street clothes he was dressed in full prison regalia—an orange jail jumpsuit.

He said nothing other than his full name, "Albert Francis Fentress Jr.," and "Yes" when Judge Raymond E. Aldrich asked if he was represented by an attorney. When it came time to enter a plea, Maroulis spoke for him: "Not guilty, Your Honor."

Then Judge Aldrich ordered the teacher back to jail, but not before announcing that he would adjourn the case for thirty days in order to give Maroulis time to conduct his own investigation and prepare a defense. The entire proceeding took less than ten minutes.

On Thursday, Fentress cooled his heels in the county jail while family and friends of the slain teen gathered at 10 A.M. for a Mass of Christian Burial at St. Martin de Porres Roman Catholic Church on Cedar Valley Road. The mass is both a celebration of life and an affirmation that it hasn't ended, just changed. The symbols of the Resurrection—holy water, the pall, the Easter Candle, incense, and white vestments—remind the mourners that the promise of baptism—everlasting life—has been fulfilled.

Hundreds turned out for the service—IBMers, fellow parishioners, schoolmates, teammates, teachers, not to mention relatives and neighbors. Gospel singers from one of Poughkeepsie's black churches sang hymns, and they all joined together to sing "Let the Circle Be Unbroken." One by one, sobbing mourners slowly passed the open casket. Some knelt and prayed; others just stood and stared before moving on. Everyone was incredulous that a life so young and so promising had been snuffed out in such a mindless orgy of violence.

At the conclusion of the mass, a long line of cars followed the hearse for the short drive to St. Peter's Cemetery on Salt Point Road. There, under threatening skies, they laid Paul to rest. His missing body parts were not buried with him. As the Masters were burying Paul, the presses were rolling at the *Journal*. When the paper hit the streets that afternoon, the citizens of Poughkeepsie got their first hint of the nightmare on South Grand. POLICE CHECKING REPORT SLAIN TEEN HAD BEEN BOUND, read the front-page headline. From "sources close to the investigation," readers learned about the clothesline that cops found looped around a post in Fentress's basement. They also learned that the teen's body bore marks that had been made by the line, and they found out that police were still baffled as to the motive behind the grisly murder.

Al Fentress was the only person who could shed light on the mystery, and he wasn't talking, so investigators looked elsewhere for answers. Paul's family was no help. They had never heard of Albert Fentress. Although their mailing address was Poughkeepsie, the Masters's home was located outside the city limits, in the Town of Poughkeepsie, which meant neither Paul nor any of his siblings had attended Poughkeepsie Middle School. None of the teen's friends knew anything about the middle school history teacher, either.

Investigators interviewed Paul's coworkers at Friendly's. Waitresses there recognized Fentress as a customer. It was possible that the two men had known each other, but no one could say for certain.

Then, on August 30, previously tight-lipped investigators let it be known that Masters's body had been dragged halfway up the basement stairs. They also revealed that Fentress had tried to remove the teen's body from the house. Still kept from the public was the extent to which Paul Masters had been tortured and sexually mutilated. That information would remain a closely kept secret for more than a year.

On Tuesday, September 4, Al Fentress was back in court. Once again he said nothing as Maroulis tried to persuade Judge Aldrich to release the teacher to a secure psychiatric facility. A psychiatrist hired by the defense, Dr. Arnold Bucove, had evaluated the teacher. His conclusion: Fentress was suicidal.

"Dr. Bucove is afraid he will make a serious effort to kill himself," Maroulis told the judge. He asked Aldrich to release the teacher on his own recognizance, or on bail set at no more than ten thousand dollars, which, he said, was all the teacher could afford, telling the judge, "I realize the charge against the defendant is most serious. Ordinarily I would not request recognizance or bail in that low an amount, but I am concerned about his welfare."

But the judge was skeptical. He told Maroulis what he thought of Bucove's diagnosis—weak and unconvincing. Nevertheless, the judge didn't close the door. He reserved decision and ordered the attorney to report back to him in two days with a detailed description of the facilities he had in mind for his client.

In the meantime, jailers were ordered to keep an eye on the teacher, but they were unable to put him in the "birdcage," the only jail cell that would enable them to maintain an around-the-clock suicide watch. It was already occupied by the defendant in another

gruesome case that sent shivers through the Mid-Hudson Valley—
one Joseph Fischer, a sinister-looking fifty-year-old drifter who had
been paroled from a New Jersey prison in June 1978 after serving
twenty-five years for murder.

He was being held without bail for the stabbing death of
seventy-seven-year-old Claudine Eggers, a retired State Department of Mental Hygiene employee with whom he had been living.
After he was arrested, Fischer told detectives he'd committed as
many as twenty murders from Maine to California, all in the year
he'd been out.

Two days later Fentress and Maroulis were in court again, and
once again Fentress stood silently while his lawyer withdrew his
request for bail. Fentress, he said, had decided to stay right where
he was, in jail. The lawyer didn't explain why.

By now investigators had received the autopsy report. It confirmed
that Paul Masters had been sexually mutilated, his penis and testicles
sliced off with a razor. That was horrific enough. What sent shivers
through everyone who was privy to the report was the pathologist's
finding that the mutilation occurred before the teen died. The report
also confirmed that the teen had been shot twice in the head at close
range. The slugs were sent to the state police lab for ballistics tests
along with the .38 that had been taken from Fentress.

When a bullet is fired, it picks up microscopic markings as it
travels through the gun's barrel. Those markings are unique to
the weapon that fired it. To determine whether or not the slugs
taken from Masters's skull came from Fentress's gun, technicians
shot off a round from the teacher's .38. Next, the fired bullet was
recovered and examined under a comparison microscope, side by
side with the slugs that were removed from Masters's skull. To no
one's surprise the bullets and the gun matched perfectly.

———

Roland Witherwax hardly ever discussed police business with his family, and on the rare occasions when he did, he was careful to spare them the most gruesome details, and he never became emotional. But when the veteran detective talked about the murder of Paul Masters, he had to fight hard to hold himself together.

"He'd been a police officer for eighteen years, and this was the first case I'd ever heard him become emotional about," said his son Wayne, recalling a phone conversation he'd had with his father about the murder of Paul Masters.

"As he was telling me details that we'd never discussed before, I couldn't tell if he was crying or not, but I remember he had to stop talking a few times."

The details were horrific. As Paul Masters made his way through the alley, Al Fentress, armed with a fully loaded .38 that he'd hidden under his shirt, was lurking behind his house, itching for a confrontation with the kids who had been harassing him. When Paul came by, Fentress confronted him and demanded to know why he was there.

Masters told him about the cops and the brawl at Krieger Elementary School, and that all he wanted to do was get back to his home on Timberline Drive. Convinced that Paul meant him no harm—and that he had no connection to the youths who had been harassing him—Fentress offered to drive him home. The teen gladly accepted, but first Fentress said he'd have to retrieve his car keys from the house. He invited Paul to come inside with him.

Once they were indoors, the teacher was able to get his first good look at Paul. He liked what he saw—a muscular teen with flawless skin, high cheekbones, bright blue eyes, and thick brown hair fashionably cut in the style of the day. He was manly but still boyish, and Al Fentress was very fond of boys.

The "scripts" he'd written earlier began running through his mind. Over and over, his own more brutal version of the rape scene from *Deliverance* played out in his head. He was aroused—and he decided that Paul wasn't going to leave.

Fentress offered the teen a drink, but not before making sure Paul was at least eighteen.

"It dawned on me I was serving him alcohol," Fentress would explain later, adding, "It would have been horrendous if I was serving somebody underage." Then he poured one for himself.

They drank vodka together and made small talk. Fentress brought out some snacks for his guest and watched as he ate, all the while imagining what he would do to the handsome young man.

They talked some more, then the teacher asked Masters if he would help him move some plywood boards that were stored in the basement. It was a ploy. After they moved just one board, Fentress drew his gun. When the teen turned around to get another board, he was looking into the face of evil, and looking down the barrel of a .38 that was just inches from his head.

Paul, his reflexes slowed by the vodka, didn't resist as the teacher tied him hand and foot to a post in the basement.

"Why are you doing this? What do you want?" the terrified teen asked. What the teacher wanted most was Paul's penis, and he wanted it in his mouth.

Excited, Fentress undid the young man's jeans and let them drop to the floor, then he pulled Masters's underpants down to his ankles. With his own organ swelling with desire, Fentress moved in. He opened his mouth and took the teen's penis into it.

He expected it to become hard, desperately wanted it to become hard, but no matter what he did—licked it, swirled it, or sucked it—the penis didn't swell.

This wasn't in the script! This wasn't how it was supposed to happen! A wave of humiliation washed over Fentress. It turned into rage, then into anger, and finally hatred for Masters for not following the script and for arousing such passion in him and then disappointing him.

Fentress stalked off, only to return a moment later with a razor blade in his hand and castration on his mind. He ordered his captive to spread his legs, then he dug the blade into the teen's scrotum.

With the first touch, Masters screamed and writhed in pain. He begged Fentress to stop.

"Don't do this. You don't have to do this," he pleaded. But Fentress was unmoved. He dug the blade deeper into the teen's scrotum, slitting it open.

"Don't fight. Just make it easier," he told Masters. "I can't stop now. Don't you see that?"

He did stop, however, but only long enough to raise his .38 to the teen's skull and pull the trigger. Masters slumped, mortally wounded but still alive.

The bloodletting wasn't over, however. Fentress went back to work—he craved the teen's testicles and removed them along with the scrotal sack. Then he went to work trying to cut off his penis. It wasn't easy, and it was messy. With blood spurting from the partially severed organ, he wielded the blade like a saw until it was completely severed.

Once again Fentress fired a round into Masters's head; then he gathered up the severed body parts and took them up to the kitchen, where he put them in a frying pan, added some cooking oil, and let them sauté. While they simmered in the pan, Fentress brought out a plate from his finest set of china, and a setting from his best silverware; then he sat down and ate the organs.

Anthropologists say that cannibalism is the ultimate form of vengeance, a demonstration of the victor's triumph over the vanquished, and eating the flesh of a slain enemy is nothing new in the annals of human history. But if Fentress felt a sense of triumph as he devoured the teen's penis and testicles, it was short-lived—he turned his attention to disposing of the body.

He decided to wrap it in a tarp he had in the garage, put it in the big Caddy's trunk, and drive it into the woods, where he'd dump it. But removing the 165 pound corpse from the basement proved much more difficult than he'd expected. He managed to drag the body halfway up the basement stairs but stopped when he stumbled. Next, he tried to clean the bloody mess in the basement with a bucket and a sponge, but the blood and gore proved too much to wipe away.

Exhausted, Fentress took a shower and put on clean clothes. Just before 3 A.M. he phoned Wally Schwartz. Within minutes of hanging up, Fentress's phone rang. It was Enid Schwartz, Wally's mother. "I shot someone," he told her.

Then he sat down in his living room and waited.

Al Fentress sat in the county jail for fifteen months. During that time he was allowed to teach history classes to other prisoners. When he wasn't teaching, he read up on the law, especially the statutes and cases that were applicable to his own. Meanwhile his lawyers maneuvered to free him.

It's the defense attorney's job to protect his client's constitutional rights, and to do whatever he can within the law and the rules of criminal procedure to make it impossible for a jury to find his client guilty beyond a reasonable doubt. In this case, that seemed impossible.

Fentress, after all, had the murder weapon on his lap when he was arrested. And he admitted to Enid Schwartz and the first cops on the scene that he had "shot someone." What's more, there was overwhelming evidence of consciousness of guilt—he tried to clean up the crime scene and dispose of the body. And overshadowing everything was the repulsiveness of the crime itself. A conviction, it seemed, was all but certain.

Maroulis had his work cut out for him, but the veteran attorney was undaunted. One month after Fentress's arrest, he went into court with a motion to dismiss the murder charges against his client, arguing that the evidence police seized from 216 South Grand was taken without a warrant and therefore constituted an illegal search and seizure, a violation of the teacher's rights.

Perhaps anticipating that his motion to dismiss would be denied, Maroulis offered an alternative motion to suppress all the evidence that police removed from the house without a search warrant, as well as all statements Fentress made to police before they advised him of his Miranda rights.

If the motion was granted, the gun, the clothesline, and the tarp, as well as Fentress's admission to Mrs. Schwartz and the police officers that "I shot someone," would be inadmissible in court, too. With no evidence, no witnesses, and no admission of guilt, there would be no case against the teacher.

Maroulis also contended that the attorney-client confidentiality privilege had been violated when the first attorney Fentress called, Wallace Schwartz, called his mother, who then called police.

Attached to the motion was a signed and carefully worded affidavit from Fentress. It was the accused cannibal killer's first on-the-record statement about what happened.

On Aug 20, 1979, shortly after 2 a.m., I called my attorney, Wallace L. Schwartz, at his home in Hartsdale, N.Y., and sought his advice regarding a serious legal problem which had just occurred. Shortly after that telephone conversation terminated, I received a call from Mrs. Enid Schwartz (of Poughkeepsie), the mother of my attorney.

Sometime after my conversation with Mrs. Schwartz, I observed a car with no lights on going by my house. It was a police car. At that moment I was seated on a hassock, and could see out the living room window to the street. I was waiting for the arrival of my attorney.

As I sat there, I could see another police car drawing up with its lights out. I then heard the police coming up on my lawn and heard someone call my name.

I looked up at the door and two policemen were standing in the vestibule. Another policeman was by the window and he inquired, "Do you have a gun?" I said I did.

The affidavit then went on to relate the conversation he had with the cop at the window and what happened next: "The policeman took the pistol and they all came in, fanned out and started searching the house. One of them asked, 'What's happened here?' I answered him candidly." But Fentress didn't say what he told them.

Then he claimed that officers continued to question him after he arrived at police headquarters, even though he made it clear to them that he would make no statement until he could confer with his attorney. At some point, he said, he asked a cop to call Maroulis, but the cop refused.

If Al Fentress was hoping he'd found a get-out-of-jail card, he was in for a bitter disappointment. The motion to dismiss was denied, as was the motion to suppress. What's more, the court turned a deaf ear to his claim that there had been a breach of attorney-client confidentiality.

Maroulis appealed, but New York's Court of Appeals, the state's highest court, turned him down, too. Then he tried to bring the case to the U.S. Supreme Court, but the high court wouldn't take it.

Fentress didn't have many options left. He could go to trial, but given the horrific facts of the crime, conviction and a life sentence seemed certain.

He could offer to plea bargain, but the DA was in no mood to cut a deal with a defendant whose crime included torture, sodomy, castration, and cannibalism. Besides, even if the DA agreed to the lesser charge of manslaughter, Fentress would be looking at fifteen years in a state penitentiary where he'd be rubbing elbows with hardened convicts who were not likely to hold a flesh-eating homosexual in high regard.

Or he could invoke the insanity defense.

The idea that insane defendants should not be held responsible for their actions by reason of mental illness has been a part of Anglo-American law since the nineteenth century, ever since 1843, when Daniel McNaughton attempted to assassinate Britain's prime minister, Robert Peel, because he believed the prime minister was conspiring against him. McNaughton killed the prime minister's secretary, Edward Drummond, by mistake, was acquitted by reason of insanity, and was sent to a mental institution where he remained for the rest of his life.

Under New York law, Fentress could enter a plea of not responsible by reason of mental disease or defect, the equivalent of not guilty by reason of insanity. To succeed, Maroulis would have to prove that Fentress either didn't know his criminal behavior was wrong, or that he was unable to stop himself from committing a criminal act. If he could do that, the teacher would be remanded to one of the state's mental hospitals, where he'd receive treatment until he was deemed cured. When that day arrived, he'd be free to leave.

It was his best hope, but it was a difficult mountain to climb, especially if the case went to a jury. For one thing, Fentress didn't appear insane. In fact, he appeared very normal. Looking at him, no one would ever have thought that he was capable of killing another human being, let alone dismembering and eating the body parts. What's more, he had no history of mental illness. Besides, during all the months he'd been in the county jail neither he nor his attorney raised the issue of his mental state.

And there was yet another hurdle to overcome: His case had been handed off to another judge—Albert M. Rosenblatt, a former Dutchess County district attorney. He had served six years as the county's top prosecutor before taking the bench in 1976. Not surprisingly, he had a reputation as a tough law-and-order judge. When he wasn't on the bench, the judge could be found playing squash—he was nationally ranked—or on the ski slopes— he was a certified ski instructor.

Fourteen months after he was arrested for the murder of Paul Masters, Al Fentress was back in court, this time to change his plea from not guilty to not responsible by reason of insanity. The law required that psychiatrists for both the defense and the prosecution evaluate him. If both agreed that he was insane when he murdered and mutilated Paul Masters, Judge Rosenblatt would have no choice but to commit the history teacher to a mental hospital. If the shrinks disagreed, the question of insanity would be left to a jury to decide.

Once again the defense hired Dr. Arnold Bucove, while the prosecution called on Dr. John Train of Larchmont. The doctors would examine Fentress separately, then testify as to their diagnoses at a hearing in open court.

On Friday, October 31, 1980, Halloween Day, an overflow crowd squeezed into Judge Rosenblatt's fourth-floor courtroom. Countless more were turned away. They came to hear what the two psychiatrists had to say. Among them were the Masters and dozens of their friends who turned out to show their support for the still-grieving family.

Security at the courthouse was tight, tighter than it had ever been. There had been rumors of a possible attempt on Fentress's life, so everyone who entered the courthouse was patted down by deputies, then required to walk through metal detectors.

It had been more than a year since Paul was murdered, and the Masters still did not know all the horrific details of their son's death. They knew that he had been mutilated, but they didn't know how, and they were still in the dark about the circumstances that brought Paul and Fentress together. They were about to find out from the mouth of prosecutor Tom Dolan and the psychiatrists.

The fourth-floor courtroom in the venerable courthouse was already crowded when deputies brought Al Fentress in. He took a seat at the defense table, between his attorneys, Maroulis and cocounsel Thomas O'Neill. Dressed in a three-piece suit, his hair neatly combed, Fentress looked more like a lawyer than his lawyers. He showed no emotion as he waited for the proceedings to begin.

The hearing was really a formality. Under the rules of discovery, Fentress was already aware that the two psychiatrists were in agreement that he was out of his mind and, therefore, legally insane when he butchered Paul Masters and devoured his remains. What's more, they also agreed that he was dangerous. The psychiatrists recommended that Fentress be remanded to a maximum-security psychiatric facility.

With a nod from the judge, Tom Dolan rose to speak. He and Maroulis had met earlier and stipulated to the facts of what happened on South Grand on August 20, 1979. Now the prosecutor was going to read the stipulation into the record.

Masters, he said, had been at Krieger Elementary School "as an observer." He fled the scene when police arrived and was confronted in the alley by Fentress.

"At the time of this confrontation, Fentress was armed with a loaded .38-caliber pistol, which was a licensed firearm. Fentress, apparently on the mistaken impression, thought Masters, who it should be noted was a completely innocent victim in this entire matter, was an intruder."

At this point, Dolan was interrupted by a question from the bench.

"He was under the impression that Masters was an intruder?" the judge asked.

"That is correct. Erroneous impression. Masters is completely innocent in this entire affair."

"He is a stranger to Fentress?"

"Yes, sir. Prior to August 20, 1979, neither man was known to each other."

"Go ahead."

In that brief exchange, Judge Rosenblatt put an end once and for all to the sordid rumors that had swirled around the case from day one—that the two men had known each other and that the teen had participated willingly in a sadomasochistic orgy that somehow had gotten out of hand.

Dolan continued. "Fentress approached the victim Paul Masters and engaged him in conversation. When it became apparent that Mr. Masters was not a threat or an intruder, the defendant invited him in for a drink. After a conversation during which both men consumed a quantity of alcohol and had something to eat, Fentress enlisted Masters's help in moving some plywood in his basement."

The prosecutor paused, his voice quivering, his hand shaking. He cleared his throat and went on.

"He then removed the trousers and underwear from Masters and attempted to fellate him. When he was unsuccessful, he used a razor blade to castrate the victim, who was alive and conscious."

From the spectators came muffled sobs. Bobbie Masters hunched over and let out a loud moan. Even total strangers had tears rolling down their cheeks.

Dolan himself turned pale, then continued. "Prior to the completion of the mutilation, Fentress shot Masters in the head, right side of the head at contact range with the .38-caliber revolver. A second shot was fired moments later. Fentress then completed the castration and placed the removed organ in the frying pan with oil for cooking. When the cooking was completed, he ate the remains."

Several onlookers, nauseated by what they had heard, left their seats and rushed from the courtroom. Bobbie Masters burst into tears. After a brief pause, the prosecutor continued. He recounted Fentress's unsuccessful attempt to remove the body from the house and to wipe away the blood, his phone call to Wallace Schwartz, and his conversation with Enid Schwartz, including his admission to her and to police "that he had either shot someone or killed someone in his home."

Then Dolan disclosed the results of the autopsy, which "found the cause of death instantaneous with two penetrating gunshot wounds of the skull and the traumatic amputation of the penis and scrotal contents."

The prosecutor then concluded by saying, "If Your Honor please, were there a trial in this case, those are the facts the People would prove beyond a reasonable doubt."

"Is it your claim here that based on your view of the evidence as prosecutor and that of your office and of the psychiatrist who you engaged, that you could not convict the defendant of the charge?" Judge Rosenblatt asked.

"While we could factually prove he committed those acts, we could not convict him of the charge because of the defense of insanity."

Maroulis stood and addressed the bench. "Your Honor, the defense states for the record that the facts are substantially correct and we take no exception to them."

With that, the court was ready to hear from Dr. Train, the psychiatrist who had examined Fentress for the prosecution.

He began by describing the teacher as a very intelligent man who had always strived to be superior. But deep down he was really very insecure and incapable of living up to the image he had created for himself. Fentress feared that he was really "a nonentity," so he acquired impressive and expensive possessions, which, the psychiatrist said, "were as important to him as the essence of his being."

"As long as Mr. Fentress could be an outstanding teacher, an unusually outstanding person, he could function," Dr. Train said. But he was incapable of absorbing stress. It undermined the "carefully constructed image which masked his anxieties and protected himself from his fears." Under stress, Fentress's personality disintegrated into psychosis.

Harassment from gay-bashing teens pushed the teacher over the edge. They stole his prized stamp collection and vandalized his car. Not long before the murder, they burned "FAIRY" on his lawn. That led him to feel an "unfamiliar rage," and he began fantasizing about taking revenge against the perpetrators. The rage, Train said, stemmed from his inability to "absorb the stress or lack of respect he thought the vandalism signified."

But that wasn't all. Also contributing to the psychosis that led him to kill was the discovery that he had "homosexual tendencies." Train said Fentress told him of three meaningful relationships he'd had with women, and of two homosexual encounters he'd had that left him "disgusted with himself."

Fentress told the doctor that he heard noises in the street the night of the murder and went out to investigate. Fearing that he was about to be attacked, he armed himself with his .38. When he met Masters, thoughts of *Deliverance* and the "scripts" he'd written began running through his mind once again.

He admitted a sexual attraction to Masters, which the teen did nothing to encourage, and then rage at the teen "for making him feel he was a homosexual." At that point, Dr. Train said, Fentress suffered a complete personality breakdown that resulted in "primitive cannibalistic behavior."

He only snapped out of it when he tripped while trying to carry Masters's body up the basement stairs. It was the stumble on the stairway that snapped him out of his psychotic state, the psychiatrist said.

The defense psychiatrist, Dr. Bucove, concurred, and both doctors testified that they were absolutely certain that Fentress could not have faked insanity because the clinical techniques they used in their respective evaluations assured them that he was being truthful.

But the proceeding wasn't over. Instead, it was continued until Monday, when a third psychiatrist, this one representing the Masters family, would take the witness stand to render his opinion on the mental state of Albert Fentress. It was a departure from the usual procedure, but Judge Rosenblatt stretched the rules and agreed to the Masters's request for a third evaluation from a psychiatrist hired by them. In this case, Rosenblatt explained, "The victim's family should be heard."

On Monday, November 3, Dr. William Johnston took the stand. "There is no doubt in my mind that he was psychotic" when he butchered Paul Masters and ate his body parts, the psychiatrist declared. In other words, Fentress was out of his mind, unable to think clearly, respond emotionally, communicate effectively, or understand reality.

What's more, the teacher suffered from "an obsessive-compulsive personality." His mental state "could be described as fragile for approximately two years prior to the incident." Then Dr. Johnston said, "Albert Fentress really was two personalities. The personality that was doing these things could not be controlled by the other personality. It was beyond his control to stop."

Dolan had a question for the psychiatrist. "Is this a clear-cut case of insanity?"

"This is a clear case, in my opinion."

After Dr. Johnston stepped down from the witness stand, Judge Rosenblatt looked over to the defense table. He ordered Fentress to step forward. The time had come for the teacher to own up to what he had done.

As he stood up and stepped forward, every eye in the courtroom was on him.

"If looks could kill, he'd have been struck dead right then and there," recalled Dave Gettleman, Paul Masters's football coach, who was in the courtroom that day.

Under oath and in a clear voice that indicated neither sorrow nor remorse, Fentress said, "I understand that I was the instrument and the cause of the death of Paul Masters."

"And do you reaffirm what you told the psychiatrists?" Rosenblatt asked.

"I very painfully affirm that."

When Fentress finished speaking, Judge Rosenblatt announced that he accepted Fentress's plea and declared the middle school teacher not responsible by reason of insanity. Then he tried to assure everyone that the cannibal killer wouldn't be walking the streets anytime soon.

"This court believes there is no real possibility of the defendant's release for a number of years, particularly in the face of diagnostic testimony, which has established that the defendant's present condition is such that he may, under certain conditions, be capable of repetition of his act, in the throes of an illness which all three psychiatrists described as all but incurable."

A phalanx of deputies led the teacher from the courtroom. Within hours he was turned over to the state's Office of Mental Health, which sent him to the Mid-Hudson Psychiatric Center, a fortresslike maximum-security facility in New Hampton that's home to the state's most dangerous criminally insane offenders, but his treatment and custody, indeed his life, would remain under court supervision.

For the moment, the people of Poughkeepsie could breathe a sigh of relief. They thought the case was over, but the fact of the matter was that it was just beginning.

Nineteen years later the cannibal wanted out.

After nearly two decades in state mental hospitals he was cured, no longer a danger. He said so, and his treatment team said so.

At fifty-seven, his hair was grayer now, and there were deep lines in his face, but Al Fentress was still trim and fit-looking, and very well dressed.

Fentress had been confined on Long Island since 1985, when he was transferred from Mid-Hudson to the unfenced Kings Park Psychiatric Center. Initially diagnosed as schizophrenic, his diagnosis had been revised by doctors: When he butchered Paul Masters and ate his organs, Fentress was suffering from a "brief reactive psychosis" brought on by stress. The ex-teacher, they said, was no longer a dangerous man.

That's how Dr. John Train, one of the psychiatrists who had testified about Fentress's mental state in 1980, saw it. "They've had him under a microscope for so long, and he has never shown any troubling behavior," the doctor declared in 1994. "His treatment was excellent. He is no longer mentally ill or dangerous."

Thanks to the insight gained from two decades of treatment and psychotherapy, the "brief reactive psychosis" Fentress had suffered—the one that led him to lure Paul Masters into his home, torture, sodomize, and butcher him, then eat his genitals—was now considered just a one-time thing, a mere spasm. That Albert Fentress no longer existed and he wasn't coming back.

"If there was the smallest possibility that I could do something like that again, I would never have made an effort to be released," Fentress said.

The psychiatrists, psychologists, and social workers on his treatment team agreed, and they were recommending that he be allowed to reenter society through a state-operated halfway house with little supervision. He'd be required to attend weekly treatment sessions and would have to observe an 11 P.M. curfew, but he would be free to get a job and he wouldn't have to register as a sex offender—that law wasn't passed until 1995.

So on Tuesday, April 6, 1999, he was in court, this time in Riverhead, the seat of government for Suffolk County, Long Island's easternmost county. Under New York law, psychiatric patients, no matter how heinous or depraved their crimes, cannot be detained if they are no longer mentally ill, so Fentress was petitioning the court for release. It would be up to the state to prove that he was still mentally ill and that he would pose a danger to the community if he were to be released.

That job fell to Laurie Gatto from the state attorney general's office and Assistant Dutchess County District Attorney Wayne

Witherwax, Fentress's former pupil and the son of Detective Sergeant Roland Witherwax, the lead detective on his case.

The younger Witherwax was a college student home for summer break in August 1979, when his father got the phone call that sent him racing to Fentress's house on South Grand. He'd been handling the case since 1992, the year Tom Dolan was elected to the county court bench.

"I was the one in the office who was the most familiar with the case, so I volunteered to handle it," Witherwax explained.

He'd been sparring with his former teacher since 1993, when Fentress first went into court to petition for permission to leave Kings Park on unescorted day trips.

To the staff at the psychiatric center, Al Fentress was a model patient. They rewarded his exemplary behavior by allowing him to roam the grounds freely, and by taking him off the grounds to shop in local stores and to visit Albert Sr. and Elizabeth in Melville, a thirty-minute drive from the hospital.

He'd been on hundreds of supervised trips to beaches, baseball games, and museums. He even wangled his own private room, one of only two in the thirty-six-bed unit where he was confined. Thanks to his parents, the room was air-conditioned and complete with a bed, a desk, and a dresser.

To his fellow inmates and the residents of Kings Park, a village of sixteen thousand on the North Shore of Long Island, he was known simply as "The Cannibal." When local residents got wind of the plan to allow Fentress to leave the grounds unescorted, they rallied. Scores of protesters formed a human chain. They carried signs that said "Confine the Cannibal" and "Keep Kings Park Safe."

A judge denied the cannibal's request to be allowed off the grounds unescorted, but not before local politicians were swept up in the anti-Fentress fervor, too. The publicity even brought

Fentress a new moniker—"New York's Hannibal Lecter," after the fictional cannibal of the same name portrayed by Anthony Hopkins in 1991's *The Silence of the Lambs*.

When the state closed Kings Park in 1995, Fentress was transferred to Pilgrim State Psychiatric Center in Brentwood. A year later he filed his first request for permission to move to a halfway house.

Doctors who testified for the state said that although he'd been a model patient, there was always the chance he could become psychotic again. After a three-day hearing, Fentress's bid was denied again. Disappointed but undaunted, he tried again the following year, only to be denied yet again.

Now on April 6, 1999, he was back in a courtroom, hoping that a six-person jury could be persuaded to turn him loose.

"Mr. Fentress is not ready to be released," declared Gatto, the assistant attorney general, in her opening remarks. "He's vulnerable and susceptible to the same psychotic behavior that emerged in 1979."

Witherwax argued that Fentress's behavior in the "cocoonlike" environment of a state psychiatric center was no indication of how he'd fare on the outside.

"What about the stresses of the real world that are out there, that he'll have to face if he's released?" he asked rhetorically.

Pitted against them was Kim L. Darrow, an experienced attorney from the state's Mental Hygiene Legal Services Office. He had been appointed to represent Fentress. Not surprisingly he saw things differently.

"Mr. Fentress is a better, a more healthy man today than in 1979. He can safely be moved to a supervised, state-operated community center," he declared.

In Darrow's view, Fentress's treatment had been a rousing

success. He was a model inmate who tutored other patients, ran a successful desktop publishing workshop with his fellow patients, and never hurt anyone.

The lines were drawn. With the jury paying rapt attention, each side presented its own mental health experts to support its case during a proceeding that would stretch over three weeks.

Dr. Juliana Kanji was the first to take the stand. Testifying for the state, the diminutive psychiatrist, a 1977 graduate of Khyber Medical College in Peshawar, Pakistan, described Fentress as "extremely intelligent and fully capable of taking care of himself." Then she added, "But he still does have a mental illness."

On day two of the trial Dr. Frederic Gannon testified that he saw no improvement whatsoever in Fentress's mental state since that steamy night in August 1979 when he murdered and mutilated Paul Masters.

"For 18 years there's been no change," the psychiatrist declared.

"He ought to be embarrassed, regretful, but it's the other way around. He's quick, impulsive, unrevealing, guarded and defensive."

He was targeted by neighborhood troublemakers because he was "effeminate," the doctor said. "They picked on him because of his homosexual nature."

On day three, the chief medical officer for the state's Board of Mental Health, Dr. John Oldham, took the stand. He testified that Fentress would be unable to adjust to the stresses of everyday life. He'd "come apart at the seams, presenting a danger to himself," and to others.

"You can do fine in a given environment, but if you leave it you won't necessarily stay that way," he explained.

During cross-examination, Darrow poked a hole in Oldham's

testimony that was big enough to drive a bus through—he got the doctor to acknowledge that he'd never met or interviewed Fentress or anyone on his treatment team. Oldham admitted that he'd based his opinion solely on his review of Fentress's medical file. It was a stunning admission, one that resonated with the jury.

Monday, April 12, was the fourth day of the proceeding. On this day jurors heard from the state's final expert, Dr. Abraham Halpern, an eminent psychiatrist from Mamaroneck. He said he feared that Fentress would, if stressed, lapse again into a psychotic state.

"All the positives that one sees in Mr. Fentress's adjustment to the hospital are related to the fact that he is in a structured situation," the psychiatrist said. "The only major question is, what happens when these controls are lifted?"

"Has there ever been a misadventure?" Darrow asked on cross-examination.

"No."

"He has abided by all the rules in the hospital?"

"Yes. But he did not break any rules so far in the hospital because he did not want to. He was seeking his ultimate release."

The next day the jury heard testimony from members of Fentress's treatment team. They all echoed the opinion of Lawrence Panza, a supervising psychologist at Pilgrim State and the first to take the stand in support of Fentress's release.

"He has been so horrified by his own actions that he's always concerned about any stress or anxiety and will seek to disarm it appropriately," Dr. Panza said. "He does not have a mental illness."

Dressed in a blue blazer, necktie, and slacks, Fentress listened attentively and took notes. In less than twenty-four hours he would take the stand in his own behalf. He'd have to overcome the devastating testimony of the state's psychiatrists who, in the course of their testimony, had revealed the depraved details of his crime.

Thursday, April 15, was a sunny but blustery day on Long Island. It was also income tax day, but that was of no concern to Al Fentress. He was finally getting his chance to persuade a jury that he deserved his freedom.

The confessed cannibal killer and his escort, a staffer from Pilgrim State, arrived in court early. Dressed in a blue blazer and gray pants, Fentress looked more like a gentle grandfather than a heinous cannibal killer.

If he was nervous, it didn't show as he walked to the witness stand. He had had many years to prepare for this moment. If the jurors were hoping to hear the gruesome details of the horrific crime from his lips, they would be disappointed. Fentress never mentioned it. Instead he spoke at length about his daily routine and the life of good works and prayerful contemplation he had been living.

"I get up at about five-thirty," he said. "My day starts with a prayer." Then he showers, watches the news on TV, and has a cup of tea. He shaves, dresses, eats breakfast while reading the *New York Times*, then walks without an escort to the computer center, where he teaches other patients. He gets along with everyone—staff and other patients. Every Sunday he attends Roman Catholic Mass.

Throughout the two hours he spent on the witness stand, the cannibal was mostly calm and articulate. He even shed tears, but they weren't for Paul Masters. He broke down when his attorney asked about his parents. They had both passed on—Elizabeth in

1995 and Albert in 1998—and he missed no longer being able to visit with them.

He was still close to his younger brother and sister, but he didn't go to their homes. They both wanted to be at the hearing to show their support, he said, but he asked them to stay away because he feared media coverage would upset his nieces and nephews. "They both have children and my interests should not be above those children."

Then he recalled the last conversation he had with his mother a few days before she died from cancer.

"She told me that one of the things that was very much on her mind was that she was never able to speak to Mrs. Masters," he said, choking back tears.

Barbara Masters, Paul's mother, died in 1995 at age sixty-six, haunted until she drew her last breath by the horrific death of her youngest child at the hands of Al Fentress.

He continued: "God counts the tears of mothers, that's a Jewish saying. I was aware that even if I never got the chance to speak to Mrs. Masters, I knew she and Mom would be speaking shortly."

Then he stopped talking, lowered his head, and began sobbing. He pulled a white handkerchief from his jacket and began dabbing his eyes.

It was a heartrending performance, as good as any Fentress had ever given to his eighth graders, and one that moved the jurors, some of whom were seen wiping their eyes, too. Judge Harry E. Seidell even called a short recess to give Fentress time to compose himself before Gatto and Witherwax began their cross-examinations.

When court resumed, it was Gatto, the assistant attorney general, who went first, but the thirty-seven-year-old Fordham Law School graduate took the good cop approach, leaving the bad cop role for her colleague, Dutchess County Assistant District Attorney Wayne Witherwax.

He tried to question his former teacher about the slaying but was thwarted by a ruling from the bench. Because Fentress's attorney didn't ask the cannibal about the murder during his direct examination, the state couldn't ask him about it during cross-examination.

"Our cross was limited to the scope of the direct testimony," Witherwax explained to reporters during a break in the proceeding.

"Mr. Darrow was careful not to ask about the facts of the crime. He was careful that his questions limited Mr. Fentress's exposure in cross-examination."

Witherwax and his ex–history teacher got into a heated exchange when Fentress told the prosecutor that he was being persecuted by the Dutchess County district attorney.

He said he had been "troubled" when he learned that a former student, the son of the lead detective on the case, was working hard to keep him confined.

"I had some ethical questions about that," the cannibal killer said angrily. "You were a former student of mine. In 1993 I was notified that you had taken on the case. The last time I saw you, you were not a grown man. Your father was also the lead detective."

His testimony ended with a final question from Witherwax. "You said you didn't want your brother and sister here because you didn't want them to be subjected to the stress of the media, is that right?"

"Yes."

"You didn't think about the stress and shame you would put your family through when you killed Paul Masters, did you?"

"Objection!" Darrow shouted.

"Sustained," said the judge. And on that note Fentress walked away from the witness stand.

When Judge Seidell instructed the jury, he told them that they had to answer two questions during their deliberations: Is Albert Fentress suffering from a mental illness that requires care and treatment? And is he a danger to himself or to others? If Fentress was to be released to a halfway house, five of the six had to answer no to at least one of the questions.

On Thursday, April 21, after more than six hours of heated deliberations that lasted over two days, the jury announced that it had reached a verdict. As they filed into the courtroom to deliver their decision, the six men and women gave no hint of their decision. The jury foreman handed a slip of paper to the clerk, who handed it to Judge Seidell. He handed it back and the clerk announced the verdict.

As to question one—Is Fentress suffering from a mental illness?—by a vote of six to zero the jury said yes.

Fentress's shoulders drooped; he lowered his head. He sighed. Before the clerk continued, he took a deep breath and held it.

As to the second question—Is he a danger to himself or the community?—by a vote of five to one the jury said no.

Al Fentress finally had his get-out-of jail card. He hugged Darrow, who had a message for the community: "You don't have anything to worry about," he said. "He's already been in the community hundreds of times." But he wasn't free yet. It would be at least several more weeks until his release could be arranged.

Meanwhile Gatto and Witherwax were stunned. "We were perplexed by the verdict," Witherwax recalled. "We couldn't understand why, if they believed he was still mentally ill, they didn't think he was still dangerous."

Keith Twining had an explanation. After shaking hands with Fentress and congratulating him, the thirty-three-year-old juror told reporters, "The horrific nature of the crime didn't sway us. What convinced me was the fact that he remained consistent with his behavior for the past nineteen years." He added that he thought Fentress had the potential "to be a good citizen and an asset to the community."

Albert Fentress was just a few weeks away from freedom. It was so close the confessed cannibal killer could taste it, but first Judge Seidell would have to issue conditions for release. Meanwhile powerful voices demanded that the cannibal be kept right where he was.

On of them was George Pataki, New York's governor. "Justice can never be achieved as long as individuals like Albert Fentress can commit vicious crimes and hide behind an insanity plea to avoid the prison time they deserve," he declared.

New York State Attorney General Eliot Spitzer deplored the verdict, too. "Given the unspeakable crime which he committed, and his mental condition, we feel Fentress remains a danger and therefore should not be released."

The *Poughkeepsie Journal* called the verdict "ludicrous." The crime, the paper said, "rates as the worst in local history—far more heinous than ordinary murder."

Dutchess County District Attorney William Grady blasted the verdict. "It is beyond my comprehension; the man is a cannibal," he fumed. "It's an utter outrage that a killer who is still mentally ill will be released into a community without supervision to wander about freely."

It didn't happen. Witherwax and Gatto filed a motion to set the verdict aside, which is just what Judge Seidell did on June 10. The judge called the verdict "irrational."

"To believe the petitioner was mentally ill but did not need inpatient care and treatment, the jury would have to believe that outside the hospital setting the petitioner would somehow, on his own, develop self-control and not pose a danger to others," he explained.

"There is simply no valid line of reasoning and permissible inferences which could possibly lead rational men to the conclusion reached by the jury on the basis of the evidence presented at the trial."

Darrow appealed Judge Seidell's decision, and the appeals court ordered a new trial for the cannibal.

The stage was set for yet another court appearance, but the proceeding wouldn't turn out the way Fentress hoped.

On Tuesday, December 4, 2001, Al Fentress was back in state supreme court in Riverhead. It was opening day in his latest bid for freedom. Just eighty miles away in Manhattan, hundreds of workers were going about the grim task of pulling bodies—many of them residents of Long Island—from the smoldering ruins of the World Trade Center. But the sun was shining, the weather was unseasonably warm, and Albert Fentress's prospects for freedom never looked brighter.

A new jury had been impaneled and a different judge, James M. Catterson, was on the bench. Wayne Witherwax, Fentress's longtime nemesis from the Dutchess County DA's office, had left the prosecutor's office and would no longer be opposing his bid. In his place was Ed McLoughlin, an intense prosecutor with a rapid-fire style and a knack for going for the jugular. Assistant State Attorney General Laurie Gatto wasn't there, either. Instead Denis McEligott would handle the case for the attorney general's office.

In his opening argument, McLoughlin reviewed the facts of the case for the five-man, one-woman jury. He told them how in 1979 Fentress had lured eighteen-year-old Paul Masters into his home in Poughkeepsie, gave him vodka to drink, then tied him up, sodomized him, shot him in the head, sautéed his genitals in oil, then ate them. The panel remained stone-faced.

McLoughlin continued. Fentress, he told them, was found not guilty by reason of insanity and was committed to state mental hospitals. Now he was making a bid for release. "We think he needs more work," the prosecutor said. "He's not ready, and we're asking you to leave him where he is."

"Albert Fentress did commit these horrifying crimes," said Fentress's attorney, Kim Darrow. "He knows it. We know it. Nobody denies them.

"But that is not what this is about. We are not here to judge his guilt but to decide if he is ready to be released from the psychiatric facility. And the law provides that if and when treatment yields results, and he is no longer a threat to society, he must be released."

He reminded the panel that Al Fentress was not on trial for murdering Paul Masters. The issue for them to resolve was whether or not the ex-teacher had been cured enough to function beyond the confines of a mental institution.

Dr. Amy Klein, deputy clinical director at Pilgrim State, was the first to testify. "The same basic risk factors he had in 1979 when Paul Masters was killed are still there," Dr. Klein said. "If it happened once, there's still a risk of it happening again."

On cross-examination, Darrow asked if Fentress had ever acted "inappropriately" during his confinement.

"No."

"Has he ever committed a violent act?"

"No."

Next to testify was New York City psychiatrist Michael Stone. He didn't pull any punches. Fentress, the doctor said, "remains dangerous and needs further treatment to have some grasp of the forces that prompted him to do what he did."

Based on his own examination and review of the records, Stone concluded that the ex-schoolteacher was a sexual sadist, a personality disorder "that doesn't go away." And he didn't believe Fentress's claims that his fantasies were triggered by the movie *Deliverance*.

"I believe he had such fantasies much longer than two or three days," the psychiatrist said. "They were in his head for months or years."

He disagreed vehemently with previous diagnoses that Fentress had suffered a brief psychosis brought on by stress and regressed to a state of primitive cannibalistic behavior when he murdered Paul Masters.

"The fact of the matter is there is no such thing as a person under stress regressing to a cannibalistic state," Dr. Stone declared. The psychiatrist called Fentress "a self-hating homosexual" who was acting out a "revenge fantasy" when he murdered the teen.

A psychologically "significant" event, one that Fentress relived for the psychiatrist, occurred when he was a child. His father caught him masturbating and threatened "to cut his balls off." The attack years later on Paul Masters "was the little boy grown up and getting back at the father," Stone said.

It had been a bad day in court for the cannibal.

The next day would be even worse.

On Wednesday Al Fentress took the stand. After recounting his life as a patient at Pilgrim State, it was DA McLoughlin's turn to cross-examine him. The prosecutor started off slowly and methodically, gradually easing into questions concerning Fentress's sex life prior to the night Paul Masters was murdered, and his treatment since. McLoughlin's tone was pleasant, his manner friendly. He was setting a trap.

Fentress testified that he had been completely honest and forthcoming with his therapists over the years. As a result, his problems with repressed homosexuality were all in the past.

The ex-teacher acknowledged that he performed oral sex on Paul Masters before killing him, and he admitted that he engaged in two other consensual homosexual encounters prior to the murder, but they were consensual. He said he told his doctors all about them and he emphatically declared that he'd never abused anyone, certainly not a minor.

It was the declaration McLoughlin was hoping for. The DA pounced. "Is it true that in the spring and summer of 1979 you orally sodomized [a ten-year-old neighbor] up to twenty times?"

It was as if a bomb had exploded in courtroom 205A. Fentress's jaw dropped. His face flushed. "Good grief," he stammered.

Darrow rose to his feet shouting, "Objection!" Immediately McLoughlin announced he had a secret witness.

Darrow complained to the judge that the prosecutor had "ambushed" him by not notifying him about the witness prior to the start of the trial, and he asked the judge to bar the man from testifying.

McLoughlin calmly explained that he had a sworn statement from a now thirty-three-year-old former neighbor detailing the abuse that occurred during tutoring sessions in Fentress's home in 1979. The man had come forward just days before the trial got under way and was ready and willing to testify.

The stunning revelation stopped the proceeding dead in its tracks. Judge Catterson adjourned the hearing until Monday. As Fentress hurried from the courtroom, he denied the allegation.

"I'm shocked," he told reporters angrily. "The district attorney was reckless."

Back at the state hospital in Brentwood, a very distressed Al Fentress sought out Sylvia Marks, a social worker and confidante.

"He said there was a bombshell at the courthouse," Marks remembered.

Fentress, she said, told her that the prosecutor from Dutchess County had a surprise witness, a man who claimed the ex-teacher had abused him more than a dozen times while tutoring him in math when he was ten years old.

What Al Fentress said next, she said, "knocked me for a loop."

"He said he never tutored anyone," Marks recalled. The social worker couldn't believe her ears—"He denied the tutoring, not the molestation."

Newspapers in New York pounced on the story. CANNIBAL STUNNED BY GHOST FROM PAST, blared the *New York Post*.

SHOCKER CLOUDS FENTRESS TRIAL, boomed the *Poughkeepsie Journal*.

Long Island's *Newsday* was only a bit less strident: NEW ALLEGATIONS MAY KEEP KILLER AT PILGRIM.

New York Attorney General Eliot Spitzer chimed in: "This information undermined Fentress's claim that the killing was an isolated incident and that he had never abused anyone else," the

AG declared. "It demonstrated conclusively that Fentress had lied to his doctors, his lawyers, and the court."

When the trial resumed on Monday morning, there was a notable absence: Al Fentress didn't show. If he had, he would have been required to take the witness stand so that McLoughlin could complete the cross-examination he'd started on Thursday.

Through his lawyer, Fentress denied the explosive claim. Darrow then informed the judge that Fentress had decided to withdraw his bid for freedom because there was not enough time to investigate the young man's allegations.

"He's extremely disappointed that a false allegation has temporarily derailed his case," the lawyer said.

Ninety days later, Fentress was back in court for a hearing. This time he wasn't fighting for his freedom. Instead, he was fighting to stay at Pilgrim State, where he enjoyed unsupervised grounds privileges and weekend furloughs. Prosecutors demanded that he be moved to a maximum-security facility like the austere Mid-Hudson Psychiatric Center, where he'd been from 1980 to 1985. Not surprisingly, Fentress didn't want to go.

All his years of therapy had been for naught, the prosecutors said, because Al Fentress never told his therapists that he'd abused anyone other than Paul Masters.

Fentress's lawyer opposed the move. "He is no longer a physical danger to others," the attorney declared. He filed an appeal. The legal wrangling dragged on for eight months, until Monday, September 23, 2002, when Judge Catterson would hear the state's motion to send Fentress back to a secure facility.

Laurie Gatto was in courtroom 205A for the attorney general's office, Ed McLoughlin was there for the Dutchess County DA, and the neighbor who was ready to testify in December to the abuse was on the witness stand.

For years Curtis St. John didn't talk about what had happened to him when he was a ten-year-old in Poughkeepsie living just two blocks from Albert Fentress. Over the years he managed to keep up with the comings and goings of the schoolteacher. He first contacted the Dutchess County DAs in 1992, after he read in the newspaper that the cannibal had petitioned the court seeking un-escorted furloughs from the Kings Park Psychiatric Center. An investigator thanked St. John and told him his testimony wouldn't be needed. When he learned in December 2001 that a jury would consider Fentress's bid for freedom, he again put in a call to the DA. This time prosecutors were very interested in what the married father of two had to say.

Choking back tears, St. John recounted how Fentress lured him into his house on South Grand by offering to tutor him in math, and abused him. He recalled their first session: "We were on the couch when Mr. Fentress ran his hand up my leg."

In later visits the teacher forced him into oral sex, he said. The abuse continued until the teacher was arrested for killing Paul Masters. St. John told no one about the abuse until 1992.

During the December trial, Dr. Amy Klein, a psychiatrist from Pilgrim State, had testified that Fentress still suffered from the same "basic risk factors he had in 1979." She didn't want to see him released then and she certainly didn't want to see him released now.

As far as she was concerned, the cannibal's failure to honestly talk about his pedophilia with his therapists undermined twenty-three years of psychotherapy.

"Psychotherapy is effective only if both players are willing to participate, and the key is an honest, open relationship with the therapist," she explained.

"So honesty is important?" Gatto asked.

"Obviously. Otherwise what's the point?"

On Tuesday McLoughlin called Michael Stone, a clinical professor of psychiatry at Columbia University. Stone had testified in December, too. Like Dr. Klein, he believed that Fentress had not been cured. His lack of truthfulness rendered treatment "null and void," the psychiatrist declared. He said St. John's testimony was consistent with his previous diagnosis of Fentress.

"Choosing someone who was too young to give consent, like a ten-year-old boy, can be part of the progression of sexually sadistic acts," he added.

In December, Stone had said Fentress was a sexual sadist. Now he broadened his diagnosis to sadistic pedophilia with narcissistic and obsessive/compulsive personality disorders.

"He's self-centered with very little empathy for others."

On Wednesday Al Fentress took the stand in a preemptive strike. A second ghost from his past, a former student who'd read about St. John's testimony, had come forward, too. He was scheduled to testify on Thursday. Fentress, it appeared, was trying to do damage control in advance of the former student's testimony. In a sworn statement, the student, now a thirty-five-year-old father, told prosecutors that he was eleven years old when Fentress molested him.

From the witness stand the cannibal denied abusing St. John, and he insisted he had no recollection of molesting the other boy.

McLoughlin pressed him. Is it possible he molested both youngsters but repressed the memory?

"It's entirely possible," Fentress replied.

"Do you now believe their stories are true?"

"Yes . . . I think they are two highly credible individuals at this point."

"Could you have molested other boys?"

Fentress hesitated. He avoided answering directly. Instead he muttered, "I pray there were no others."

At long last Al Fentress had been unmasked; the veil of deception he'd hidden behind had been ripped away, revealing him for what he had been all along—an evil sexual predator.

The gruesome murder and castration of Paul Masters had not been a one-time lapse into a stress-induced psychosis. Fentress had been a wolf in sheep's clothing all along. He preyed on children, betrayed their trust and the trust the community had placed in him. For twenty-three years he duped dozens of well-meaning therapists who went to bat for him, declaring him worthy of special privileges that allowed him to roam free while he was a patient at Kings Park and Pilgrim State. They even put their careers on the line when they pronounced him cured and recommended his release.

It was anticlimactic, but on Thursday the second man took the stand, breaking the silence he'd kept for twenty-three years. He was still in great pain, he said, and he requested that his name not be revealed. The news outlets covering the proceeding cooperated.

His testimony was gripping. He had been a lonely Poughkeepsie Middle School student in September 1978 when he joined the school's chess club. Fentress, he said, lured him to his home with an offer to teach him the game.

"It started with him tickling me," the man recalled, his voice breaking. "At some point, he reached into my pants." The encounters progressed to kissing, then to oral sex.

"He enjoyed kissing me," the man said. "He would hold my head. He would force his tongue into my mouth." Then he said Fentress "coerced" him into oral sex. The encounters, which ended in the spring of 1979, took place beneath the teacher's prized possession—his personally signed photo of Richard Nixon.

On Friday Judge Catterson issued his ruling. He ordered the cannibal back to Mid-Hudson. Fentress, the judge said, "possesses both a dangerous mental disorder and is a physical danger to himself and others."

He said the cannibal reminded him of author Hannah Arendt's words about Nazi war criminal Adolf Eichmann when he stood trial in Israel: "The deeds were monstrous, but the doer was quite ordinary, and not even monstrous."

Fentress's attorney asked Catterson to stay the ruling pending an appeal, but the judge declined.

"I will not substitute my judgment for the psychiatrists at Pilgrim," he declared. Later that afternoon Al Fentress was in a van on his way to the Mid-Hudson Psychiatric Facility. In less than three hours he was there.

Since opening its doors in 1974, the facility has housed some of New York's most dangerous offenders, men and women who were judged either incompetent to stand trial or criminally insane. There are no open wards at Mid-Hudson, and the campus is closed, which means Fentress will not be allowed to roam the grounds unfettered like he did at Kings Park and Pilgrim, and he won't be getting any furloughs—they're not allowed.

EPILOGUE . . .

- *Burt and Barbara Masters,* Paul Masters's parents, left Poughkeepsie and moved to San Jose, California, not long after Fentress was declared not guilty by reason of insanity. Barbara succumbed to cancer in 1995 at age sixty-five, heartbroken until the day she died. She never stopped believing that Al Fentress's claim of insanity was nothing more than a ruse to escape prison. Burt Masters remarried and is living in Hawaii. His second wife is named Barbara.

- *Roland Witherwax* retired as a detective lieutenant in April 1983 and moved to Florida, where he died in 2001 at the age of sixty-two.

- *Wayne Witherwax* left the District Attorney's Office and is a law clerk to a county court judge in Dutchess County.

- *Curtis St. John* has devoted his spare time to counseling men who, like him, have been victims of sexual abuse. Prosecutors say his courage in coming forward was what convinced Judge Catterson to decide against releasing Albert Fentress.

- *Judge Tom Dolan* stepped down from the bench in 2010. His advice to lawyers: "Be on time. Be prepared. Tell the truth."

- *Albert Fentress,* the middle school madman, is still at the Mid Hudson Psychiatric Center.

3

JOHN WEBER
The Husband from Hell

"I was surprised, it tasted good."

That's what John Weber told an investigator in Phillips, Wisconsin, a small town of fifteen hundred about one hundred miles south of Lake Superior. But he wasn't talking about jailhouse food. Instead he was describing one of his sister-in-law's breasts, which he had cooked and eaten, along with other body parts.

On a chilly November night in 1986, seventeen-year-old Carla Lenz, a beautiful and shapely high school senior, vanished from her home seven miles south of Phillips. Her older sister, Emily, was married to John. He had been questioned when Carla first went missing, as had all her relatives, but the six-foot-six-inch factory worker was never a suspect.

John Ray Weber came into the world on November 4, 1963. He was the second of two children born to Lawrence and Marguerite Weber. The marriage was Marguerite's second. John and

Albert Fentress on December 4, 2001, during a hearing at the Suffolk County courthouse.

Photo by Karl Rabe. Reprinted by permission from the Poughkeepsie Journal.

Exterior of Albert Fentress's home at 216 South Grand Avenue in Poughkeepsie.
Peter Davidson

Paul Masters encountered an armed Albert Fentress in the alley behind the middle school teacher's house.

Peter Davidson

Albert Fentress talks to the media on September 25, 2002, in the Suffolk County courthouse. On the witness stand the confessed cannibal acknowledged he may have molested at least two young boys in the months and weeks preceding his murder of teenager Paul Masters.

Photo by Karl Rabe. Reprinted by permission from the Poughkeepsie Journal.

Paul Masters was a star football player for the Spackenhill High School Spartans.

Photo courtesy of Burt Masters

Paul Masters's gravesite at St. Peter's Cemetery in Poughkeepsie, New York.

Peter Davidson

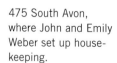

Above: John Weber's mug shots were taken September 5, 1988, the day he was arrested for beating his wife, Emily. *Photo courtesy Price County Sheriff's Office*

Right: John Weber as he looked in 2006.

Wisconsin Department of Corrections

475 South Avon, where John and Emily Weber set up house-keeping.

Photo courtesy Craig Moore

The exterior of Gary Heidnik's house of horrors at 3520 North Marshall Street in Philadelphia.

Photo by Sam Psoras. Reprinted by permission from the Philadelphia Daily News.

A sheriff's deputy holds the door of the holding area open as Gary Heidnik is taken into court.

Photo by Michael Malley. Reprinted by permission from the Philadelphia Daily News.

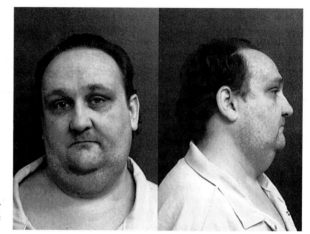

Nathaniel Bar-Jonah's intake photo when he arrived at the Montana State Prison.

Montana Department of Corrections

1216 First Avenue South, Great Falls, Montana, the home of Nathaniel Bar-Jonah in 1996. Officers found bones in the garage behind the triplex, but they weren't Zach Ramsay's. *Photo by Stuart S. White. Reprinted by permission from ZUMA Press.*

Nathaniel Bar-Jonah leaves court, August 1, 2001, in Great Falls, Montana.

Photo by Stuart S. White. Reprinted by permission from ZUMA Press.

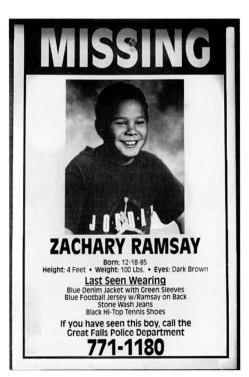

MISSING

ZACHARY RAMSAY

Born: 12-18-85
Height: 4 Feet • **Weight:** 100 Lbs. • **Eyes:** Dark Brown

Last Seen Wearing
Blue Denim Jacket with Green Sleeves
Blue Football Jersey w/Ramsay on Back
Stone Wash Jeans
Black Hi-Top Tennis Shoes

**If you have seen this boy, call the
Great Falls Police Department**

771-1180

Posters with Zachary Ramsay's description plastered the city of Great Falls after his disappearance.

Photo by Stuart S. White. Reprinted by permission from ZUMA Press.

The house Marc Sappington shared with his mother and where he murdered Terry Green and Alton "Freddie" Brown. *Wyandotte County Appraiser's Office*

A more recent photo of Marc Sappington.
Kansas Department of Corrections

his older sister, Kathy, had four half siblings from their mother's previous marriage.

The Webers were a well-known and established family in the Phillips area. They owned property in town and an eighty-acre spread ten miles to the north, and at one time they operated a food market in Phillips—Weber's Grocery. Lawrence and Marguerite worked hard to create a wholesome and loving home for their children, but almost from the beginning it was clear that there was something wrong with John. He was the family misfit, his behavior often bizarre or downright destructive.

He was nothing like his older siblings. They were popular and successful at almost anything they did. His older half brother, Leslie Ray Alm, graduated with honors from the United States Military Academy in 1973, when John was ten. Les was a star distance runner and the winner of the coveted Army Athletic Association trophy, which is awarded each year to West Point's most outstanding athlete. He served five years as a commissioned officer in the United States Army, earned a Ph.D., and is currently a university professor and department chairman. Another sibling, a half sister, was a straight-A student through high school and college.

As for John, he was the kid the other kids at Phillips Elementary School picked on. He was easy to pick on, too, because he never stood up for himself. He whined and cried easily and often. He wasn't athletic and he didn't do well in school. Marguerite referred to John as the "dummy" of the family. On several occasions John ran away from home.

He was a chronic bed wetter. His parents tried everything. They even installed a special device that would sound an alarm when he started urinating in bed, but nothing they did helped.

He also liked to set fires—he lit his first when he was just four years old and would have burned the house down on more than one occasion if alert family members hadn't quickly extinguished the flames. When he was in the eighth grade, his school desk mysteriously went up in flames.

And he was a thief. He regularly stole money from Weber's Grocery, the mom-and-pop store his parents ran until 1973. John's paternal grandfather had left it jointly to his wife, John's grandmother, and Lawrence Weber, John's father.

Not surprisingly, the other children in Phillips didn't want to play with John. As a result he spent a lot of time alone in his room, where he fantasized about an imaginary friend. He first appeared when John was a fifth grader, and he never left. Whenever John had a mishap or got into trouble, he'd blame his imaginary pal. His sister Kathy would hear him sometimes, speaking in two distinct voices and carrying on serious conversations, even arguments, with his make-believe buddy. She even caught him talking and gesturing first as himself, then as someone he called "Natas," which spells Satan backward.

As he matured, John's fantasies turned sexual and very bizarre, and many of them involved his sister Kathy. When he was home alone, he liked to dress up in her clothes and pretend that he was a woman. He'd fantasize about tying her up and torturing and raping her.

When John was thirteen, Kathy came across a stack of bondage magazines while she was cleaning his room one day. The X-rated publications were filled with photos of women gagged and bound with ropes or chains. There were also photos of women being whipped, and pummeled with fists and paddles.

At first, fifteen-year-old Kathy didn't know what to do. She showed them to Marguerite, who promptly threw the X-rated publications in the garbage. But that didn't put an end to John's affinity for hard-core pornography. He rebuilt his collection, but this time around he was more careful about where he stashed it.

As he grew older, John's fantasies grew darker and even more sadistic than the ones depicted in the bondage magazines. He'd imagine shoving knives, bottles, and safety pins into women's rectums and vaginas. He spent hours writing down his sick fantasies in spiral notebooks that he hid away. Sometimes he'd copy sexually explicit stories word for word from the magazines, adding his own personal twist—he'd insert the names of girls he knew, most often his sister Kathy or one of her friends, or one of his schoolmates.

For his birthday one year, John was given a tape recorder. He wasted no time making voice recordings of his perverted fantasies. They turned him on. To satisfy himself, he'd look through bondage magazines and masturbate.

More often than not Kathy was the object of his lust. From the time John was ten until he turned fifteen, her bras, swimsuits, and panties would disappear. One day she found some of them in his room all cut up.

At times his lust would turn into wrath—on at least two occasions he put his .22-caliber rifle to Kathy's head and threatened to pull the trigger. Both times she managed to calm her younger brother down and talk her way out of the life-threatening situations.

On another occasion, he smashed a beer bottle over her head.

"I was extremely afraid of him," she said. At times she was so scared she stayed awake all night. Kathy had good reason to fear her younger brother: On the night he bashed her over the head with a beer bottle, he had loaded the back of the family's Ford Bronco with clothesline, chains, plastic tape, scissors, a shovel, an axe, and his .22.

"Everything was ready for me to be hauled away in it," Kathy recalled.

It took a while, but the Webers finally came to the realization that John was seriously mentally ill. They committed him to a clinic in Marshfield, which admitted him to its Child-Adolescent Unit. He was treated by Dr. Harold Fahs, a clinical psychologist. According to Dr. Fahs, John was uncooperative and resisted treatment. The psychologist even offered an ominous prediction: John, he said, would one day wind up in jail for seriously harming a woman.

In the summer before his senior year of high school, John was again admitted to a hospital for psychiatric treatment. Doctors at the Wausau Hospital Center in Wausau prescribed antipsychotic drugs. Despite the medications, John was a difficult patient for them to treat, too. He lied to his doctors and was less than honest with them during therapy sessions. His therapists said John was a classic sociopath.

After five weeks of intense inpatient treatment, John was transferred to a group home in LaCrosse. While there, he enrolled at Logan High School for his senior year and graduated in 1981. Within days he enlisted in the U.S. Army for a three-year hitch.

Despite his long and well-documented history of mental health issues, John managed to find a home in the Army. He did well in basic and was trained as a helicopter mechanic. He served honorably for three years, first at Fort Carson in Colorado and then in Germany. While in the service, he developed a serious drinking problem and even experimented with LSD and marijuana. He also picked up a two-pack-a-day smoking habit. When his hitch ended in 1984, John returned home to Phillips. He moved back into his old room in his parents' house at 417 South Avon Avenue. Kathy had moved out, so John was the only one living at home with Lawrence and Marguerite.

Tiny Phillips—population fifteen hundred—is the county seat of Price County, 1,252.6 square miles of forests, lakes, streams, and rivers that's home to fifteen thousand men, women, and children. They are 97 percent white, 54 percent female, and 193 miles from St. Paul, Minnesota, the nearest city with a population of two hundred thousand or more. It's also logging country and a hunter's paradise. From the time he was a young boy, Lawrence would take John hunting for deer and grouse, and fishing for trout, walleye, and sturgeon. Sometimes they would camp out in the woods. As soon as he arrived home from the Army, father and son were trekking through the woods in full hunting gear or casting their fishing lines in one of Price County's streams.

After a few weeks of rest and relaxation, John went looking for work. He landed a job at the Cayouga Wreath Factory in nearby Fifield, where he worked alongside Caroline Lenz and her son Gene Jr. Through them he met eighteen-year-old Emily, Gene Jr.'s twin and the oldest of Caroline and Gene Lenz Sr.'s two daughters. He also met the Lenzes' other daughter, Carla.

John was attracted to both of the Lenz daughters, but he decided he was in love with Emily, a five-foot-four-inch, 113-pound beauty whose curly ash blond hair reminded him of actress Farrah Fawcett. She was warm, friendly, and outgoing, while he was soft-spoken, sullen, and withdrawn.

Despite the differences in their personalities, John, twenty-two, and Emily, nineteen, were married on August 6, 1986, almost two years after first meeting in the fall of 1984. Carla was Emily's bridesmaid. The Lenzes approved of the marriage wholeheartedly and welcomed John into their family with open arms. He impressed Gene Sr. as a hard worker. The Lenzes might have felt differently if they'd known about his mental history or his drinking problem, but nearly two years would pass before they would learn what was on their son-in-law's mind and in his heart.

John and Emily set up housekeeping at 475 South Avon, a block away from Lawrence and Marguerite's home. The house was owned by the Webers, who rented it to the young couple for two hundred dollars a month.

Their marriage got off to a rocky start. They bickered constantly. Again and again, Emily caught John in lies about his drinking, and lies about his collection of raunchy bondage magazines. A few weeks before the wedding, she intercepted a letter John had written to Carla. In it he apologized for trying to kiss her and begged her not to tell Emily. When Emily confronted him, he said he had been drinking when he wrote it, and he assured her that there was nothing between him and her younger sister.

There had been a more sinister incident that raised some eyebrows around Phillips. About a month before the wedding, John bought a 1977 Pontiac Sunbird from a local teenager named John Kenney Jr. Weber became enraged when the old car's transmission didn't work properly. Two days after John purchased the car, the teen was run over by a freight train. He had been lying on the tracks and didn't move as the train barreled toward him, its engineer frantically blowing the whistle. An autopsy indicated that Kenney was drunk. His death was ruled an accident.

"He got what he deserved," John told Emily, who chalked the teenager's death up to an unfortunate coincidence.

John began drinking more. He was working as a laborer at Winter Wood Products, a factory that manufactured tables, park benches, and wheelbarrow handles. He also worked a second job at Marquip, a factory that produced machinery for the paperboard and carton industry. After a shift, he'd join his colleagues at a nearby bar, where he'd have five or six beers before heading home; then at home he'd knock off a twelve-pack almost every night.

And he began wetting the bed again. What's more, he was unable to perform sexually with Emily—the only way he could achieve orgasm was by masturbating.

Emily was understanding and tried to be reassuring, but John felt humiliated. In October, less than two months after they walked down the aisle, the couple split up. Emily moved back in with her parents, and John turned to Carla for marital advice. She was a good listener and was eager to help her sister and brother-in-law patch up their marriage. Carla, recalled Caroline Lenz, "was always willing to listen to other people's problems."

At about eleven o'clock on the night of November 12, 1986, Carla answered the telephone. The teen was at home looking after her nine-year-old brother, Joe, while their mother, Emily, and Gene Jr. worked the night shift at the Phillips Plastics Corporation. Gene Sr., a long-haul trucker, was on the road and wasn't expected home for a few more days.

After hanging up the phone, Carla put her jacket on and left the house. She told Joe that she'd be gone for a few minutes, but when Caroline, Gene Jr., and Emily arrived home from work,

Carla was nowhere to be found. They searched the house and the surrounding area, then called the Price County Sheriff's Department to report Carla missing.

From the outset, Sheriff Michael Johnson suspected foul play. For one thing, Carla took neither clothes nor money, and all her makeup was still in her room. She'd even left her driver's license behind. She was getting along well with her parents and siblings, and as far as anyone knew she wasn't involved in a serious relationship with a boy. What's more, she was doing well in school. She had even completed all her homework assignments the night she vanished.

Johnson and his deputies scoured the area. They handed out flyers and put up posters with a photo and a detailed description of the missing teen. The FBI, Wisconsin State Patrol, and surrounding police agencies were alerted. A reward was offered. John pitched in, too, distributing flyers and offering suggestions as to what might have happened to his sister-in-law. He even pointed his finger at men he thought might have had something to do with Carla's disappearance.

"There's no sense worrying about her," John told the Lenz family one day. "She's probably dead."

Incredibly, almost no one ever suspected John Ray Weber. However, one person had a hunch that he knew more than he was letting on—his sister Kathy. Years later she admitted her suspicions.

"Carla and I looked very similar," she said. "As soon as I saw her picture in the paper I knew that he had something to do with it." Kathy, however, kept her suspicions to herself.

"I just felt it was sick of me to think that way," she explained. "I felt guilty for even thinking those thoughts."

One year to the day that Carla disappeared, a second Phillips woman vanished. Shelly Hansen was twenty-three, single, and pregnant when she went missing. As far as anyone knew she was happy about her pregnancy and looking forward to having her baby. The day she disappeared Shelly was even showing pictures of the fetus—she'd had an ultrasound in the morning—to her friends and anyone else who happened to cross her path. Her car was located, but it gave no clues about what had happened to her—no blood, no signs of a struggle. A ten-thousand-dollar reward was offered, but no one ever came forward with information about her whereabouts.

The unexplained disappearance of two young women on the same date just one year apart sent shudders through the close-knit community. Things like that didn't happen in Phillips. Authorities and townspeople feared that a serial killer was in their midst.

Two months later, Emily and John agreed to give their marriage another try, but the reconciliation was short-lived. They separated again in May. Emily told her husband that she was ready to begin her life over again without him and that they should end their marriage.

John took it hard. He moved back into his parents' home, convinced that Emily had been cheating on him. He filed divorce papers in January 1988, but just weeks before the divorce would have become final, the couple agreed to get back together. This time they sought the help of a marriage counselor, who steered them to a Minneapolis urologist, a specialist in impotence.

The doctor diagnosed John's problem as the result of poor circulation. He prescribed papaverine, a powerful medication that widens blood vessels, allowing more blood to flow into them. Before making love, John would inject the base of his penis with the medication. It was painful, but it worked, at least for a while, and it gave John a much-needed boost to his ego.

But he was still drinking. Although he wasn't a nasty drunk—instead of becoming violent he would withdraw and brood—on at least one occasion he roughed Emily up, pushed her head against the bathtub, and wouldn't let her leave the house or use the phone.

Despite the outburst, as the 1988 Labor Day weekend approached, John and Emily seemed to be doing well. They talked about building a home on an isolated eighty-acre plot of land north of Phillips that his parents owned. Before the holiday weekend ended, John would use that hope as a ploy to lure Emily to the remote spot, where he planned to torture, mutilate, and kill her.

Until Sunday night, the Labor Day weekend had been an uneventful one in Phillips.

Patrolman Alan Lobermeier was on duty at the police station when the phone rang and the caller identified himself as John Weber. He said he was calling to report that his wife, Emily, had been kidnapped and beaten up on Saturday night while walking past the Normal Building in downtown Phillips, a three-story structure that at one time had served as a training center for schoolteachers but had been converted to offices for the Price County Health Department and Department of Human Services.

John told Lobermeier that Emily's abductors had driven her to a wooded area, beaten her, and left her naked. She managed to walk home, arriving there in the wee hours of the morning all bruised and battered. He told Lobermeier that he had cleaned his wife's wounds in the bathtub, then phoned his mother-in-law, who came to their house and drove Emily to the nearest hospital, Flambeau Medical Center in Park Falls, twenty-seven miles from Phillips. Emily was in the Intensive Care Unit, in critical condition. John said he was calling from the hospital.

Lobermeier asked John to stop by the police station to fill out a report when he returned to Phillips later in the evening. Then he notified Craig Moore, Phillips's thirty-nine-year-old police chief. Moore was at home, but he left immediately and arrived at the station a few minutes later.

Originally from Michigan, Chief Moore grew up in Phillips and graduated from Phillips High School. He had been a cop since 1972. He joined the Wisconsin State Patrol not long after he came home from Vietnam, where he served with the U.S. Army's 9th Infantry Division. He was awarded two Purple Hearts for wounds he received in combat. In 1976, he became a detective with the sheriff's department in Manitowoc County, south of Green Bay. Three years later he moved to Phillips to become the city's assistant chief of police.

He didn't stay there long. Three years later he was appointed chief of police in Greybull, Wyoming, a cowboy town of twelve hundred near the Bighorn National Forest. He stayed there until 1987, when he returned to Phillips as the new chief of its four-man department.

The mustachioed Moore was a seasoned investigator, and he wasted no time taking charge of the case. After conferring with Al Lobermeier, the chief placed a call to his counterpart in Park Falls to request that one of their officers be dispatched to the hospital to interview and photograph Emily. Then he headed for the location where John claimed the abduction had taken place. He expected to find some indication—a purse, a shoe, or some other item—that someone had been forcibly snatched from the street and shoved into a car, but he found nothing.

Next he drove over to John and Emily's residence at 475 South Avon and knocked on neighbors' doors, asking if they'd seen or heard anything unusual. No one remembered anything out of the ordinary, so Moore returned to the station.

John walked in at nine thirty. He was distraught and nervous. Moore had seen the lanky factory worker around town from time to time, but had never had any dealings with him. Carrying a yellow legal pad and some printed forms, he brought John into a windowless interview room on the main floor. Even before he sat down, John began repeating what he had told Lobermeier on the phone three hours earlier, and then some.

He said that he and Emily were at home Friday night watching television. At about ten thirty she announced that she was going to walk downtown for a bite to eat. Emily was gone for an hour when John turned in for the night, and he didn't wake up until seven thirty the next morning.

Moore stopped him. He began reading from one of the printed forms he had brought into the room. It was the Miranda warning.

"Are you accusing me?" John asked indignantly.

"No."

"Then why are you reading me my rights?"

Moore calmly explained that it was just standard operating procedure, and John shouldn't interpret it to mean that he was being accused of anything. As he read, Moore put a check mark next to each of the rights, then he passed the paper over to John for him to sign. John signed, handed the paper back to the chief, and went on with his story.

"When I woke up, Emily was on the top of the covers in the nude, on her side. She was covered with dirt and leaves and twigs. There were pieces of duct tape in her hair, and cuts all over—her breasts and other places, and her face was bruised and swollen. Her eyes were swollen shut."

John was rambling, so Moore slowed him down. He offered

him a cigarette, lit it, then lit one for himself. Then he said, "Let's take it from the top, John. What did Emily tell you happened?" he asked.

Emily, he said, told him that she was walking downtown, near the Normal Building, when she heard a car approach. She heard it come to a screeching stop, the doors opened, and two men grabbed her from behind. They put duct tape on her eyes and mouth and shoved her into the backseat.

John told Moore that all the while Emily was in the car, a hunting knife was pressed to her throat. The men drove to a secluded spot in the woods, where they ripped off her clothes, then beat her and tortured her. When they were done, they pushed her out of the car and left her on the side of the road naked. Somehow she managed to get to her feet and find her way back home.

He discovered her in the morning when he woke up at about half past seven. He helped her to the bathtub, where he washed her wounds. With scissors he cut away the duct tape. He helped Emily back into bed, then called his mother-in-law, Caroline Lenz.

John played the part of the concerned husband well, but the chief wasn't buying his story. Moore's experience and instincts told him it was a big lie. Good cops are keen observers of human behavior, and although he was a small-town police chief, Moore had big-city law enforcement skills.

"Right off the bat I smelled a rat," he said later.

For one thing, John was nervous, too nervous, as he told the tale. For another, Moore couldn't comprehend how a woman could be snatched off a street without someone seeing something and reporting it. He also found it hard to believe that a bruised and battered woman could stumble naked through town without being spotted by at least one good citizen who would phone police—even in the wee hours of the morning in a small town.

"There are always people out, especially on a holiday weekend in early September," Moore explained later.

And there were other bits and pieces that didn't pass the chief's smell test: John never expressed any interest in Emily's condition; he seemed more concerned about how the chief planned to go about tracking down Emily's attackers than he was about his wife's pain and suffering, and he wanted to know what would happen to the assailants when they were finally captured and brought to justice.

But what puzzled Moore most was the fact that John didn't call authorities or seek medical help until more than twenty-four hours had passed after Emily's alleged abduction.

John tried to explain that away. "I wanted to, but Emily wouldn't let me—she didn't want anyone to see her in that condition." That explanation held no water with the chief. A married man himself, Moore believed any loving husband would have immediately sought medical care.

When the interview ended, Moore asked John if it would be okay to look through his house. "There may be fingerprints on the tape," the cagey chief explained. John readily agreed, not realizing that by agreeing he was consenting to a police search of his home.

At the house the chief collected and bagged several pieces of duct tape that he found in a wastebasket in the bathroom. From the couple's water bed he took the top and bottom sheets, both of which contained bits of twigs and clumps of mud and leaves. He also took several swabs from around the drain in the couple's bathtub.

So far John's story was checking out, and Emily told the same story to the Park Falls cop who interviewed and photographed her in the hospital. Moore, however, was still skeptical. He wanted to hear for himself what the battered woman had to say. But he would have to wait. Emily's condition was critical. She had been beaten, stabbed, and cut over almost every inch of her body, including her vagina and rectum.

Emily couldn't see. Her eyes were swollen shut, and her lips were split and puffy, and she had internal injuries, including broken ribs. She was in excruciating pain. Her doctors wouldn't allow Moore to speak with her until her condition improved.

It had been a busy five and a half hours for Craig Moore. At 11 P.M. he was back at headquarters with the items he'd removed from the Weber home, all of which he logged in and locked up in the evidence room.

Craig Moore got his first look at Emily on Labor Day, September 5. John was already at the hospital when Moore arrived around noon. He was sitting in the visitors' waiting room, fidgeting and chain-smoking. After consulting with Pat Woods, Emily's ICU nurse, Moore walked over to Emily's bed. In all his years as a cop, he had never seen anything like Emily.

"She was one massive purple bruise," the chief recalled. "She had literally been beaten to a pulp. The nurse told me that if Emily had not gotten medical treatment when she did, she would have died."

Moore had never met her, but looking at her now he guessed that Emily weighed at least two hundred pounds. She actually weighed half that, but the savage beating had caused her entire body to swell to double its size.

He introduced himself. "Emily, I'm Chief Craig Moore from the Phillips Police Department," he said gently. "Do you think you're strong enough to tell me what happened to you?"

Moore had a tape recorder with him and he clicked it on. With great difficulty Emily told a less detailed but essentially similar story to the one John had told him the day before. When she finished, Moore thanked her and left her bedside, but he didn't believe a word she'd said.

Craig Moore is a very patient man. He was convinced Emily was holding back, and he believed that what was stopping her from telling the truth was fear. Emily, he surmised, was scared to death, and rightfully so. With her eyes swollen shut, she couldn't see. She didn't know who was in the room with her. As far as Emily knew, John was there, too.

The next time Moore approached Emily, he assured her that only he and a nurse were with her. John, he said, was in the waiting room and he promised her that no one would harm her. Then he asked Emily if she believed in God.

"Yes," Emily whispered.

Craig Moore is a sincerely religious man, but it wasn't the first time that he had invoked the Almighty to get to the truth.

"Then pray with me," he said, taking her hand in his. "Dear Lord, please protect this woman and give her the strength to tell the truth. Amen."

With that, Emily began to reveal what had really happened to her. Over a period of three hours she told Moore all about the torture and defilement she had endured at the hands of her husband. What Moore was hearing was far worse than anything the chief had suspected or could ever have imagined.

She told him she had spent the Friday before Labor Day at home alone on South Avon. She had cleaned the house and was doing other household chores when the phone rang at about 6 P.M. It was John.

They'd had a tiff the night before. John had been feeling horny and wanted to have sex, but Emily wasn't in the mood. She had told him, "Tomorrow night, John. I promise."

They'd had some words; then John had gone off to sulk and guzzle beer.

Now he was on the phone asking if she'd like to go for a ride with him out to his parents' eighty-acre spread off State Road 13. "I have a surprise for you," he said. "It's about us moving up there. I'll pick you up in an hour." He refused to say another word about the surprise until they got to the property.

An hour later John drove up in his yellow 1970 two-door Oldsmobile Cutlass. Before they headed out of town, he stopped at a store and purchased a spiral notebook. Along the way Emily pressed him for a hint about the surprise, but he wouldn't tell her anything until they were on the Weber property.

"I don't want to spoil the surprise," he said teasingly.

They drove north along State Road 13. They passed the Price County Airport and the huge Marquip plant. From there on it was a straight drive to the Weber property. The road neither curves nor bends, and the lay of the land is pancake flat. There's not much to look at along the way except trees, lots and lots of trees.

When they reached Rock Creek Road, John turned left onto a dirt driveway. They'd arrived at the property. He brought the Cutlass to a stop in front of a barn about a hundred yards from the highway and told Emily to wait for him inside while he prepared the surprise.

"Don't peek," he warned playfully. "You'll spoil it."

Emily was excited and she did as John asked. He was gone for about fifteen minutes before returning to pick her up. She climbed back into the Cutlass and they drove off, following the driveway for about a half mile before turning into the woods. As John steered the car carefully through the trees, Emily figured that he was taking her to the spot where they would build their dream house.

John brought the car to a stop in a clearing and told Emily to close her eyes. Again, Emily did as he asked. As she waited for him to tell her to open her eyes, she heard him poking around for something on the backseat. The next thing she knew, she felt something long and hard and cold pressing against her neck.

"Is this going to hurt?" she asked. She opened her eyes. John's favorite hunting knife—the one her parents had given him for his birthday—was pressing against the left side of her neck. It was twilight, but Emily could see John's eyes, and the look in them told her that she had reason to fear for her life. He was livid. The veins in his neck were pulsating. His mouth was contorted, and his hazel eyes glowered with hate. She'd never seen him like this.

"Have you been cheating on me?" he snarled.

"No, John, of course not." She tried to convince him that he had no reason to be jealous, that he was the only man in her life.

He told her he didn't believe her, and that he had brought her into the woods so that she could watch him blow his head off. Then he ordered Emily to open the spiral notebook he'd bought before they drove out of town. He handed her a clipboard that contained two letters he wanted her to copy. One was to John; the other was to her parents.

Then John punched her hard in the mouth with his fist. "I'll cut your tits off if you don't do what I tell you," he shouted.

His words were chilling. With a knife against her throat Emily did as she was told. As she scribbled, her hand shook. It dawned on her that she was in mortal danger.

The letter to her parents was an apology for leaving without saying good-bye, and for not being able to tell them where she'd gone or when she'd be coming back. The letter to John stated that she was very sorry but she couldn't stay married to him any longer, that she was the cause of all the strife in their marriage and that she hoped he'd be able to find someone who would treat him better than she had. It added that her parents probably wished that she had disappeared instead of Carla.

A "PS" asked John to tell all their friends that he had been right about her all along.

After she finished copying the letters, John had her sign two birthday cards—one to him and the other to her father. Then he gave her envelopes to address. He told Emily to write only her name in the space for the return address. He also had her sign a blank check drawn from their joint account. He ordered Emily to make it out to cash for $250.

Then he told her, "I'm going to get rid of you, just like I got rid of Carla."

The words stopped Emily cold. She stared at her husband in disbelief. Ever since her sister went missing, the Lenz family had believed that Carla was abducted by a stranger. They had never suspected that John had anything to do with her disappearance.

"Oh, you didn't know I killed Carla, did you?" John asked, a cunning grin crossing his face. They'd been married for two years, known each other for almost four, but until that moment Emily had never realized how evil John was.

It dawned on her that no one knew they'd gone to the woods. If she screamed, there'd be no one around to hear her. He could kill her right then and there, bury her, and mail the cards and letters, and no one would be the wiser. She feared she would vanish just like Carla, and that John would get away with it.

Realizing that she was on the verge of losing her own life, Emily made up her mind—she wasn't going to die without a fight.

If she got the chance to run, she would. And if she got the chance to kill John, she wouldn't hesitate.

As she was thinking about her options, John got out of the car. He stomped around to the passenger side and yanked the door open. When she was too slow in exiting, he pulled her from the vehicle by her hair.

"Strip," he commanded. While John watched, Emily reluctantly began peeling off her clothes. She unzipped her brown and gold jacket with the words "Winter Wood Products" on the back and let it fall to the ground. Next, she pulled the Olympic sweatshirt she was wearing over her head and let it fall, too. She kicked off her sneakers, then slipped off of her jeans. It was drizzling now, and the air was cold and damp. All Emily had on was a bra and white panties.

When John cupped his hands to light a cigarette, Emily decided the time was right to make a run for it. She took off, but John took off after her.

"You'd better get back here or I'll kill you for sure," he screamed.

Emily managed to run about a hundred feet. She was barefoot and half naked, and she realized that she couldn't outrun her lanky husband or a bullet. She stopped dead in her tracks. John caught up to her, grabbed her by the crotch, and dragged her back to the car. He reached into the backseat and pulled out a roll of duct tape, which he wrapped around her head so that it covered her eyes and mouth. Then he pulled Emily's arms behind her back and taped her wrists tightly together. With his hunting knife he cut the straps on Emily's bra, then slashed off her panties.

Emily was now stark naked, and she couldn't see, speak, or use her hands. She was bound and gagged, and John could do to her whatever he wanted—his wildest sexual fantasy brought to life.

He shoved her to the ground. Emily fell hard, landing on her back. He jumped on top of her. Straddling her, he began slashing away at her breasts. She could actually feel her skin shredding.

He drove an inch-and-a-half safety pin through her left breast, then twisted it several times before snapping it shut. He picked up the knife again and slashed away at her chest and abdomen. At one point he put the knife down and pummeled her with his fists. When he was finished battering Emily's front side, he turned her on her stomach and began slashing away at her backside with the hunting knife.

John was having the time of his life making Emily suffer, and there was more to come. He'd brought along a wheelbarrow handle from his job at Winter Wood Products. He shoved it into her vagina and pushed it up as far as it would go. Then he slowly twisted it several times before pulling it out. He turned her over on her stomach and did the same to her anus.

"Now are you in the mood?" he snarled.

Somehow, through it all, Emily remained conscious. Every inch of her body ached, but she had an iron will to live that couldn't be broken, at least not by John Weber. She made up her mind—she vowed to stay alive if only to bring him to justice for killing her sister.

Adrenaline took over. She managed to get back on her feet. She pulled and tugged at the duct tape that bound her hands until it came loose, then she ripped it from her mouth. With her hands and mouth now free, Emily was able to scratch and bite. She tried to gouge his eyes out, but John knocked her down. He stomped and kicked her again and again with the heavy steel-toed workman's boots he was wearing. When he bent down to pick up a shovel, Emily climbed back up on her feet. Wielding the shovel like a baseball bat, John whacked her over the head with the metal end at least twenty times. Each time he hit her, she fell down, and each time she got back up.

"You're going to be a tough one to kill," he screamed.

"Stop it, stop it, just leave me alone!" she yelled back. "I'm not going to let you kill me. I'm not going to die."

At some point Emily passed out. She wasn't sure just when, but when she came to, she was still in the woods. She was wearing John's jacket, and he was cradling her in his arms.

"John was talking in a nice voice, like he really felt bad," Emily told Moore.

Then she heard another voice, but no one else was around. It was a completely different voice, she said. "It was mean and lower, and it kept saying, 'Don't let her live.' "

John referred to the mean voice as "Natas." He said, "Natas, I've got to let her live. I can't kill her."

The two voices were going back and forth, arguing about killing Emily. "It was like I wasn't even there," she recalled. At one point, the argument became so heated that John smashed his fists into the ground.

He must have won the argument, however, because as soon as the first rays of sunlight poked through the trees, he helped Emily to her feet and led her back to the Cutlass. They drove back to Phillips, arriving there more than twelve hours after they'd driven away the evening before.

John was no longer his wife's tormentor. Now he was her caregiver. He helped her out of the car and into the house. He filled the bathtub with warm water and gently lowered her into it. He washed and bandaged her wounds, then led her to their bed, where Emily, exhausted from the ordeal, slept for the next ten hours. While she slept, John concocted the abduction story.

When Emily woke up, John was on the edge of the water bed. He wasted no time reciting the story he wanted her to tell.

Even before he left Emily's bedside, Chief Moore had made up his mind that he was going to arrest John right then and there, despite the fact that the case was out of his jurisdiction. The crime scene wasn't a downtown street in Phillips—it was the Weber property on Highway 13, which meant it was a case for Price County Sheriff Wayne Wirsing. But John was in the visitors' waiting room just a few yards down the hall, and there was no telling what he might do once he found out that Emily had revealed the truth about what he'd done to her. So Moore decided not to worry about jurisdiction. "I'm not a territorial person," he explained later. "I don't believe in jurisdiction. I believe in getting the job done."

Craig Moore isn't a big man. At six foot four, John had at least six inches on the chief, and he was heavier and younger. Moore was concerned about how the lanky factory worker would react to being arrested, so he picked up the phone at the nurse's station and called for backup. Within minutes Park Falls Police Officer Josef Jeske walked into the hospital.

Moore explained the situation to Jeske, who positioned himself in the lobby next to the entrance. If John was going to make a run for it, he would have to run through the beefy cop. With Jeske blocking his only way out, the chief cautiously approached John. He ordered him to turn around, put his hands on the wall, and spread his legs. He was under arrest.

At first John defiantly ignored the chief's commands. Moore watched as John's eyes looked to the doorway. The Cutlass was just beyond it. For an instant it seemed that John might flee, but he changed his mind as soon as he spotted the Park Falls cop. He meekly turned around and did as he was told. Moore frisked and cuffed him, then marched him out the door.

As he led John through the lobby and into the hospital parking lot, Emily's parents were walking in.

"I don't know what's going on, but they've arrested me for Emily," John yelled to his in-laws. An irate Gene Lenz Sr. blocked Moore's path. He demanded an explanation.

The last thing Moore wanted was a confrontation while escorting a prisoner. To pacify the Lenzes, he said he'd be happy to talk with them, but they would have to wait until he had John securely locked inside his patrol car. In the meantime he ordered them to move out of his way.

After locking John in his police cruiser, which was equipped with a steel mesh partition that separated the front and backseats, Moore walked back to where the Lenz family was waiting. He told them that John was under arrest for the aggravated battery of Emily and that there might be additional charges filed against him, including charges related to the disappearance of Carla. In the meantime, he suggested that they visit with Emily; she would be able to fill them in. Moore then turned away and headed back to his police car.

He steered the vehicle south toward Phillips, where John was turned over to Sergeant Dan Greenwood of the Price County Sheriff's Department. The handcuffs were removed and John was fingerprinted and photographed. He was ordered to remove his clothes and don a jail jumpsuit. When that was done, Greenwood escorted his prisoner to a holding cell on the main floor of the Price County Safety Building. As soon as the door clanged shut behind him, John lay down on the cot, curled up into a fetal position, and fell asleep.

While John slept, Chief Moore phoned Lawrence Weber, John's father, and told him what was going on. Mr. Weber consented to a police search of his property. Next Moore assembled a team of investigators from three agencies for the search—his own department, the Price County Sheriff's Office, and the Wisconsin State Patrol.

The lawmen rendezvoused at the Weber property. Freshly made tire tracks led them to the spot where John had beaten Emily with the shovel. They even found the shovel lying next to a freshly dug hole that measured twenty-eight inches deep by thirty-four inches by twenty-six inches. While it seemed much too small for the body of an adult woman, investigators theorized that it was a work in progress.

At another location, investigators found an empty Miller Draft beer can, a partially used roll of silver duct tape, Salem Lights cigarette butts, a blue baseball cap, a flashlight, and a hacksaw. A few feet away they found more duct tape and a wooden wheelbarrow handle, which appeared bloodstained.

Trooper Bryan Vergin of the Wisconsin State Patrol drew detailed maps of the locations where Emily was attacked. He carefully noted the position of every item that investigators collected.

Moore was a tenacious lawman. Even though the case was not in his jurisdiction, he continued to work it. He had been working it almost around the clock since he'd met with John Weber on Sunday. It was now 11 P.M. on Monday, and he was driving back to headquarters with a stack of evidence that corroborated Emily's story. An hour later he was at the home of Price County Judge

Douglas Fox. He stood by while the judge signed two search warrants—one for a second search of John and Emily's house at 475 South Avon, and the other for the Cutlass.

In the wee hours of September 6, a team of investigators came together to search John Weber's 1970 Olds Cutlass. Among them were Chief Moore, Sheriff Wirsing, and District Attorney Paul Barnett. Moore had ordered the car impounded when he arrested John. A tow truck brought it from the Flambeau Medical Center parking lot to the sheriff's garage at the Safety Building. Now the investigators were getting ready to examine every inch of the vehicle.

It was a slow process. First, Sheriff's Deputy Keith Johnson photographed the car inside and out. Johnson noticed that the door handle on the passenger's side of the coupe looked like it was stained with blood. He photographed the handle; then it was removed from the door, bagged, and marked. He also took photos of every other item that was removed from the car.

In the glove compartment they found a partially used roll of duct tape similar to the one found at the grave site, and similar to the tape Moore removed from the wastebasket at 475 South Avon. They also found the hunting knife that they believed John used to slash Emily.

When they looked underneath the Cutlass, they noted that mud flaps were hanging over three of the four tires. Only the left front tire was missing a flap. A flap found on the Weber property matched the three that were on the car. They scraped bits of grass and soil off the car's undercarriage. Like everything else, those items were photographed, bagged, and marked.

Opening the trunk was like opening a window into John's twisted and depraved psyche. For one thing, it was a massive mess, but it also turned out to be a treasure trove of evidence and more.

Amid dozens of empty beer cans and the cartons they came

in, investigators found the clothes Emily had been wearing when John forced her to strip, including her tattered bra and torn panties. They also found the clipboard that held the originals of the messages John had had Emily copy, as well as the birthday cards and the envelopes.

There were also a couple of chilling "to do" and "need to buy" lists. Among the entries for "PH 1" (which investigators figured meant Phase One) were "bondage for legs," "saw," "duct tape," "oil for ass," "pins," "needles," and "checkbook."

Another page contained notations for the second phase: "Take shot in dick just before PH2. 3cc." "Burial spot. Compost heap?" "Make sure compost heap is same as before execution."

As the team dug deeper into the trunk, they came across a black bag. Inside they found the blue spiral notebook into which Emily had copied the messages John had written out for her. Also in the bag were a box of stickpins, three Dutch Master cigars, and two more wheelbarrow handles, one of which had what looked like a notch carved into its handle. They also found a green duffel bag that contained torn bras of various sizes, soiled men's and women's underwear, a vibrator, and a stuffed rabbit with a hole in its crotch.

They took more than a hundred porn magazines from the trunk. The magazines ran the gamut from soft-core publications like *Playboy* and *Penthouse* to hard-core publications with graphic photos and articles featuring bondage and sadistic acts of violence against women. Many of the magazines were tattered and dog-eared; John, it seemed, had gotten his money's worth out of them.

But the most significant evidence the team would take from the car was discovered by Chief Moore. It was an audiocassette that was sticking out of the tape player. At first Moore thought that it was a music tape, but just to make sure, he turned the ignition key to accessory and pushed the tape in. In about ten seconds he heard John's voice. What John had to say for more than fifty minutes sent chills through every lawman who heard it. More important, it revealed in graphic detail what had happened to Carla Lenz.

John spoke in a mellow voice, slowly at first, and it was clear he was talking directly to one person: Emily.

"If you do exactly as I tell you, when I tell you, and what I tell you, you will be all right," he promised. "I need to explain something to you, and I want you to listen closely and understand. I have a lot to tell you, so sit back and relax."

John said that when he and Emily were having marital difficulties in the weeks after they married, he sought advice from Carla.

"The first time I talked to her I knew right away that she had a crush on me, and I knew how she felt. So I would go out and I would talk to her, and we would go for rides."

Then his tone began to change. His voice was still mellow, but it took on a sinister edge.

"I know what happened to Carla. I know real well," he said, drawing out the word "real." "The same thing is *not* going to happen to you. You are going to live. However, you may be a little sore—and you will definitely remember me. So I will explain what happened."

John said he phoned Carla at around 11 P.M. on November 12, 1986. He said he invited her to go for a ride. She said yes. He grabbed a "kit" he'd prepared a few weeks earlier and drove his Pontiac Sunbird to Storms Road. Carla was already walking down the road to meet him. She climbed into the car and John headed for his parents' property on State Road 13. When they arrived, John told Carla that he was thinking of leaving for Colorado. He asked if she would go with him.

"She said no, and that she wanted nothing more than to see me and you back together again, so I told her that I had a surprise for her, and that she would need to close her eyes and turn away."

Carla smiled and did as her brother-in-law asked. When she closed her eyes, John reached into his "kit." He pulled out his .25-caliber pistol. Carla was still smiling when he grabbed her hair and shoved the muzzle of the gun into her mouth.

"She didn't know what to think," John said. "I told her she should do exactly as I said or she would die. And I told her she was going to watch me blow my head off. And she kept screaming, 'Why?' I told her to shut up; when she wouldn't, I slammed a sock into her mouth."

Carla was as feisty as her older sister, and she fought back. She managed to spit the sock out of her mouth; then she made a grab for the gun. She tried to wrestle it away from John, but she was no match for her brother-in-law. He pinned her to his lap. Then he told her he didn't want to live anymore.

"What do you want from me?" Carla asked.

"Before I blow my head off, I want to see you strip."

When Carla said no, John put the gun to his head and pulled the trigger.

"No, John, don't," she begged. But nothing happened; the safety was on.

"Well, maybe I'll kill you first, then me."

Carla wasn't ready to die, so she reluctantly agreed to take off her clothes.

"She started with her jacket," John said. "She had that purple jacket on, and she took that and her shirt off, and then her shoes and then her pants, and then she asked how far."

"All the way," he told her.

John watched as Carla pulled her panties down, then took off her bra.

"She had her arms across her tits and I couldn't see them very well, but I could see her muff, and it looked like it was black. But actually it was brown, and she had it trimmed up."

John reached back and removed a roll of duct tape from his "kit" and rolled it over his sister-in-law's mouth and eyes—"about three wraps so she could not see," he said. Then he pushed her face-first into the dashboard, yanked her wrists behind her back, and bound them with tape, too.

"I knew she couldn't get out of that," he said.

John then set about torturing the teen. He played with her breasts, pulling on her left nipple "as far out as it would go." He bit it, "hard." He pinched it, "real hard."

The violence and degradation continued, and it got worse, much worse. The lawmen couldn't believe what they were hearing.

John went on. He said he pushed his fingers into Carla's vagina. He tugged at her pubic hair, pinched her clitoris, and hit her with a plank across her buttocks thirty to forty times. Then he told her, "Now you are going to give me a blow job, and if I feel one tooth, I'll cut your tits off."

He "fucked her face for a good ten to fifteen minutes," he said. He ordered her to lick the crack of his ass, and she did. Then he told her to hold her mouth open. "If you close it even once, I'll cut your tits off," he warned. "Then I pissed in her mouth."

The tape went on and on. He took the ends of two wheelbarrow handles, rolled them in the snow, then forced one into her

vagina. "I fucked her with it, first slow and deep and then fast."
Then he pushed another one deep into her rectum. "It went in
real hard, and real stiff," he said.

He took a cigarette and burned her clitoris "long and hard."
He took a safety pin, "one of the big ones," and "poked her ass
about twenty times." He used the same pin again and stuck it
through one of her nipples. Then he shoved a beer bottle into her
rectum "and pushed it in as far as the neck."

He filled a hypodermic needle with lighter fluid and injected
it into her left nipple, "all the way in."

He pulled off the tape that covered her eyes. "I want you to
see this," he told her.

With his hunting knife he cut off her right nipple and showed
it to her. Then he sliced off her right breast. At that point, he said,
Carla went into spasms. "I showed her tit close up, holding it by
the nipple," he said. Then he kicked a beer bottle "all the way up
her ass." He had to do it "three or four times before it disappeared."

Incredibly, Carla was still alive. "So I stepped on her throat
until she died." Instead of burying his sister-in-law in the grave
he'd dug two days earlier, John stored Carla's corpse and her
severed breast in the Sunbird's trunk. While cops and Carla's
family, including John, scoured the county looking for the missing teen, he drove around with the body. On the second day after
Carla died, John sliced off a chunk of her left leg, skinned it, and
froze it along with the severed breast. "That night I made some
patties and I ate her leg," he said. He did the same with her breast.

A few days after he cannibalized his sister-in-law, John buried
what was left of her on his parents' property.

"Now you know what happened to Carla."

As far as the investigators were concerned, they had just heard an astounding confession to an unspeakable crime by a savage madman. It turned their stomachs, but there was much more to come.

John's monologue continued, but this time he was telling Emily what he dreamed about doing to her.

In a hate-filled diatribe, he vowed to make his wife suffer, but he wouldn't kill her. He wanted her to live. He was going to "make her fuck herself" and "fuck herself up her ass." Her ass, he promised, "will be sore and your cunt will probably be sore and your tits will be sore.

"Women are nothing," he growled. "They flaunt their bodies and think they can get anything they want by being a cock tease. I pay them back and I'm definitely paying you back.

"There will be others, many others," he promised. As for Emily, "I will cut off your tits and then start at your ankles, and make another cut just below your knee and another one by your rotten pussy."

He would break every toe, "maybe even a few fingers." And "maybe I will cut off your head."

Finally the tape ended. Moore removed it from the Cutlass's tape player, tagged it, and bagged it. It was past 3 A.M. What started as an assault and battery case on Sunday had by Tuesday turned into the most gruesome murder investigation in the history of Price County.

Despite the tape, Moore and the other investigators knew they had their work cut out for them. To convict John for the murder of his sister-in-law, they would have to prove that she was indeed dead. They decided to interrogate John in hopes that he would confess and either take them to Carla's remains or tell them where on his parents' property they were.

John was sound asleep in his cell in the Price County Safety Building when Moore and two other investigators and a jailer came for him. It was a few minutes after 4 A.M. The jailer waited for John to get off his cot before he unlocked the cell door and placed handcuffs on his wrists. The lawmen waited while John relieved himself, then they led him to an interrogation room in the building's basement.

The interrogators agreed it would be best if Chief Moore questioned John one-on-one while they watched from behind a two-way mirror. Before the questioning began, Moore once again read the Miranda warning from a printed form. And once again the chief checked off each of the rights and passed the paper across the table for John to sign. He signed it and passed it back to the chief. Then John asked about Emily.

Moore told him that she was doing as well as could be expected. Then the chief clicked on his tape recorder and asked, "What really happened, John?"

"I'm not really sure," John said, explaining that he had been drinking Miller beer "in the gold can." He told Moore he remembered sitting in the car and talking with Emily, telling her that he "knew what was going on with that Johnston guy," referring to Dan Johnston, whom John believed Emily was dating during one of their separations.

At that point, John said, he lost control and began beating her, but he couldn't recall exactly what he did to his wife. He did, however, remember taping her eyes, hands, and mouth.

John broke down in tears when Moore asked him if recalled sexually assaulting Emily with a wheelbarrow handle. He nodded his head to indicate that he did. He said he remembered that it was dark and raining hard, and that they spent the night in the woods because it was so dark they could not find their way back to the car, so he gave her his jacket and cradled her in his arms to keep her warm.

He remembered he had a knife and a shovel and that he hit Emily with the shovel to kill her "because of the way she treated me." And he remembered asking her, "Who's better, Danny or me?"

When Moore turned John's attention to Carla, John stopped talking.

"I heard the tape," the chief told him. John insisted that he had made it only to frighten Emily, and that he never played it for her. "I didn't kill Carla," he declared.

Then Moore asked about Shelly Hansen, and John denied knowing her. He lied. The chief would learn later that they had worked together at Marquip, and that he had been seen with her at several bars in town in the weeks before she vanished.

Moore turned John's attention back to Carla. Again, John denied that he had had anything to do with his sister-in-law's disappearance. But Moore wasn't about to give up. He felt that if he could keep John talking, eventually he would reveal where Carla was buried. The chief then turned to the tactic that had worked so well with Emily.

"John," he asked solemnly, "do you believe in God? Because I would like to gather whatever is left of Carla and give her a Christian burial so the good Lord can grant her some peace. You understand what a Christian burial is, don't you?"

When John nodded that he did, Moore asked if he would like to take a ride with him to his parents' property so that he could point out the location of Carla's grave. John said no, but he offered to draw a map that would lead them to his sister-in-law's remains. Immediately, Moore took out a pink statement form, turned it over to its blank side, and gave it to John, who very slowly sketched a rough map of the property. He indicated where investigators would find the grave—a hundred yards from Rock Creek Road, not far from the barn.

Chief Moore led John back to his cell. As soon as the door clanged shut, three investigators—Moore, Assistant Chief Dennis Dosch, and Price County Chief Deputy Sheriff Tim Gould—were on their way to the Weber property.

Dawn was just breaking over the horizon as the lawmen drove north on Highway 13. They walked back and forth in a grid pattern in the area John indicated. An hour after they began searching, Dennis Dosch found what appeared to be a grave.

The lawmen radioed the sheriff's department, then marked the area around the grave with yellow crime scene tape. The Wisconsin State Crime Laboratory in Madison, the state capital, was notified and a team of technicians was dispatched to Phillips. They would take charge of excavating the crime scene as well as collecting and bagging the evidence.

Meanwhile, John was meeting with John Reid and James Lex Jr., attorneys from the public defender's office that covered Price and three other Northwoods counties—Taylor, Langlade, and Lincoln. They were beside him later that day when he appeared before Judge Douglas Fox. The judge found probable cause to hold John for the aggravated battery of Emily and set bail at $200,000.

Back at the Weber property, the excavation of the grave had begun. It was a painstakingly slow process. Before any digging could start, the entire area around the grave site was photographed from a variety of angles. Using hand tools, technicians carefully sifted each bit of sandy soil they dug up. As they worked, they uncovered a purple jacket, a bra and panties, and a hypodermic needle. Then they uncovered the skeletal remains of a human being from beneath a foot and a half of sandy soil. A tuft of matted hair was still attached to the skull. The technicians noted that part of the left leg and left foot were missing.

The skeletal remains were carefully collected and placed in a body bag, then driven to the University of Wisconsin Hospital and Clinic in Madison, where a dental odontologist, Dr. Donald Simley II, armed with X-rays supplied to him by Carla's dentist, confirmed they were the remains of Carla Lenz.

Cadaver dogs were brought in to search the property for other bodies that might have been buried there, but a two-day search yielded nothing.

Investigators tracked down John's 1977 Pontiac Sunbird, which had been sold and resold. Armed with a warrant, Sheriff Wirsing impounded it and had it towed to the Wisconsin State Crime Laboratory in Madison, where criminologists pored over the vehicle with a fine-tooth comb. A search of the trunk yielded hairs that matched in color and texture hairs that were still attached to Carla's skull.

Two weeks after John's arrest, Lawrence Weber walked into the Price County sheriff's office with a carton filled with some of his son's belongings. Among the items in it were two .25-caliber handguns and several pads and notebooks into which John had written out in meticulous detail his diabolical scenarios for kidnapping and torturing women. Based on the writings, detectives concluded that John had been actively stalking a Phillips High School cheerleader. They also concluded that before he was taken into custody, no young woman in Price County had been safe from John Weber.

Investigators sought and were granted another search warrant for John and Emily's home on South Avon. They feared they would find more human body parts—from Carla or other victims—but they didn't. Nevertheless, the suspicion that the woods held more victims of John Weber's depravity plagued them. They tracked John's travels over fifteen years and alerted law enforcement agencies wherever John had been. Several looked at John as a person of interest in unsolved cases involving dead or missing young women, but lawmen were never able to make a connection that could stand up in a court of law.

Price County investigators interviewed John's friends and coworkers. One of them reported that John had expressed a keen interest in Satanism. Certain rock-and-roll records, John told him, contained hidden messages from the devil.

It didn't take long for news of John Weber's arrest to get out. Price County District Attorney Paul Barnett hoped to prevent the fact that John had admitted on tape to cannibalizing Carla from becoming public knowledge. He worried that if it got out, it would only inflame passions and taint the potential jury pool. He was right. As soon as he filed his eight-count criminal complaint—it would eventually blossom to eighteen charges—with the circuit court on September 9, the cat was out of the bag.

Word of the grisly crimes spread like wildfire through the tiny town and beyond. Newspapers in Madison and Milwaukee carried the story. It even made headlines in the supermarket tabloids— HUSBAND DIGS HIS WIFE'S GRAVE WHILE SHE WATCHES, blared the *Weekly World News*, which also carried photos of Carla, Emily, and John.

It wasn't long before John was being compared to the infamous Edward Gein, a recluse who'd lived in an isolated farmhouse in Plainfield, 150 miles south and east of Phillips.

Beginning in the late 1940s, an inordinate number of women had vanished without a trace from Plainfield and the surrounding area. Investigators were baffled until November 16, 1957, when Bernice Worden disappeared from her store in the morning. That's when lawmen learned that fifty-one-year-old Gein had been her first and only customer of the day. They paid a visit to Gein's dilapidated old farmhouse.

Dozens of disemboweled and headless carcasses hung throughout the ramshackle house. Mrs. Worden was one of them. Her newly severed head was found sitting on a shelf wrapped in plastic. Dozens more heads were scattered throughout the house. When investigators opened Gein's refrigerator, they found every shelf filled with human organs in glass jars.

There were more gruesome discoveries: lampshades, trousers, and seat covers made from human skin, soup bowls carved from skulls, and belts studded with human nipples.

In addition to killing and cannibalizing living and breathing humans, Gein admitted digging up the graves of newly deceased women and cannibalizing them, too. After removing the bodies, he carried them to his truck, carefully restored the grave sites, and drove back to his farmhouse with his treasure. A judge declared Gein—the inspiration for the character of Norman Bates in the novel and film *Psycho*—insane and sent him to a facility for the criminally insane. Dubbed the "Mad Butcher of Plainfield," he died in 1978 from natural causes.

Not surprisingly, John Weber quickly became the most vilified man in the history of Price County, the perpetrator of its most monstrous crime. Following his arraignment, he was transferred from his holding cell to a regular cell in the Safety Building. It had a bunk and, high up on the wall, a small, heavily barred window that looked out on the street. From it he was able to watch Carla's funeral procession as it left the Heindl Funeral Home for the cemetery where she was laid to rest. And he would listen to drive-by curses—every now and then a pickup truck or a Bronco would pull up under his cell window and one or more of the occupants would shout out epithets.

A preliminary hearing was held on October 10. Because Judge Fox recused himself—he had been involved in the Weber divorce proceedings—Circuit Court Judge Gary Carlson was on the bench. The bearded jurist came over from nearby Taylor County. He would preside over the case through to the end, but this day the purpose of the proceeding was to determine if there was enough evidence to hold John for trial.

An overflow crowd turned out for the proceeding, and security was tight. After ruling on some preliminary motions, including a defense motion for a gag order, which the judge denied, Carlson ordered deputies to bring John into the courtroom. The lanky defendant shuffled in, his hands and legs in shackles. A deputy walked directly in front of him while another followed behind. They escorted him to the defense table, where he took a seat next to his attorney, James Lex. The deputies took seats directly behind John.

Emily was the first witness. She was still bruised, and tears rolled down her cheeks as she recounted what John did to her the night of September 3. For most of the time she avoided eye contact with John, who showed no emotion. She spoke in a barely audible voice until DA Barnett asked about her injuries and her hospital stay.

"I was in the ICU for sixteen days; I was in a great deal of pain," she said firmly. She glared at John but he never raised his eyes.

When her testimony was over, Emily stepped down from the witness stand. She walked past John and out of the courtroom without breaking stride. She was followed to the stand by Chief Moore. He in turn was followed by an investigator from the Sheriff's Department and a criminologist from the state crime lab. The last witness was Dr. Simley, the forensic dentist who had positively identified the skeletal remains taken from the Weber property as those of Carla Lenz.

At the conclusion of his testimony, Judge Carlson ruled that there was probable cause to hold John for trial. He continued bail and appointed a battery of psychiatrists to probe John Weber's twisted psyche.

John shuffled out of the courtroom and was led back to his cell. He whiled away the next five months sleeping, crying, and writing letters.

In a letter to his parents, Weber apologized for breaking their hearts. He said he planned to commit suicide before the trial in order to spare them more heartache. He admitted that he had intended to kill Emily when he attacked her, and he admitted killing Carla, but denied torturing the teen. He wrote that he lost control and strangled her when she refused to run away with him. He closed by comparing himself to Charles Manson and John Wayne Gacy. "I'll bet they make a TV movie out of this," he wrote. "I always wanted to be a star."

In a letter to his in-laws, Weber apologized "for all the pain and suffering I have caused your family," but he wanted them to "understand my side of this." What happened, he wrote, was beyond his control. "I literally became someone else. I refer to it as my dark side." He wrote that his heavy drinking "didn't help matters any and by no means is that an excuse." He never loved or respected himself. He thanked God that Emily was spared. "She is a wonderful woman, capable of a lot of love if given the chance. I never gave her or myself that chance."

In a letter to Emily, Weber wrote he still loved her. It was his love that made him stop beating her, he said. And he apologized for accusing her of cheating. The accusation didn't come from him, he wrote; it came from "Natas."

None of the letters were ever delivered. Instead, they were confiscated during a search of Weber's cell.

The trial was slated to begin on March 6, 1989, but it wouldn't be held in Phillips. Instead, Judge Carlson granted the defense motion for a change of venue. *The State of Wisconsin v. John R. Weber* would be tried in Room Five of the Marathon County Courthouse in Wausau, ninety miles south and east of Phillips. The jury would be chosen from among the 126,000 citizens of Marathon County, with Judge Carlson presiding.

Because the case involved the insanity defense, it would be a bifurcated proceeding: a guilt phase in which the state would have to prove beyond a reasonable doubt that John was guilty of the charges against him, and a responsibility phase during which the jurors would hear testimony as to John's mental state. In this phase the defense would have to prove that John either didn't know his criminal behavior was wrong or that he was unable to stop himself from committing his criminal acts.

To convict in the guilt phase, the jury would have to reach a unanimous decision. In the responsibility, or sanity, phase, an eleven-to-one decision would be good enough.

The legal sparring was well under way before the court got down to the task of picking a jury. The defense filed a flurry of motions, including a motion to move the trial out of Wausau due to pretrial publicity, which the judge denied; a motion to permit references to Natas during the guilt phase (denied); a motion to suppress references to Ed Gein and cannibalism during the guilt phase (granted); a motion to waive the defendant's right to a jury trial in phase one (denied).

With the motions disposed of, John's attorneys made a surprising announcement: Weber was pleading guilty but not responsible by reason of insanity to nine of the charges against him—the first-degree murder of Carla and her kidnapping, and the seven charges for the attack on Emily (attempted murder, kidnapping, sexual intercourse by threat of force with a dangerous weapon, two counts of sexual contact by threat of force to degrade or humiliate, unlawful imprisonment, and aggravated battery).

He was pleading not guilty to the remaining charges related to Carla—three counts of sexual intercourse by force; four counts of sexual contact by threat of force, one count of unlawful imprisonment, and one count of sexual mutilation.

In other words, John admitted kidnapping and murdering his sister-in-law, as well as doing all those horrible things to his wife, but because he was out of his mind he was not guilty by reason of insanity. As to the charges that he raped and mutilated his sister-in-law, he pleaded not guilty.

One by one, Judge Carlson read each of the charges Weber was pleading guilty to out loud. As he finished each charge, he asked Weber if he did in fact commit the crime. Each time John answered, "Yes." The judge then announced that he was accepting the pleas, declared John guilty of the crimes, but deferred sentencing to a later date.

By lunchtime Tuesday, a jury of nine women and five men, including two alternates, had been sworn in and seated. The judge informed the panel they would be sequestered, their phone calls and newspapers would be censored, and their TV viewing would be restricted. With that the jury was dismissed for the day and bussed to a local motel. Opening arguments were set for the next morning.

Before he gave the go-ahead for opening statements, Judge Carlson read the remaining nine charges out loud. The jurist pulled no punches. He recited all the gruesome details the prosecutor had written into the criminal complaint against Weber—"Inserted wheelbarrow handles and beer bottles into the vagina and anus"; "cut off the nipple of one of the breasts"; "forced to engage in fellatio with the defendant."

The savagery of the words that rained down from the bench rang in the ears of every juror and spectator, many of whom moaned or gasped with each horrific sentence and phrase. Meanwhile, the words didn't have the same effect on John, who sat unshackled between his attorneys at the defense table. Dressed in jeans and a checkered sport shirt, he appeared oblivious to the proceeding as he busied himself with a stack of papers.

When Judge Carlson finished reading through all the charges, he called on Price County DA Paul L. Barnett to make his opening statement. The prosecutor rose and walked to an easel that had been positioned fifteen feet from the jury box. He placed a blown-up photograph of a smiling Carla Lenz on it, then took three steps back and began speaking. He reviewed the charges against Weber. With each gruesome charge, he'd turn and look at the photo. Then he'd turn back to the jury and move on to another gruesome charge, then turn and face the photo again.

The bespectacled Barnett brought the pretty high school senior to life for the jurors. They couldn't help but feel her pain. The effect was devastating, and Public Defender Lex knew it.

When Barnett finished, Lex approached the bench for a conference. Speaking quietly so the jury wouldn't hear, he moved for a mistrial based on the prosecutor's use of the photo. The motion was denied.

It was now Lex's turn to present his opening statement. The defense attorney admitted that John kidnapped and murdered Carla, and that he kidnapped and assaulted Emily.

"On November 12, 1986, John Weber kidnapped and murdered his sister-in-law," he declared.

"On September 3, 1988, Mr. Weber kidnapped, sexually assaulted, and physically assaulted his wife, Emily Weber."

He reviewed the nine charges to which Weber was pleading guilty, then he declared that the DA "has no physical evidence directly proving John Weber is guilty of the remaining charges against him."

Weber, he said, "is guilty of what he has done. It does not necessarily follow that he is guilty of what he is charged with."

With that, the opening statements were over and the court was ready to hear its first witness. The bailiff called Emily to the stand. All eyes except two followed her as she entered the courtroom, walked past the defense table, and was sworn in. Once again, John avoided eye contact with her.

After Emily was sworn in, Barnett asked her to tell the jury how she and John first met, what brand of cigarettes he smoked—"Salem Lights"—and what kind of beer he drank— "Miller."

The DA inquired about the guns he owned—"a .410-gauge shotgun, a .22-caliber rifle, and a .25-caliber pistol," and why he owned them—"he was an avid hunter."

Then Barnett turned the questioning to the night Carla disappeared.

"Would your husband have known that Carla and Joe were home alone that night?" he asked.

"Yes," she replied.

"Would it have been unusual for your sister Carla to have left home at that time of night after the three of you had gone to work?

"Yes."

"And why was that?"

"She wouldn't leave Joe at home alone."

"Since your brother Joe would have been nine years old at the time this occurred, do you have an opinion as to whether Carla, after the rest of the household members have left for work, would have voluntarily stayed out of the home for a period of time other than a short period of time?"

"She would have never left the house unless it would have been for a very short time."

Barnett then brought up the evening of the assault, even though John had pleaded guilty to the charges relating to the assault on Emily. The young prosecutor was setting up the groundwork for the cassette tape that Moore had found in the Cutlass. When it was played, the jurors would hear from John Weber's own lips how he tortured and mutilated Carla. It was remarkably similar to the attack on Emily: He lured both women to the same isolated location—his parents' property on Rock Creek Road; he enticed both of them to close their eyes while he reached for a weapon; he slashed their clothes, then mutilated and tortured them in much the same way. Barnett saw a pattern, and he wanted the jury to see it, too.

He asked Emily to recount her ordeal from the moment John phoned her with the alluring promise of a surprise on Rock Creek Road. After John had told her to close her eyes, she felt something cold and hard against her throat, she said. It was a hunting knife.

"He asked if I was seeing anybody. I said no."

"Was that the truth?" Barnett asked.

"Yes."

She went on, recounting how John tortured and mutilated her, raped her with a wheelbarrow handle, stabbed, slashed, punched, and pummeled her, clobbered her with a shovel again and again, and told her, "I'm going to get rid of you just like I got rid of Carla."

Jurors wept, spectators wept, even cops wept. The judge called a recess and let the jurors leave the courtroom to regain their composure.

When the proceeding resumed, Emily identified John's hunting knife as the one used to coerce, slash, and puncture her.

On cross-examination, Lex established that Emily had never seen the wheelbarrow handle during the attack because her eyes were taped shut. He also managed to get Emily to admit that her husband had never before laid a hand on her.

Lex's cross seemed little more than an exercise in futility. All he could do was hope to plant a few seeds of doubt about some of the elements of Emily's story.

On redirect, Barnett asked Emily about John's drinking on the night of the attack. She said she saw him guzzle one beer while at the property. Finally, she was asked about her suffering as a result of the beating and about the bedside interviews she gave to Chief Moore, who followed her to the witness stand.

It was Thursday afternoon when Moore was sworn in. He identified himself as the chief of police of Phillips. He recounted his experience in law enforcement and his specialized training as an investigator.

The chief's testimony, which carried over through Friday afternoon, centered on the investigation from the time he first was made aware that John Weber had reported that his wife had been attacked in downtown Phillips, through the collection of evidence from the Cutlass and the subsequent interrogation of Weber in the basement of the Public Safety Building.

Barnett zeroed in on the more than one hundred pornographic magazines investigators found in the trunk. He wanted to draw a direct line from the X-rated magazines to the attacks on Emily and Carla. He wanted to establish that the attacks on the sisters were inspired by the magazines.

"How would you characterize the nature of those magazine contents?" he asked.

"I would say those magazines were pornographic in nature," the chief replied. "Some of the magazines pictorially spoke of bondage; I believe one was of spankings. And overall, the majority of the magazines dealt with some type of sexual gratification."

"Sexual gratification from what kind of acts?"

"Sexual intercourse and oral sex."

Then Barnett wanted to know if there were photos of anal insertions.

"Yes," the chief said, "there were."

Next, Barnett asked Moore to identify the tape recording he made of John's interrogation. The jury was provided with a written transcript and followed along as the hour-long tape played.

After a brief cross-examination by John Reid, Chief Moore stepped down from the witness stand.

He was followed to the stand by the team that conducted the postmortem examination of Carla's remains, forensic anthropologist Dr. Kenneth Baker, then forensic pathologist Dr. Robert W. Huntington III.

Dr. Huntington was followed by a ballistics expert who'd examined John's twenty-gauge pump-action shotgun and determined it had fired a shell that was found at the grave site. The final witness of the day was criminologist Barbara LeMay of the state crime lab. She testified that a clump of matted hair found in the trunk of the Sunbird matched Carla's, which meant that Carla's lifeless body had indeed been riding around Phillips with John after he killed her.

When the criminologist stepped down, Judge Carlson dismissed the jury, but not before announcing that he would hold court the next day, Saturday, when *The State of Wisconsin v. John R. Weber* would enter its sixth straight day.

Saturday, March 11, 1989, was cold and threatening. The first witness to take the stand was Dr. James Sergeant, Emily's doctor at Flambeau Medical Center. He first saw her in the emergency room on Sunday, September 4, 1988.

Barnett wanted to know if the doctor had a principal diagnosis based on his initial observation of Emily.

"She had so many diagnoses I am not sure what we settled on for principal diagnosis," the doctor said. Reading from his records, Dr. Sergeant reported that Emily had multiple concussions and facial swelling under the skin. Her eyes were swollen shut. There were also swelling and blood clots in the lower abdomen and the labia, lacerations of the leg, puncture wounds of the buttocks, cuts and abrasions in the vaginal area, and swelling caused by internal bleeding. She'd also suffered contusions to her liver and pancreas, which were causing severe abdominal pain. There were abrasions to the mucous membrane lining of her vagina caused, he said, by "forceful rubbing against it with something that was not perfectly smooth."

"Could the injury to Emily's vagina have been caused by the insertion of a wooden wheelbarrow handle?" Barnett wanted to know. The doctor said it could have been, and that could also have been the cause of similar abrasions inside her anus.

Sheriff's investigator Richard Heitkemper followed the doctor to the witness stand. He testified about the tight chain of custody during the transfer of Carla's remains from the grave site to Madison for the postmortem. The next to testify was Sheriff Wirsing. He testified to the impounding of the Sunbird and the gathering and processing of evidence from it.

Lawrence Weber was called next as a witness for the prosecution. He testified that he'd turned in to a sheriff's deputy a .25-caliber pistol that belonged to his son. Barnett took the opportunity to ask John's father if it was true that his son's job at the Winter Wood Products factory involved making wheelbarrow handles. The elder Lawrence answered, "Yes."

The judge ordered a recess for lunch. When court reconvened, an edited version of John's Cutlass tape, dubbed the "Weber Fright Tape" by the press, would be played for the jury.

Court reconvened following an hour-long break for lunch. Before the bailiffs brought the jury back in, Judge Carlson had some words for the spectators. He warned them about what they were going to hear.

"You will find it extremely disturbing," he said. He advised those who were squeamish to leave right then. And he said he would tolerate "no sharp intakes of breath, no crying or sobbing, no noises, no nothing. If there is, the deputies will immediately remove that person from the courtroom."

The judge ordered the bailiffs to bring the jury in, and John Weber, escorted by deputies, left the courtroom. Judge Carlson instructed the jurors that it was the defendant's right not to be there if he so chose, and that his leaving the courtroom should be ignored when they deliberated his guilt or innocence.

Then the judge warned the panel about the gruesome tape that they were about to hear. "The playing of the tape is not going to be a comfortable experience for anybody," he declared. "If any of you at all feel uncomfortable, please don't hesitate to let me know. Or let the bailiffs know."

The judge ordered the tape recorder switched on. Everyone in the courtroom was able to hear John Weber calmly and gleefully reveal the horrors he had inflicted on his sister-in-law as well as what he dreamed of doing to his wife. When side one ended, the cassette was flipped over and the jurors heard the other side. Some members of the panel couldn't take it. Mercifully, the judge allowed a couple of recesses so they could regain their composure.

When side two ended, Judge Carlson sent the jurors back to their motel. They would be back on Monday to listen to the defense case. In the meantime, they would spend the rest of the weekend with the diabolical voice of John Weber and his sadistic perversions ringing in their ears.

Monday morning probably came around much too soon for the jurors. They were in the jury room waiting to be called into the courtroom when the defense team announced that it would not put on a case. With the defense resting, phase one of the trial was about to head into its final phase—closing arguments.

Prosecutor Barnett went first. "We don't have Carla Lenz here to testify of her own firsthand personal knowledge regarding what occurred, but we believe, ladies and gentlemen, that through the introduction of circumstantial evidence, coupled with the defendant's own description of what occurred on that night, that we have established proof beyond a reasonable doubt."

He called on them to consider John Weber's pattern of behavior. "He threatened to blow his head off when he confronted Carla in the car. That's the same thing he said he was going to do when he had Emily out there. That's a pattern, ladies and gentlemen.

"You remember he said, 'Maybe I will kill you first and then myself,' if she didn't strip? He made the same threats to his wife, ladies and gentlemen. He forced Emily Weber to strip at knife-point, his own wife."

Barnett went on, pointing out other similarities in the attacks— the bloody wheelbarrow handle and the mutilation of genitalia, breasts, and buttocks, as well as the location and John's threats to blow his head off.

He finished his summation by talking about the motive for the attack on Emily. It was, said Barnett, "jealousy, and anger because he felt that she had done him wrong, had abused him in some respects."

Carla had rejected him, too, he said, and Weber was sick and tired of being rejected. Then the prosecutor asked the jury to find John Weber guilty on all charges.

It was Lex's turn. "Ladies and gentleman, John Weber is guilty of some vile and disgusting acts. No question about that," he began.

The tape, he said, was a fabrication, made to frighten Emily. He then tried to pick apart some of the forensic evidence, observing that hair but no blood was found in the Sunbird's trunk. "If John Weber had cut the breast off a living person, it would generate a lot of blood," he declared.

Following a brief rebuttal by Barnett, Judge Carlson gave the jury its instructions and ordered the panel to begin deliberating immediately. Two jurors were selected at random and were excused from deliberations. But they weren't free to leave. They were on standby in case one of the impaneled jurors became incapacitated and unable to participate in deliberations.

At 12:53 P.M. the jury filed out of the courtroom. At 3:15 P.M. one of the bailiffs informed Judge Carlson that the jury had reached verdicts. When they returned to the courtroom, the judge asked the foreman if verdicts had been reached on all counts. He said they had been. Judge Carlson read them out loud one by one. John Weber was guilty on all counts.

The judge scheduled the sanity phase for the next morning.

A bitter cold front from Canada swept through the upper Midwest on Tuesday, March 14. A blizzard was predicted for later in the week. It was going to be a tough few days, especially for the defense team. John Weber was guilty of all eighteen counts he had been charged with. It had been proven beyond a reasonable doubt that he was a cold-blooded killer, a rapist, and a sexual sadist. Persuading the same jury that had convicted him of nine of those counts that he was not responsible for his crimes by reason of insanity would be a very formidable task.

Unlike the guilt phase, the burden of proof in the responsibility phase falls on the defense, which is why the defense gets to make their opening statement first.

Attorney John Reid began by explaining that John Weber was suffering from a mental defect when he attacked first Carla then Emily. His client, he said, was a sexual sadist who derived sexual pleasure from torturing and humiliating women.

"Since a very young age, John Weber has built an elaborate mechanism, an internal device to deal with his illness, and to hide the extent of that illness from other people—his family, his friends, his wife, and the doctors who have attended him."

He promised that the defense would show that John has been mentally ill since preschool. He was mentally ill when he murdered

Carla, and mentally ill when he beat Emily to within an inch of her life. If his crimes were the result of his illness, he could not be held responsible.

In his opening Barnett said the state would prove that John was intoxicated during both attacks, which the prosecutor said were motivated by hatred and jealousy. John, he said, meticulously planned each attack weeks in advance, then got drunk so he could carry them out. The attacks were choices within his control, and therefore he was legally responsible for them.

The jury would hear testimony from eighteen witnesses, among them Emily, Marguerite and Lawrence Weber, two psychiatrists, and Kathy Weber, John's sister. And they would once again listen to the "fright tape," only this time it would be an unedited version.

Lex called Emily to the stand. Through her the jury learned about "Natas," John's alter ego.

Next up was Chief Moore and the "fright tape." Before it was played, Judge Carlson informed the jurors that they did not hear the entire tape when it was played for them during the guilt phase—segments related to John's mental state had been deleted, as had segments related to cannibalism.

Moore switched the tape recorder on. This time John remained in the courtroom. Almost as soon as it started playing, John covered his ears with his hands. He sobbed and moaned as his own voice recounted horrific acts of mutilation and degradation. Jurors wept, too.

Several times Carlson called a recess so that John, jurors, and spectators could regain their composure. He would be forced to call another recess after John was heard to say, "That night I made some patties and I ate her leg."

When the tape ended, Carlson adjourned court for the day.

Once again, shaken jurors ended their day with the diabolical voice of John Weber and his sadistic perversions ringing in their ears.

Sixty-seven-year-old Marguerite Weber took the stand on Wednesday. Before questioning began, she looked over her at her son and mouthed "I love you."

Reid began by asking her about John's bed-wetting; then he asked about the discovery of X-rated magazines in her son's room. Reid wanted to know if they were hard-core.

"Very," she said. "I only had to read about three lines and I destroyed them." But that didn't put an end to John's fascination with hard-core porn. Over the years his mother found more magazines, and they were nothing like *Playboy*.

"It just kept happening," said Marguerite, who wept the entire time she was on the stand.

In addition to the magazines, which she referred to as "stinky magazines," Marguerite testified to discovering detailed plans written in John's handwriting for sexually abusive acts against Kathy, one of his female teachers, and a female schoolmate.

On cross-examination, Barnett managed to elicit from Marguerite the fact that she disapproved of John's marriage to Emily.

"In your mind, do you consider Emily to be at least partly the reason John finds himself in the predicament he's in?" the prosecutor asked.

"I do."

"Why is that?"

"Because they fought forever and ever and ever over everything."

Then Barnett asked if she thought that the attack on Emily was sparked by anger.

She replied, "Yes."

When he testified on Thursday, Lawrence Weber recounted John's troubled early years and echoed Marguerite's sentiments about Emily. He had hoped his son would marry Carla, he declared, in response to a question from the prosecutor during cross-examination. On redirect, Lawrence answered questions about John's drinking and about his days in the Army. Then on recross, he recounted a conversation he had with his son during which John confessed that, while stationed in Colorado, he had killed an Army buddy's dog with his bare hands. When Lawrence left the witness stand, he stopped briefly at the defense table and lovingly patted John on the back.

On Friday, the eleventh day of the trial, Kathy Weber took the stand. She smiled and waved to her brother before beginning her testimony. Through her Reid tried to paint a picture of two John Webers—the evil John who smashed a beer bottle over her head and would have killed her, and the good John who was kind to animals and helpful to his neighbors.

"You couldn't find a person with a bigger heart," Kathy declared. "He would do anything for anybody. He shoveled all the neighbors' walks and mowed their lawns, the elderly women who couldn't do it themselves. He'd go and do it. He was so good-hearted."

She recounted hearing John arguing with "Natas." Asked what went through her mind when she heard that Carla had gone missing, Kathy said, "My heart sank."

She knew her brother had something to do with it. "I didn't know what, but I knew he was involved."

Why didn't she report her suspicions to the police? Reid asked.

"I just felt that it was sick of me to think that way, to put the blame on somebody who's trying to do better." She added, "I felt guilty for even thinking those thoughts."

Kathy was followed to the stand by Dr. William J. Crowley, a psychiatrist and clinical professor of psychiatry at the Medical College of Wisconsin. Dr. Crowley had been hired by the defense to examine and evaluate John. He diagnosed Weber as a sexual sadist, "clearly a seriously disturbed individual," who was suffering from a borderline personality disorder. John, he said, knew that his behavior was wrong but was overwhelmed by his sadistic impulses and incapable of resisting them when he attacked Carla and Emily.

The next day, Saturday, Dr. Robert Miller took the stand. Dr. Miller had examined and evaluated John for the prosecution. The psychiatrist had a keen professional interest in multiple personality disorder. He did not believe that John had more than one personality. He did agree with his colleague, though, that John was a sexual sadist, but he was not suffering from a mental disease or defect as defined by law. John's mental problems, he said, did not render him "unable to understand what he was feeling," nor did they make it "impossible for him to control his behavior." In other words, John was not insane.

After a five-minute break, Judge Carlson called for closing arguments. Predictably, Defense Attorney John Reid argued that his client was not legally responsible for his actions and asked the jury to so find. He reminded the panel of John's conversations with "Natas." John, he said, should not be sent to a prison but to a mental hospital. He could not be released until a court determined that he was no longer a danger to the community.

"I think you know what that means," he added, implying that it would never happen.

In his closing, DA Barnett called John Weber "a fraud, a liar, and a manipulator, someone who consciously, willfully, intentionally, and deliberately kept to himself the person he really and truly is."

There is no doubt, the prosecutor declared, "that John Weber is legally responsible, legally culpable for his acts."

Once again, Judge Carlson ordered the jury to begin deliberations immediately. At 5:28 P.M. they filed out of the courtroom. An hour and a half later they announced that they had reached a decision. Nine minutes later they were back in the jury box.

The Lenzes and the Webers were seated in the courtroom when Judge Carlson announced the jury's decision. By a vote of eleven to one, the panel had decided that John was not insane when he attacked and murdered Carla. And by a vote of eleven to one, they had reached the same finding with regard to Emily, who showed no emotion.

The judge thanked the jurors for their service and announced that he would sentence John on March 22 in Price County.

"You must never be free. You must never be in a position where this can happen again." With those words, Judge Gary Carlson sentenced John Weber to life in prison plus 164 years and nine months.

Asked if he had anything to say, John spoke up. "It doesn't do much good to say I'm sorry because I can't take back the hurt and pain I caused not only to the Lenz family but to my own."

Then he was led away.

EPILOGUE . . .

- *John Weber* was remanded to the custody of the Wisconsin Department of Corrections. After a brief stay at the Dodge Reception Center, the convicted cannibal killer was transferred to the maximum security Columbia Correctional Institution in Portage. He was joined there by another Wisconsin cannibal, Jeffrey Dahmer, following his conviction in 1992. Dahmer was murdered by an inmate on November 28, 1994. In February 2001, John Weber was transferred to the maximum-security Green Bay Correctional Institution.

- *Emily* divorced John shortly after he was convicted. She still lives in Wisconsin, as do her parents and Marguerite and Lawrence Weber.

- *Circuit Court Judge Gary Carlson* is still on the bench.

- *Price County District Attorney Paul Barnett* left Phillips to become an assistant attorney general in Madison.

- *Chief of Police Craig Moore* retired in January 2005. He believes the woods around Phillips hold at least one more body that was put there by John Weber—Shelly Hansen. She disappeared one year to the day after Carla Lenz went missing. Was it just a coincidence? "Lawmen don't believe in coincidences," he says.

In July 1990, the people of Phillips got news they never expected: The state's Court of Appeals had overturned Weber's murder conviction and ten additional convictions. It ruled that Chief Moore went beyond the scope of the search warrant when he listened to the tape that he found in the Cutlass. Investigators, the court said, were limited to searching for a hunting knife and the clothing Emily was wearing when John assaulted her. Prosecutors appealed to the Wisconsin Supreme Court. Ten months later, the state's highest court reversed the Court of Appeals. In a six-to-one decision, the Supreme Court said Moore did not need an additional warrant because Weber had left the tape in the cassette player in an unlocked automobile, indicating that he had no expectation of privacy.

4

GARY HEIDNIK
Stocks and Bondage

Before the world knew anything about Jeffrey Dahmer or Hannibal Lecter, there was Gary Heidnik.

During the wee hours of March 25, 1987, an army of police forced their way into a grimy row house in North Philadelphia. A sign on the outside proclaimed it the United Church of the Ministries of God, but this was no house of worship. Instead it was a house of horror into which Gary Heidnik, a forty-three-year-old white man with a diabolical plan, lured young black women and held them as his sex slaves in a basement dungeon.

"Gary Heidnik is one of the most evil persons I ever encountered," declared former Philadelphia Homicide Lieutenant James Hansen. The detective commanded the squad of cops that stormed the dilapidated house at 3520 North Marshall Street, in the seedy Franklinville section of the city.

"I remember the stench and the heat just like it was yesterday," he said. The sickening odor hit the cops as soon as they forced the front door open. It was so bad Hansen couldn't keep from retching. Many of the cops threw up.

Once inside, the lieutenant made a beeline for the kitchen, while Sergeant Frank McClosky headed for the basement. There he found two young black women—Lisa Thomas and Jacquelyn Askins. They were both naked from the waist down. They were manacled to a pipe and bound to each other by heavy metal chains. Clamps fashioned from automobile mufflers were around their ankles. Pushing aside a board that was lying on the concrete floor, the officers uncovered a four-foot-deep pit. Inside, shackled and bent over, was another young black woman, Agnes Adams. She was completely nude.

Meanwhile the cops upstairs were in for some stomach-turning discoveries: Chunks of what appeared to be human flesh clogged the drain in the kitchen sink. When Hansen opened the refrigerator, he noticed a white trash bag on a shelf. He looked inside. What he saw next made him sick—two handless forearms. More limbs were in the freezer. What appeared to be human bones were found in a charred pot on the stove. More bones were on the floor.

The body parts—in all, twenty-four pounds of human flesh and bones—were the remains of twenty-four-year-old Sandra Lindsay, a mildly retarded black woman who'd died while shackled to the pipes in the basement. Her body had been cut up with a power saw, her flesh put through a food processor and fed to the other women. Later detectives learned that Lindsay's head and rib cage had been baked in the oven.

The survivors told a mind-boggling tale of extreme torture, sexual depravity, and cannibalism, and of how "Bishop" Heidnik, a financial whiz who'd turned a modest stock market investment into a small fortune, boasted of his diabolical plan to enslave ten or more women and father as many children as possible.

It never happened. On July 6, 1999, Gary Heidnik, the "Madman of Marshall Street," was strapped onto a gurney and executed by lethal injection.

Eastlake, Ohio, is a city of twenty thousand on the shores of Lake Erie, about twenty miles northeast of downtown Cleveland. It's where Gary Michael Heidnik was born on November 22, 1943.

His father, Michael, was a tool and die maker and a local politician who served eight years on Eastlake's City Council. His mother, Ellen, was a beautician. According to Michael, she was also an alcoholic. It was not a happy marriage. They argued all the time.

In 1946 Michael and Ellen split. In her divorce papers, Ellen accused her husband of "gross neglect of duty." In his filing, Michael called her "a wild woman" and a "boozer."

Gary was two and his brother, Terry, a toddler when their parents divorced. At first the boys lived with their mother. Three years later they were living with their father in a ranch-style home on a tree-lined suburban street.

Before she committed suicide on Mother's Day 1970, Ellen married three more times. Her last two husbands were African-American. Michael remarried, too, but neither Gary nor Terry got along with their stepmother.

They didn't get along with their father either. Michael was a harsh disciplinarian whose severe punishments frequently crossed over the line into abuse. Both boys were beaten often and for little or no reason.

"It got to the point where we'd be afraid to pick anything up because he'd beat us if we dropped something like a glass," Terry told the *Philadelphia Daily News* in 1988.

"I got beat more often and more severely than Gary did—there were mornings I woke up with ice packs around my head," Terry recalled.

As for Gary, he was a chronic bed-wetter, but instead of getting medical help for his son, Michael did his best to shame him; whenever he wet his bed his father would hang the urine-soaked sheets from Gary's bedroom window for everyone in the neighborhood to see.

And Michael was a racist; he wouldn't allow his sons to listen to rock and roll "because a lot of the musicians were black," said Terry, who struggled with schizophrenia through most of his life. His father's racist rants went something like this: "What good's a nigger? If you're gonna abuse someone, abuse a nigger. Their life's [sic] miniscule. Put them on a boat and pull the plug."

Michael vehemently denied being a racist, and he denied being a strict disciplinarian. Gary, he told reporters, was just "a regular kid." Like any father-son relationship, the senior Heidnik said, "we had our ups and downs."

But Gary was anything but a regular kid. He didn't have many friends growing up. He was remembered as very withdrawn—an average student who had a paper route, joined the Boy Scouts, but otherwise kept to himself.

The other kids even had a demeaning nickname for him: From the early grades on they called him "Football Head." The nickname stemmed from an accident Gary had when he was six or seven—he tumbled out of a tree one day and landed flat on his skull. The fall, it was said, permanently molded Gary's head into a shape that resembled a football, hence the nickname.

According to Terry, Gary was never the same after falling from the tree. "We lived on a four-acre piece of land where animals came up to the house. Gary used to feed them before the fall, but after he fell from the tree, all he wanted to do was rope them, tie them up, and hang them from the nearest tree."

By the time he entered junior high school, Gary had developed two unusual interests that set him apart from his peers: the stock market—he avidly followed the daily opening and closing prices in the *Cleveland Plain Dealer*—and the Army—he liked to wear military-style fatigues.

Michael encouraged Gary's interest in the military and even encouraged him to apply for admission to the U.S. Military Academy at West Point. Gary, Michael thought, could become a general and then President of the United States. To get a taste of cadet life, Gary enrolled at the prestigious Staunton Academy in Virginia for his sophomore year of high school. Michael managed to scrape up the $1,500 annual tuition and Gary spent two years there, leaving after his junior year.

Why he left Staunton is not known. According to the school's alumni director, Gary did well academically—his IQ was 130—and he was never a discipline problem. Perhaps he just burned out, or perhaps Michael decided not to foot the bill anymore after Gary failed West Point's entrance exam.

Whatever the reason, Gary returned to Eastlake. In September he enrolled at North High School for his senior year, but he dropped out in October. By the end of November Gary Heidnik was a soldier in the United States Army. He could become a general, he thought, but he would have to work his way up through the ranks.

His three-year hitch got off to a good start. Thanks to the discipline he'd learned at Staunton, he excelled during basic training—his drill instructors graded him as "excellent." After basic, he applied to military police school, but he was turned down. Instead the Army sent him to Fort Sam Houston in San Antonio, Texas, where they trained him as a medic. Once again he did well. He also developed a thriving side business as a loan shark, lending out money to fellow soldiers at steep interest rates.

In May 1962, the Army put him out of business when they assigned him to a field hospital in Landstuhl, West Germany. When Heidnik was forced to leave for Germany in a hurry, he had no chance to collect the thousands of dollars he had loaned out. That didn't sit well with the budding tycoon.

Nevertheless he adjusted to his new assignment and everything was going well until late August, when Heidnik reported to sick call complaining of dizziness, blurred vision, vomiting, and almost constant nausea. An Army neurologist determined that he was suffering from gastroenteritis. What's more, he said, Heidnik showed symptoms of schizophrenia.

The doctor prescribed Stelazine, a very powerful anti-hallucinogenic medication. One of its side effects is a disorder called tardive dyskinesia, a condition marked by involuntary muscle spasms of the face and body. In his medical records, one of Heidnik's Army doctors later noted that his head would twitch horizontally every few seconds.

The last thing the U.S. Army needed was a schizophrenic in its ranks, so Heidnik was put on a plane and sent back to the United States, to a military hospital outside Philadelphia. The official Army diagnosis was "schizoid personality disorder." Three months later he was mustered out on medical grounds. Eventually he was awarded a 100 percent pension for what the Army decided was a service-connected disability.

He had been away from Eastlake for only fourteen months, but after his discharge from the Army Heidnik didn't want to go back to his hometown. Instead he settled in Philadelphia and enrolled in a nursing program, which he completed in February 1964. He served a six-month internship, after which the Commonwealth of Pennsylvania certified him as a licensed practical nurse. He also took courses at the University of Pennsylvania, earning credits in a variety of subjects including anthropology, history, chemistry and biology, business and law, and he purchased a three-story house on Cedar Avenue in Philadelphia's University City section.

An astute businessman, Heidnik rented out the first two floors and lived on the third. He worked for a time at the University of Pennsylvania Hospital, often taking on double shifts while pulling in nearly $1,900 a month in disability payments and Army pension. From that point on, however, Gary Heidnik's life began to sink into psychosis, triggered, perhaps, by his mother's suicide.

Ellen did herself in by drinking a bottle of mercuric chloride. Gary had her cremated; then he took her ashes to Niagara Falls, where he sprinkled them over the falls.

From then on, Gary himself attempted suicide dozens of times. He tried to overdose on Stelazine; he drove a motorcycle head-on into a truck; he tried hanging himself, and he also tried swallowing glass. Each time he wound up in a mental hospital. Doctors diagnosed him as depressed, psychotic, and schizophrenic. He would often spend long periods not talking. Instead he'd communicate by writing notes or through sign language. At other times, he just didn't communicate at all.

With each subsequent hospital admission, Heidnik's behavior became more bizarre. For a while he constantly wore a leather motorcycle jacket, refusing to remove it even to go to bed. He stopped bathing, he smelled, and he developed some other weird traits, like rolling up one pants leg as a signal that he didn't want to talk to anyone, or giving a crisp military salute whenever anyone asked him a question.

One time he landed in a mental ward after bashing his brother, Terry, in the head with a carpenter's plane. "I got sixteen stitches for that," Terry recalled. "There was blood all over the place."

Eventually the brothers reconciled, and Terry asked Gary what he would have done if Terry had died from his wounds. Gary calmly answered: "I would have soaked your remains in a bathtub full of a special acid that would eat your flesh and bones without harming the plumbing."

In 1971 Gary Heidnik found God, or as he told it, God found him. He was on the beach at Malibu gazing at the Pacific Ocean when the Lord spoke to him.

The world, God said, was in need of a new church to minister to the mentally and physically handicapped, and he, Gary Heidnik, was to be its bishop.

By October Heidnik had it all set up. He incorporated the United Church of the Ministers of God. Among the founders were his brother Terry and Dorothy Mae Knight, a retarded black woman with whom Gary was living at the time.

Under the bizarre bylaws, which Heidnik drew up himself, the church would be governed by a bishop appointed for life, or until he decided to resign.

"His is the final word on interpretation of the Bible or the settling of religious disputes," the bylaws read. The Bible would be the church's "guiding inspiration" with one caveat: "It is to be remembered that it is only an interpretation of the original Scriptures."

As for Jesus, "The divinity of Christ is questionable but he is recognized as God's prophet and our savior, hence his claim of Divine Origin is to be played down."

Bishop Heidnik would have the final word on all secular matters. He could raise money through "loans, stocks, bingo games, business ventures and other endeavors." The bylaws also contained a provision for liquidating the church's assets. "If and when dissolution should become necessary, the total assets of the church should be given directly or sold and the profits given equally to the federal government's Peace Corps and Veterans Administration."

Heidnik bought an altar, which he set up in his living room. Every Sunday he'd hold services for a handful of people, mostly retarded men and women he'd round up from the Elwyn Institute, a not-for-profit agency that provided services for the mentally retarded. He'd preach a short sermon, then everyone would climb into the church's old van and drive to McDonald's or Roy Rogers for lunch. Sometimes they would head for the Jersey Shore or an amusement park, all paid for by Bishop Gary Heidnik.

Until he launched his church, Heidnik always claimed he was a nonbeliever, an atheist. "He told me he set the church up as a tax dodge," Terry said. He plunked down $1,500 and opened up an account in the church's name with Merrill Lynch.

It must have been a very blessed account because by 1987 it was worth a hefty $545,000—it had returned a whopping 25 percent a year, outperforming the Standard & Poor's 500 by 9 percent annually. Heidnik the stock whiz managed the account personally. The church had other assets, too: a Cadillac, a Rolls-Royce, a Dodge Dart, a van, and the house on North Marshall Street.

In addition to his mental problems, Heidnik also had legal problems. In the fall of 1976 he was arrested and charged with assault, possession of a handgun without a license, and carrying a firearm on a public street. The arrest stemmed from an incident that involved the boyfriend of Heidnik's tenant, a black man named Robert Rogers.

It seems Heidnik had a dispute with the girlfriend, a nurse. He went into the basement and shut off her utilities. When the boyfriend came over, he went into the basement to turn the power back on. The basement door was locked, however, so he pried open a window and climbed in. Heidnik was waiting for him with a rifle and a pistol.

"I'm going to kill you and say you're a burglar," Heidnik said. Then he lifted the pistol and fired. Luckily the bullet just grazed the man's cheek. "I talked him out of shooting me a second time," Rogers said. When they went outside, Heidnik was still toting his guns. When the police came, he was arrested. The charges were dropped a week later, but the court records do not indicate why.

A few months later Heidnik sold the house. When the new owners were cleaning the place out, they made a startling discovery—in the basement someone had dug a pit through the concrete and scooped out the dirt. The pit was large enough to hold an adult.

Meanwhile Gary moved into an apartment in West Philadelphia with a black woman named Anjeanette Davidson. Anjeanette was unable to read or write. Her IQ was pegged at 49. When she got pregnant, Gary refused to allow her to see a doctor. About a month before she was due to give birth, Anjeanette's older sister showed up at the apartment with the police and a court order and spirited her away. On March 22, 1978, Anjeanette gave birth to a baby girl by C-section. The baby was placed in a foster home soon after birth.

As soon as Anjeanette recovered, she and Heidnik drove to Selinsgrove Center, an institution for the mentally retarded near

Harrisburg, where another of Anjeanette's sisters, Alberta, was living. Alberta, thirty-four, had the mental ability of a five-year-old. Heidnik signed her out, promising to return her no later than the next morning, but he never did. Nine days later officials at Selinsgrove obtained a court order and went looking for Alberta.

The first place they looked was Anjeanette's apartment in West Philadelphia. When the official from the center knocked on the door, Heidnik opened it. He assured the official, a woman, that Alberta was not there. He even permitted her to walk through the apartment.

"Where is she?" the woman asked.

"I put her on a bus back to Selinsgrove," he replied.

The woman left, but she returned the next day, this time with the cops. Again Heidnik allowed her to walk through the apartment, and once again there was no trace of Alberta. This time, however, she had the cops search the entire building. To no one's surprise they found Alberta hiding in a storage room in the basement.

Back at the center, Alberta was given a thorough medical examination. Doctors found a tear on the vestibule of her vagina which indicated recent sexual intercourse. They also swabbed her mouth and throat. The swabs turned up traces of sperm in her mouth and gonorrhea in her throat. Three weeks later police arrested Heidnik and charged him with kidnapping, rape, false imprisonment, unlawful restraint, involuntary deviate sexual intercourse, recklessly endangering another person, and interfering with the custody of a committed person. He pleaded not guilty and waived a jury trial, which left his fate in the hands of Common Pleas Court Judge Charles P. Mirarchi Jr.

The judge wanted a complete psychiatric evaluation of Heidnik. The psychiatrist who evaluated him said that there was a "high probability" that Heidnik would commit similar crimes in the future. "Of particular concern is the defendant's potential for engaging in sexually assaultive crimes against females."

While the report was prophetic, Heidnik got off easy. Because Alberta was judged too retarded to testify, the rape, kidnapping, false imprisonment, and involuntary deviate sexual intercourse charges could not be prosecuted. On the remaining charges—unlawful restraint, interfering with the custody of a committed person, and recklessly endangering another person—Judge Mirarchi sentenced Heidnik to the maximum—three to seven years in the state penitentiary. "If it had been in my power to give him longer, I would have," the judge would declare ten years later.

Heidnik was sent to Graterford, a maximum-security prison facility near Philadelphia. He arrived there on January 29, 1979, and almost immediately he went mute. For months he didn't utter a single word. In June prison authorities finally decided to send him to a mental hospital, Norristown State, where he stayed until October. Then it was back to Graterford, but not for long. In May he was sent to Farview, a maximum-security hospital for the criminally insane. In all, Gary Heidnik bounced from prison to mental hospital and back to prison more than a dozen times during the four years and four months he was under the control of the Pennsylvania Department of Corrections.

During that period he came up for parole three times, and three times he was turned down. The fourth time was the charm, however, and on March 24, 1983, the parole board decided he was ready to rejoin society. Three weeks later thirty-nine-year-old Gary Heidnik was back in Philadelphia.

Within a year he bought the house on Marshall Street and befriended Cyril "Tony" Brown, a retarded black man who was employed at the Elwyn Institute. Through Brown, Heidnik met a bevy of retarded black women, and he knew just how to win them over—with lunch at McDonald's, then a drive to Marshall Street for sex.

Heidnik favored threesomes. He liked to lie flat on his back while one of the women straddled him with his penis inside her. As she pumped away he'd bite hard on one of the other woman's breasts until he climaxed. About a half hour later they would do it all again—only this time, the women switched places.

The lovemaking sessions were almost daily occurrences at Marshall Street. One of the women who participated from time to time was Sandra Lindsay. But the trysts must have left Heidnik unfulfilled, because about this time he decided to seek a bride, but not just any bride—he wanted an Asian virgin to be Mrs. Gary Heidnik. To find her he registered with an agency in Philadelphia that specialized in mail-order brides from the Philippines.

A few weeks later a twenty-two-year-old Filipina named Betty Ditso was at home in the Philippines flipping through a brochure that contained the names of American men who were looking for brides. Betty was from Mindanao, the southernmost island in the Philippines. She was the youngest of six children. Her father was a military man who died when Betty was twelve, leaving her mother and five brothers and sisters in dire straits.

As Betty read through the brochure, one entry in particular caught her eye—Heidnik's. It said he was thirty-six, a nurse living in Philadelphia. Betty's mother wanted her to become a nurse, so she decided to write to him.

At the time Betty wasn't looking for a husband, just a pen pal. They exchanged letters, then photos. After two years of weekly correspondence, Heidnik proposed and Betty accepted. He never told his bride-to-be that he was on disability for mental problems, or that he had been in and out of mental hospitals, or that he had been in prison. And he never revealed his true age.

Betty's mother wasn't too keen on the idea of her youngest child traveling halfway around the world to marry a man she'd never met. She thought he might be a witch, but Betty, who liked American movies and American music, was hell-bent on marrying Gary Heidnik. She applied for and was granted a visa, and Gary sent her a plane ticket. On September 29, 1985, Betty headed for Manila, where she boarded a plane that took her to first to Tokyo and then to Philadelphia, where Gary Heidnik was waiting for her at the gate with a bouquet of flowers.

She was shocked when she first laid eyes on her American fiancé. For one thing, he looked much older than she'd expected. For another, he was dressed all in black—black shirt, black leather vest, black pants. "He looked like Dracula," she recalled.

He suggested she stay in a hotel until they were married, but frugal Betty didn't want him to waste his money. "I trust you," she told Heidnik, so instead of driving her to a hotel he drove to North Marshall Street.

After hauling her luggage into the house, Heidnik showed Betty around. When he took her to an upstairs bedroom, Betty was in for yet another shock: A black woman was sleeping in the water bed.

Betty had never seen a water bed before. What's more, until her plane landed in Philadelphia, she had never seen a black person before. She wondered what she'd gotten herself into, but Heidnik told her that the woman was a tenant who was renting the room from him for $250 a month. That must have reassured Betty, because instead of making a beeline for the front door, she spent her first night in America in a water bed next to a retarded black woman.

On Thursday, October 3, Betty and Gary drove fifty miles to Elkton, Maryland, where they tied the knot, but they didn't live happily ever after. As soon as they returned to Philadelphia, Betty once again got the feeling that all was not right with her husband. Wherever they went, they were accompanied by a cadre of Gary's mentally retarded friends. On the first Sunday of their married life, a dozen or so retarded men and women showed up at the house for church services. They sang while Heidnik preached about King David and his many wives. A week later Betty was in the kitchen when she heard moaning and groaning coming from the master bedroom, so she climbed the stairs to investigate. When she opened the door she found Gary in the buff, in bed with three naked black women.

Betty ran crying from the room. Heidnik chased after her. "Just give me a ticket," she shrieked. "I'll go back to the Philippines."

"No," he said. "This is normal here in America. Don't you know that? I'm the boss. I'm the one who runs the show."

When she insisted he stop seeing other women, he beat her. On more than one occasion he made her stand in a corner for twelve hours. He deprived her of food and water. Several times he forced her to watch him having sex with other women. He even threatened to kill her.

Eventually Betty was able to sneak away to mail a letter she wrote in her native Tagalog to the Philippine Consulate in New York. The handwritten plea for help was simple and straightforward: Her husband, she wrote, was *"diperensiya sa utak"* (mentally ill) and she was in fear for her life. The consulate put her in touch with an attorney, who urged her to leave Heidnik and go to the police.

Three months after her plane had touched down at the Philadelphia International Airport, Betty heeded the lawyer's advice and fled. She told Heidnik she was going food shopping. Instead, she escaped to a shelter for abused and battered women, then contacted the police.

On January 27, 1986, the District Attorney's Office charged Heidnik with spousal rape, involuntary deviate sexual intercourse, simple assault, and indecent assault. Two days later he was arrested. The charges were dropped in March, however, because Betty failed to appear for the preliminary hearing. Heidnik didn't know it, but Betty was pregnant. In September she gave birth to his son. She named the baby Jesse, after King David's father, and sent her husband a postcard announcing the birth. He never replied.

Two months later Heidnik took his first sex slave—Josefina Rivera, a twenty-five-year-old prostitute who went by the street name Nicole.

It was two days before Thanksgiving, but Josefina Rivera wasn't feeling very thankful. She was out on the street, enduring a cold rain in a thin windbreaker and tight jeans, hoping to earn some more money. But traffic was light and the cars that drove past the corner of Third and Girard weren't stopping. She thought about calling it a night and going back to the apartment she shared with her boyfriend, Vincent Nelson, on North Sixth Street, but she decided to work the corner a little longer.

While Rivera waited for her first trick, three miles to the north Gary Heidnik slid behind the wheel of his 1987 Cadillac Coupe De Ville. The car was brand spanking new, pewter over white with a continental kit, custom front, and wire wheels. He'd driven it home from the showroom only nine days earlier.

Heidnik decided that the time had come to put his breeding plan into action. The basement was ready—the pit had been carved from the concrete floor; the chains and manacles were in place. Now all he had to do was fill the room with women. He was about to snare his first one.

He backed the Caddy out of his driveway, then steered it toward downtown. When he spotted Rivera, he pulled over and lowered the passenger-side window.

"You working?" he asked.

Rivera walked over to the car and peered in. "Yeah," she said.

"What's your price?"

She gave him a figure and he counteroffered. "Would you take twenty?"

She agreed, opened the door, and got in.

"I'm Gary," he said.

"I'm Nicole."

"I need to make a quick stop first," he told her. A few minutes later he pulled into a McDonald's parking lot. She followed him inside, where he ordered a cup of coffee for himself, nothing for her.

She could see him clearly now in the bright light, a tall white man with pale blue eyes and a neatly trimmed brown beard. A thick gold chain and a gold cross dangled from his neck. On his wrist was a shiny Rolex watch. He wore a burnt orange cowhide jacket with fringes on the arms, over a plaid flannel shirt. The jacket was stained and rubbed out in spots and his jeans were filthy. His hair oozed grease and he smelled badly. If she had gotten a whiff of him before, she would have turned him down, but the new-car smell masked his body odor. Josefina couldn't wait to get their business over with.

"Where are we going?" she asked impatiently.

"My house," he replied, heading for the door as he answered. Five minutes later they arrived at 3520 North Marshall Street. Turning left into a driveway, he passed a chain-link fence and steered the car into a ramshackle two-car garage. Josefina couldn't help but notice the other car that was parked inside—a Rolls-Royce.

He led her into the house through a back door that opened into the kitchen, the walls of which were covered with pennies that someone had carefully glued into place.

Heidnik never broke stride as he headed straight for the living room. He asked Rivera if she wanted to watch a movie, but she was anxious to get this trick over with, so she told him she didn't have time, she had to get back to her kids. That was a lie. Rivera *was* the mother of three, but her children, all under five, weren't living with her.

Heidnik turned and led her up a narrow stairway. At the top Rivera noticed that one of the walls in the narrow hallway had been papered with real money—one- and five-dollar bills. He led her into the bedroom, pulled a twenty-dollar bill from his pocket, and handed it to her. In a flash he was out of his clothes and on the water bed. Rivera took off her shirt and jeans and climbed in beside him.

She was skinny, but her breasts were round and firm, her legs were long, and her skin was the color of cocoa. She was the product of a Puerto Rican father and an African-American mother, but her facial features definitely favored her father. She was an attractive young woman and Heidnik was ready.

A few minutes after she climbed into the water bed, their business was over. Rivera had earned her money. She put on her shirt and was about to step into her jeans when she felt a pair of hands grip her throat. They squeezed. She started to lose consciousness. As her legs gave way, Heidnik loosened his grip. He handcuffed her right wrist, then clamped the other cuff around a bedpost. Later, he handcuffed her hands behind her back and pushed her out of the bedroom, down the stairs, through the kitchen, and into the basement, where he chained her to an overhead pipe by her feet so that her legs hung in the air. A lumpy and soiled mattress was under her back and Rivera lay down on it. Exhausted, she fell asleep.

She awoke hours later—cold, hungry, and scared. She had no idea what Gary wanted of her; she would find out soon enough. In the meantime, she surveyed the musty basement. A single bulb cast a dim light throughout the room, but it was just enough for her to make out a white freezer and a washer-dryer on one side of the cellar. She also noticed a boarded-up overhead window. She thought it might be reachable if her chains were long enough.

A battered old pool table took up most of the middle of the room. From the corner of her eye Rivera noticed that an area of the concrete floor had been broken up, as if someone had been digging a pit. She was wondering what it was for when she heard footsteps coming down the stairway. It was Gary, and he brought her an egg sandwich and a glass of orange juice. Even though she was very hungry, Rivera turned the food down.

"Suit yourself," Heidnik said, as he turned to carry the food upstairs. A few minutes later he was back, this time with a pick and shovel. He went to work on the pit, making it wider and deeper. As he worked he told Rivera of his plans.

"Society owes me a wife and family," he told her, after recounting how he had fathered four children, and how all four were snatched away from him. "I want to get ten women and keep them here and get them all pregnant. Then, when they have babies, I want to raise those children here, too. We'll be one big happy family." If Rivera didn't know it before, she knew it now: She was the captive of a madman.

Heidnik worked on the pit for a few more minutes then put down the pick and the shovel and walked over to Josefina. He dropped his pants and ordered Rivera to take his penis into her mouth. When it got hard he inserted it into her vagina, pumped until he climaxed, then left the basement.

As soon as Heidnik left, Rivera began looking for a way out. When she realized that the chain was long enough to reach the window and beyond, she hunted around for a tool she could use to pry open the boards that covered the window. She found a pool cue, which she was able to use as a lever. After prying off the boards, she hoisted herself up to the window, opened it, and crawled through to the backyard, as far as the chains would stretch. Then she started screaming, but the only one who paid any attention was Gary Heidnik.

Screaming women were not uncommon on North Marshall Street. Neither were gunfire or sirens. Neighbors rarely if ever even turned their heads, but when Heidnik heard her, he came racing out to the backyard. He tried to force Rivera back through the open window, but she resisted, so he ran back inside and down to the basement, where he grabbed the chains and reeled her in like a fish.

When he finally got Rivera back into the cellar, he beat her with a stick, then shoved her into the pit. A few minutes later he was back with a radio. He tuned it to a rock station, turned the volume all the way up, and left. Now if Rivera screamed, he was certain no one would ever hear her.

The day after Thanksgiving Sandra Lindsay wasn't feeling well. She was suffering from severe menstrual cramps and by nightfall she decided to walk to a corner store to get some Midol. It was the last time her family saw her.

Lindsay was a twenty-four-year-old dark-skinned black woman. She was mildly retarded and walked with a limp. Her speech was slurred and she wore big glasses with thick lenses. When she wasn't talking, her lower jaw hung open.

Lindsay worked at the Elwyn Institute, which is how she'd met Heidnik, through Tony Brown, her ex-boyfriend. Heidnik bought her lunch at McDonald's and took her to the Jersey shore and Great Adventure, so she joined his church.

Sometimes she slept with Brown, and sometimes she went to bed with Bishop Heidnik. At one time she was carrying Heidnik's baby, but the thought of motherhood frightened her and she aborted the pregnancy.

As she limped her way along the street, Heidnik pulled up in the Coupe De Ville. It was cold and windy. When he offered her a ride, Lindsay accepted. Later that evening he brought her down to the basement.

Rivera, who was in the pit, heard them coming down the steps. Lindsay kept telling Heidnik that she didn't want to go to the basement. "Shut up. I'm not going to hurt you," he told her.

After chaining Lindsay to the pipe, he hoisted Rivera from the pit and introduced the two women. "Nicole, this is Sandy," he said. "Sandy, this is Nicole." Then he left them alone.

Lindsay, who was wearing a blouse and a pair of eyeglasses and nothing else, explained how she had met Heidnik. She told Rivera all about Tony and sleeping with Heidnik and about the abortion.

"Gary was mad," she said. "He criticized me at church on Sunday. He said abortions were evil." She told Rivera that Heidnik even offered her a thousand dollars to have his baby, but she turned him down. "Now he says I'm going to have his baby whether I want to or not."

She couldn't understand why Bishop Gary, who had always been so nice to her, had so suddenly turned against her. She started to cry. With every sob her entire body shook. An hour later Heidnik was back. He brought crackers and water for his captives, then started digging. After working on the pit for a while, he wanted sex. With Rivera looking on, he ordered Lindsay to take his penis into her mouth. After a few minutes he inserted it into her vagina. When he finished with Lindsay, it was Rivera's turn.

Sandra Lindsay wasn't a streetwalker. She had a family, and they went looking for her. Their search led them to 3520 North Marshall Street. They knew Sandra had visited there on more than one occasion and they knew Gary lived there, but they didn't know his last name.

Heidnik had just served his captives breakfast when Lindsay's sister and two of her brothers began pounding on his front door. He peeked through the shades and waited for the pounding to stop. After a few minutes they went away. The next time Heidnik went down to the basement, he brought blank sheets of writing paper, a pen, and an envelope.

"Write what I tell you," he ordered Lindsay. "Dear Mom, do not worry, I will call."

He waited while Lindsay wrote. When she finished, he told her to sign the letter and address the envelope. "I'm going to mail this from New York," he said. "Then nobody will come here looking for you. They'll just think you ran away."

Over the next two days Lindsay's family combed North Philadelphia. On Monday they reported Sandra missing to the police.

The case was assigned to Sergeant Julius Armstrong, a seventeen-year veteran of the Philadelphia Police Department. He went to the house on North Marshall Street and pounded on the door, too. When no one answered, the sergeant left. Then he went looking for Tony Brown.

He found him at the McDonald's near the Elwyn Institute. "What's Gary's last name?" he wanted to know. Brown told him. The sergeant asked him to spell it; then he went back to the police station and punched the name into the computer exactly as Brown had spelled it. Nothing turned up. That's because Brown had spelled Heidnik incorrectly, and Armstrong did nothing more to identify the owner of the house—he didn't check the tax rolls or the utility records. Had the sergeant punched in the correct spelling, he would have learned that Heidnik had done four years in prison for kidnapping a mentally retarded black woman and hiding her in a basement. That information would have been enough to send an army of cops with battering rams to the house on Marshall Street.

To make matters worse, Jeanette Perkins, Lindsay's mother, had received the note Heidnik had forced her daughter to write. She brought it to Sergeant Armstrong, who decided that Lindsay was a runaway. He didn't exactly drop the case; he just put it on the back burner. But Perkins never believed her daughter had run away—that would have been out of character for Sandra—so she kept going back with her sons and daughters to North Marshall Street and pounding on the door, but no one ever opened it.

As November slipped into December, the captives in Heidnik's dungeon settled into a routine. Wearing nothing more than a shirt, they spent most of their time huddled together, desperately trying to keep warm. In the morning Heidnik brought them Pop-Tarts for breakfast. Sometimes he would bring them lunch—

bread and crackers. For a while, dinner was usually a well-done hot dog with some rice. If he was in a good mood he brought in fried chicken. But the food situation soon deteriorated. Heidnik had two dogs, Bear and Flaky. One day, as he fed them their daily ration of canned Alpo dog food, he decided it would be a good idea to feed the women dog food, too.

"Eat it or take a beating," he barked. The women did as they were told, and from then on canned dog food became a staple of their diet.

And every day, sometimes twice a day, Heidnik would come downstairs for sex. The routine was always the same—oral first to get him aroused, then vaginal intercourse to impregnate the women. Sometimes he'd have sex with one, while at other times he wanted sex from both. If they refused, complained, raised their voices, or in any way displeased him, he'd beat them with a shovel handle or throw them into the pit.

Around this time he added a new torture to his repertoire— while Rivera and Lindsay looked on, he screwed a large eye hook into a ceiling beam about seven feet above the floor. He'd slap a handcuff on one of the women's wrists, then attach the other cuff to the hook. From it the woman would dangle, sometimes for hours.

Hygiene was virtually nonexistent in the basement. All the women had to wash themselves with was some baby wipes. To relieve themselves they used a Porta Potti.

Three days before Christmas, Heidnik went hunting for another woman to add to his basement harem. As he cruised the streets in his Coupe De Ville, a hot-looking nineteen-year-old in a blue down jacket caught his eye. Her name was Lisa Thomas, and she was on her way to a girlfriend's house to retrieve a pair of gloves she'd left there a few days before.

Heidnik stopped the car, rolled down his window, and asked, "You want to see my peter?"

"I'm no prostitute," she replied indignantly.

Heidnik apologized, asked her where she was going, and then offered her a ride. "I'm not going to hurt you," he assured her. Thomas eyed the big car, sized up its driver, and decided to accept the offer. Heidnik drove her to her friend's house and waited outside while she retrieved the gloves. When she returned, he asked if she would like to join him for a bite to eat.

There must have been something about Lisa that especially appealed to Heidnik because instead of heading for McDonald's, he drove to TGI Friday's. As they ate, he invited the teen to accompany him to Atlantic City. When Thomas said she didn't have anything to wear, he pulled out a fifty-dollar bill and handed it to her.

"For new clothes," he said, as he passed the bill across the table. "When you finish eating, we can go to Sears and you can buy whatever you want."

After purchasing two pairs of jeans and a couple of tops, Heidnik asked if she would let him put them on her. Thomas agreed and they drove to North Marshall Street, where he invited her to make herself at home. He gave her a wine cooler. After a few sips Thomas fell sound asleep. When she awoke, she was stark naked in Gary Heidnik's water bed. As she started to put her clothes on, Thomas felt a pair of hands grip her throat. She began to lose consciousness.

"Quit choking me," she gasped. "I'll do whatever you want."

Heidnik handcuffed her and dragged her down to the basement.

"I want to introduce you to my two friends," he said. He removed the plywood that covered the pit, and Thomas watched in amazement as two women, both naked from the waist down, emerged.

"I'm Nicole," said the first one. "I'm Sandy," said the second. Then Heidnik initiated her into his dungeon harem—while Nicole and Sandy looked on, he forced Lisa to have sex with him.

On December 25, Heidnik played Santa Claus. He brought a Chinese restaurant's takeout menu into the basement and allowed each woman to choose her Christmas dinner. Two days after New Year's Heidnik went hunting again and returned with Deborah Johnson Dudley, a twenty-three-year-old black woman. No one knows what ruse he used to snare her in his evil scheme. Dudley was sassy and rebellious, and from the start she gave her captor nothing but trouble, and almost immediately she began planning her escape from the dungeon.

Meanwhile, Heidnik brought yet another woman to the basement—Jacquelyn Askins. She had been plying her trade in front of a North Philadelphia hotel on January 18 at around noon, hoping to turn a lunchtime trick or two. Heidnik drove by and she went home with him.

What followed next was the usual pattern: Sex in the water bed, a grab of the throat from behind—the Heidnik maneuver—then down to the basement.

With five women chained in the basement, Heidnik decided that he could no longer be Mr. Nice Guy—he'd have to rule with an iron hand. To keep Askins from getting out of line, he beat her even before he introduced her to the others.

"That's what you're going to get if you don't do what I tell you," he told her. Then he beat her again to make sure that she understood.

Despite his efforts at crowd control, a rebellion was brewing, and its leader was Deborah Dudley. Somehow she got her hands on a heavy chunk of iron pipe. The plan called for her to hit Heidnik over the head with it, then the four others would grab whatever they could and bash Heidnik again and again until they killed him.

The plan might have worked but Rivera, desperate to curry favor with her captor, tipped him off. To punish the women, all except Rivera, and to make sure they couldn't hear him walking about the house or coming and going through the door, he punctured their eardrums with screwdrivers.

"He used three kinds," Thomas said later. "Small, medium, and large. He twisted them in our ears until pus came."

Sandra Lindsay was dying, and everyone in the house knew it except former Army medic and licensed practical nurse Gary Heidnik. As punishment for sliding back the plywood board that covered the pit without his permission, he strung her up from the eye hook and left her hanging there for eight hours. For three days before that, Lindsay had complained of a fever, and she couldn't keep any food down, not even the bits of bread Heidnik tried to stuff down her throat.

When he finally unhooked her, Lindsay fell to the floor in a heap. "She's faking," he said. He checked for a pulse but found none. It was February 7, and Sandra Lindsay was dead. Heidnik decided to destroy her body.

He hoisted the still-warm corpse over his shoulder and carried it upstairs. A short time later, the women in the basement heard the unmistakable buzz of a power saw. About two days after Lindsay died, Heidnik bought a food processor at Sears. He used it to grind up the fleshy parts of Lindsay's body, which he mixed with dog food and served to Bear, Flaky, Rivera, Thomas, and Dudley. The body parts that he couldn't put through the food processor—the head, rib cage, hands, and feet—he tried to destroy by cooking.

And he tried to turn Lindsay's death into a learning experience for Dudley. He unhooked her and dragged her up to the kitchen. When she returned, Rivera asked her what had happened. Heidnik, she said, had shown her Lindsay's head in a pot on the stove, then warned that if she didn't stop misbehaving, the same thing would happen to her.

Meanwhile the stench of death permeated the entire house. The nauseating odor stuck to Heidnik—the women smelled it on him whenever he entered the basement for sex. It even seeped out into the neighborhood. It was so bad, in fact, that neighbors put in a call to the police. They were worried about Heidnik.

It was bitterly cold in Philadelphia on February 10. Officer Julio Aponte was only an hour into his four-to-midnight shift when the call came over his car radio. "Check on the well-being of a person and a foul odor at 3520 North Marshall Street," the dispatcher ordered. Three minutes later Aponte parked his blue and white patrol car in front of the ramshackle house.

Three neighbors were waiting for him at the curb. They told the young cop that they were concerned about the home's owner, Gary Heidnik. No one had seen him in several days. He'd tried to commit suicide once before, they said, and they feared that this time he'd succeeded and his body was rotting away inside. How else to explain the sickening odor coming from the house?

Aponte pounded on the front door, but no one answered. He walked around the back, peeped into the windows, but the shades were drawn tight. He heard loud rock music blaring inside but saw no sign of life. The neighbors demanded that the cop break in, but he wouldn't do that without a go-ahead from his supervisor.

Aponte was back in his car talking to the dispatcher when the front door opened.

It was Heidnik, and he was very much alive. Aponte looked Heidnik up and down. As far as he could tell, he was all right. He was coherent and rational. When the cop asked about the odor, Heidnik answered, "I just burned my dinner, that's all."

The response satisfied Aponte, who got back in his patrol car and drove away.

It was a close call. If Aponte had been a bit more aggressive, or a bit more inquisitive, Heidnik's reign of terror would have ended right then and there. But it didn't, and even before the patrol car was out of sight, the Madman of Marshall Street was conjuring up a new, more diabolical torture for his captives—electric shock.

He cut off the plug end of an electrical extension cord and exposed the wires, stripping off about a quarter of an inch of the insulation. Then he plugged the other end into an outlet. He touched the bare end of the cord to the women's chains and watched them jump. He thought this was very funny, so he did it again. Heidnik had a new tool with which to terrorize the women, and he wielded it without mercy. If they defied him or displeased him in any way, they could expect to receive a jolt delivered through their chains.

On March 18, 1987, he ordered Dudley and Thomas into the pit. He had grown tired of Dudley's insolence and he was going to punish her. When she began screaming, he ordered Rivera to attach a garden hose to a faucet and fill the hole with water. As the other women watched, Rivera pushed the electrical cord toward the trapped women's chains. The cord, with electricity running through it, made direct contact with Dudley's chains.

"He's killing me," she yelled. Those were the last words she ever uttered.

"I don't want to hear that bullshit," Heidnik said, after Rivera told him Dudley was dead. He walked over to the pit, where he saw Dudley lying facedown in the muddy water. He pulled her out, then left her body on the concrete floor.

"Aren't you glad it wasn't one of you?" Heidnik asked nonchalantly. He then went upstairs, but he returned a few minutes later with blank writing paper and a pen, which he handed to Rivera.

"Write," he commanded. "Put the date at the top, March 18, 1987, and the time, 6:30 P.M." Then he told her what else to write: "I, Nicole Rivera, and Gary Heidnik killed Debbie Johnson by applying electricity to her chain while sitting in a pool of water in a hole in a basement of 3520 Marshall Street."

He had Rivera sign it, he signed, and then he ordered Askins and Thomas to sign it as witnesses. Heidnik told Rivera, "If you ever go to the cops, I can use this as evidence that you killed Debbie."

Dudley's body remained on the cellar floor overnight. The next morning Heidnik put it inside the basement freezer. Her body, he decided, didn't have to be sliced, diced, and cooked, because, unlike Lindsay, no one could connect him to Dudley. He decided to dump the body just as soon as he thought of a suitable location.

After Dudley's death, Rivera's lifestyle improved dramatically. Heidnik freed her from her shackles, and he permitted her to don clean clothes. They had sex in the water bed instead of the cellar. He took her along when he brought his Rolls-Royce into a garage for repairs, and he bought her a new wig and new clothes. She even accompanied him when he went looking for a suitable spot to dispose of Dudley's body, and again when he actually dumped it off a dirt road in a state forest in the remote Pine Barrens of South Jersey.

One day Heidnik took Rivera to the McDonald's near the Elwyn Institute, where they ran into Tony Brown. "Do you know where Sandy is?" Brown asked. "Her family is looking for her."

"They probably stashed her away somewhere so they can cash her Social Security checks," Heidnik replied.

He later confided in Rivera, "If I ever get caught, I'm going to act crazy. I'm going to go into court and salute everybody." And he revealed that he'd been hoodwinking his psychiatrists for years. "I've learned so I can keep getting my government checks," he told her.

With his harem now down to three, Heidnik decided to restock it. On the evening of March 23, he and Rivera hit the streets in the Coupe De Ville. It wasn't long before they spotted twenty-four-year-old Agnes Adams standing on a corner hoping to hook a customer.

They both knew her—Rivera from working the streets, and Heidnik from having done business with Adams twice before, the most recent occasion in February, while he had four sex slaves chained in the cellar. Back then he had brought her to Marshall Street for a noontime blow job, after which she left. This time, however, she would be staying.

While Rivera waited in the kitchen pondering her future, Heidnik took Adams upstairs to the bedroom. They had sex, he gave her the Heidnik maneuver, and she wound up in chains in the basement.

Meanwhile, Rivera decided to make her break. She wanted to see her family, she told him. If he allowed her to do that, she'd bring him another woman that very night. At first Heidnik resisted, but Rivera pressed on, reminding him how much she'd already helped him, and besides, he had the letter.

After some hemming and hawing, Heidnik agreed. They devised a plan: He would drop her off, she would visit with her family, then get the woman she had in mind and meet him at a gas station on Sixth and Girard. As they drove downtown, Heidnik warned Rivera that he would kill the women in the cellar if she didn't return.

As soon as she was out of the Cadillac, Rivera bolted for Vincent Nelson's apartment. At 11 P.M. she rang the bell and pounded on the door until Nelson answered. Rivera was crying and shaking and began telling a wild tale about torture and chains, and a dungeon, and about arms and legs in a refrigerator and a head in a pot, and a man named Gary who was waiting for her in a Cadillac on Sixth and Girard.

At first Nelson didn't believe her, but after about thirty minutes he came around. "We're going up there and we're going to mess this dude up," he told her. He grabbed a hammer and the two of them set out to kill Heidnik.

They'd gone about a block when Nelson had second thoughts. He decided it would be better to call the police. At a pay phone he dialed 911, then he handed the receiver to Rivera.

Within minutes a police car pulled up. As Officers David Savidge and John Cannon listened to her story, they found it hard to believe, too, until Rivera showed them the cuts and scabs the muffler clamps had left on her ankles. The two cops got back into their car and drove to Sixth and Girard, where they pulled behind a pewter-over-white Coupe De Ville that was parked in front of the King Serve and Save gas station and mini-mart. With guns drawn, Savidge and Cannon approached the car. Heidnik saw them coming but offered no resistance.

"What's this all about? Didn't I make my child support?" he asked.

"No," Savidge said. "It's about kidnapping, rape, and murder." Then he put the cuffs on Heidnik.

Four hours later a squad of cops broke through the front door of 3520 North Marshall Street. Gary Heidnik's reign of terror was over. The next day Rivera led detectives to the isolated spot where Heidnik had dumped Dudley's body.

For the next three weeks, cops combed through the grimy house and dug up the ground around it. They were convinced there were more bodies, but none were ever found.

Heidnik went on trial on Monday, June 20, 1988, in Room 653 of Philadelphia's stately City Hall. He faced a myriad of charges: first-degree murder, kidnapping, rape, aggravated assault, involuntary deviate sexual intercourse, indecent exposure, false imprisonment, unlawful restraint, simple assault, making terroristic threats, recklessly endangering another person, indecent assault, criminal solicitation, and possession and abuse of a corpse.

Early on District Attorney Ronald Castille announced that he was going for the death penalty, and early on he assigned one of his top deputies—Charles Gallagher—to the case. Gallagher was a dedicated civil servant, the son of a cop and the brother of a nun.

Fifteen months had passed since Officers Savidge and Cannon took Heidnik into custody outside the Serve and Save, and much had happened since. For one thing, the media attention had been relentless, and with good reason. The gruesome case had everything: sex, murder, race, bondage, torture, religion, cannibalism, even money. The media didn't know which angle to cover first.

Heidnik hadn't even been in jail twenty-four hours when he was punched in the face by another prisoner. He had to be treated for a broken nose. A week later he tried to hang himself with a T-shirt. Then he hired A. Charles "Chuck" Peruto Jr., a flamboyant and very quotable criminal defense attorney whose father,

A. Charles Sr., was regarded as the dean of Philadelphia's criminal defense lawyers.

Chuck Jr. had gone to work for his father when he first graduated from the University of Delaware law school, but he decided to hang out his own shingle two years later. He was a tenacious advocate for his clients and a brilliant courtroom tactician. Reporters loved him—they could always count on him for a headline-making quip. A sharp dresser, he favored custom-made suits and shirts and expensive Italian shoes. And he was always impeccably coiffed—his beard was short and trimmed, while thanks to hair spray every hair on his head remained perfectly in place.

Heidnik and the thirty-two-year-old attorney met for the first time at the Philadelphia Detention Center. Their meeting lasted more than two hours. Peruto listened to all the sordid details directly from Heidnik's mouth. It was the worst story he'd ever heard. He told Heidnik he'd take the case for a fee: $100,000.

He was shocked when Heidnik agreed.

On April 23, 1987, Gallagher, Peruto, and Heidnik were in municipal court for a preliminary hearing. The purpose of the procedure was to determine if authorities had probable cause to hold a defendant for trial. To demonstrate that they did, Gallagher called Lisa Thomas, Josefina "Nicole" Rivera, and Jacquelyn Askins, as well as two doctors from the medical examiner's office. The women testified about their ordeal—the stick beatings, screwdriver ear-gougings, and daily rapes—and about the deaths of Lindsay and Dudley. When Gallagher asked each one if she knew why Heidnik had kept them prisoner in the basement, they all had the same answer: He wanted to impregnate ten women and raise all the children in the basement.

Dr. Robert Catherman from the medical examiner's office testified that Deborah Dudley was electrocuted. His colleague testified to the human body parts found in the kitchen refrigerator: "Two forearms, one upper arm, two knees, and two segments of thigh."

Relatives of the women wailed loudly with every gruesome disclosure from the witness stand. As for Heidnik, he wasn't moved at all, not even when the women pointed their fingers at him. During the entire two-hour procedure he mostly stared into space. Occasionally he'd lean over and whisper in Peruto's ear.

At the end of the hearing, Judge Charles Margiotti ordered Heidnik held without bail. He would stand trial for two murders, six kidnappings, five rapes, and one count of solicitation to murder and one count of abuse of a corpse.

As he exited the courtroom, Peruto told waiting reporters he would claim insanity. "Heidnik," he said, "is absolutely crackers."

Assistant DA Gallagher saw it differently. He pointed out that Heidnik was very methodical in his seduction and enslavement of the women, and his efforts to dispose of the two corpses demonstrated that he knew what he was doing was wrong. "The prospects of him succeeding with the insanity defense are slim," Gallagher declared.

One month later, Peruto and Heidnik were in court again, this time in common pleas court for a status hearing in front of Judge Charles L. Durham, who also served as the court's calendar judge. He would set the trial date and assign the case to one of the common pleas court's justices.

Heidnik seemed oblivious to the proceedings as Peruto entered a not-guilty plea in his behalf. Sitting in his chair next to Peruto, Heidnik blinked constantly and twitched his head. Whenever the judge asked him a question, he responded with a snappy military salute. After the proceeding, Peruto said he had no doubt that Heidnik was "completely insane."

In April 1988, Judge Graham announced that Common Pleas Court Judge Lynne M. Abraham would try the case. She was a former assistant district attorney who almost never engaged in plea bargaining with criminal defendants. In fact, she'd been dubbed a "tough cookie" by then Mayor Frank Rizzo. The nickname stuck. In 1975 Abraham became the first woman elected to Philadelphia's Municipal Court. During her campaign she stood on street corners handing out "tough cookies." Four years later she was elected to the state's common pleas court, where she presided over criminal trials. Nearly every lawyer who appeared before her agreed—she was a tough cookie, and not likely to be ruffled by the sordid details of the Heidnik case. During her five years as a prosecutor, Abraham had tried dozens of homicide cases and developed a keen interest in forensics; it wasn't unusual for her to show up at the city morgue to observe autopsies.

The following month, Abraham held a hearing on Peruto's motion for a change of venue. To demonstrate that Heidnik couldn't get a fair trial before a Philadelphia jury, Peruto came to court armed with videotapes of the extensive news coverage of the sensational case. As soon as deputies finished setting up a television set and VCR on a metal stand, Heidnik was brought shuffling in.

He was pale, gaunt, and dirty. His clothes seemed two sizes too big, his beard was long and scraggly, and he needed a haircut and a shower. But unlike in his previous court appearances, when he'd seemed uninterested and uninvolved, as soon as he sat down he turned his chair toward the screen and waited for the bailiff to turn the TV on.

Then he listened intently as newscaster after newscaster

referred to him as a "maniac" and a "torture killer." He watched as relatives of the women declared, "He's guilty," "He should be electrocuted," "He should die." He heard his brother Terry comment on his suicide attempt: "I'm not surprised. What's he got to live for?"

And he paid close attention as the women recounted how he raped, tortured, and abused them, and how two of them, Sandra Lindsay and Deborah Dudley, died. There was Agnes Adams telling a reporter, "He raped me. Yes, he did. He put screwdrivers in my ears." And there was Lisa Thomas talking about how Heidnik dismembered Lindsay: "We knew he was burning her body up. We could smell it."

After two hours, the show was over. Even though the tapes demonstrated the enormity of the story and the extent to which the media had covered it, Judge Abraham was unconvinced. She believed a panel of twelve jurors untainted by the news coverage could be found in Philadelphia—at least she wanted to give it a try—so she reserved ruling on Peruto's motion and set jury selection for the next day.

For three days they conducted voir dire, then Abraham threw in the towel. They would travel clear across the state to Pittsburgh, she announced, select a jury, and bring them back to Philadelphia, where they would be sequestered for the duration of the trial. In two days they had a jury—six men and six women, and six alternates, and they were all white. A week later the trial began.

Gallagher's opening was brief, less than twelve minutes. He told the jury and a packed courtroom how Heidnik went trolling for women and brought them to North Marshall Street, where he plied them with food and sex. He assaulted them. He choked them. He handcuffed them, and he took them into his basement, where he put muffler clamps on their ankles. He starved them. He tortured them. He repeatedly had sex with them. He killed two of the women, the prosecutor said, dismembered one of them, then cooked and fed her to the others, and he did it all "in a methodical and systematic way, and he concealed them in a methodical and systematic way." To head off the insanity defense, Gallagher declared that Heidnik "knew exactly what he was doing, and he knew it was wrong."

Peruto had been thinking about his opening for days. He decided to hang his hat on two hooks: insanity and intent. "My client is not innocent," he said. "He is very, very guilty." He went on to say that the case was not a "whodunit." Anyone "who puts dog food and human remains in a food processor and calls it a gourmet meal and feeds it to others is out to lunch."

He finished his nine-minute opening by saying, "Understand two things. One, Gary Heidnik didn't want anyone to die, and two, because of his mental illness he couldn't tell right from wrong."

Josefina Rivera was the third witness Gallagher called to the stand. She followed a tearful Jeanette Perkins, Sandra Lindsay's mother, and Sergeant Julius Armstrong. Before she began, Abraham had a stern warning for the spectators: "If anyone interrupts, they will be jailed," she said sternly. "I won't permit any outbursts no matter how sad or bizarre the testimony."

In a low but steady voice Rivera, dressed in a sundress and wearing a wig, described how Heidnik captured her, how he enslaved her, and the depravity he forced her to endure for four months. Despite the gory details, no one made a sound as she recounted how Sandra Lindsay, Lisa Thomas, Deborah Dudley, Jacquelyn Askins, and Agnes Adams were added to the harem.

"What did you do to pass the time?" Gallagher asked.

"Nothing much, outside of having sex; we just stayed in the hole. Three times we were down in the hole and we ran out of air and we couldn't breathe. We started screaming and hollering and Gary came down and beat us."

In the beginning they weren't allowed to bathe or wash their hair. "We just had baby washcloths," Rivera said. But the situation changed after Christmas. "Then everybody had a day to go bathe. He would take your chains off the sewer pipe and take you upstairs and put you in the tub with the chains, and after that he would take you in a little bedroom and have sex with you."

Rivera answered questions about the deaths of Lindsay and Dudley. "He had Sandra on bread and water and he kept her chained with one arm over her head. She had been throwing up and she said she wasn't feeling good."

After Lindsay collapsed, Heidnik picked her up and carried her upstairs. "We heard an electric saw and then smelled a terrible odor," Rivera recalled. "He smelled like it and so did the food he brought us."

Dudley was nothing but trouble for Heidnik, she recalled. After Lindsay died, Heidnik took her upstairs. When she returned in less than five minutes, she was very subdued. According to Rivera, Dudley said, "He showed me Sandra's head cooking in a pot and her ribs were cooking in a roasting pan in the stove, and her legs and arms were in the freezer."

During his cross-examination, Peruto tried to establish that Heidnik was out of his mind. "Why was he keeping you captive?" he asked.

"He wanted us to have children."

"Why did he pick the cellar?"

"He said he didn't want to do it in the conventional way because the city kept taking [the babies] away."

"How many women did he say he wanted, and how many babies?"

"He wanted ten women to have ten children, all in the basement."

Peruto tried to discredit Rivera. "Your boyfriend is your pimp, isn't he?"

"No," Rivera shot back. "I never worked for anybody but myself."

"Did you get any of your information from the media?"

"I was there. I don't need to get it from the newspapers," she snapped bitterly.

Day two of the trial began with Rivera still on the stand. On redirect, Gallagher made the point that Heidnik knew what he was doing. First, the prosecutor asked Rivera what Heidnik did as soon as they returned from New Jersey after dumping Dudley's body.

"He stopped to buy a newspaper so he could check his stocks," she said. Then the Assistant DA asked if she knew where he got his sordid ideas from.

"From the movies," she said. Specifically, *Eating Raoul*, *Mutiny on the Bounty*, and *The World of Susie Wong*.

Eating Raoul, Rivera said, provided the inspiration for chopping up a body, grinding it up in a food processor, mixing it with dog food, and feeding it to his captives. From *Mutiny on the Bounty* he learned "the right way to hit somebody." He liked *The World of Susie Wong* "because he liked the way Oriental women treat men."

Later in the day, Gallagher called Lisa Thomas, Jacquelyn Askins, and Agnes Adams. Thomas and Askins testified about the degradation and torture they suffered at the hands of Gary Heidnik. Adams was in the subterranean dungeon for only two days, and she wasn't there when Thomas and Dudley died. Adams testified about her two previous visits to Marshall Street, before she was taken prisoner, and how Heidnik later had sex with her, drugged her, and dragged her to the basement.

Before the day ended, Judge Abraham issued an order: Gary Heidnik, she commanded, take a shower. He hadn't taken one in seven weeks, and his body odor was fouling the courtroom. Even Peruto, who had to sit next to him, was complaining. Besides, Philadelphia was in the grip of a one-hundred-degree heat wave, and the courtroom was barely tolerable.

The next day, Heidnik was cleaner but still not quite clean enough. He had taken a shower and his shoulder-length hair and beard had been washed and combed, but he still smelled badly because he hadn't bothered to wash the Hawaiian shirt or baggy pants he'd worn to every court appearance for a year. As far as anyone knew, they had never been washed.

Whether Heidnik bathed or not didn't matter to Gallagher. He was about to rest his case, but before he did he called Dr. Robert Catherman, the deputy medical examiner, to the stand. Dr. Catherman testified that Deborah Dudley had been electrocuted. He was followed by Officer Julio Aponte, who told the jury about the pungent odor that permeated North Marshall Street on February 10. Asked why he didn't investigate further, the officer testified, "I asked him what the foul odor was, and he said he was cooking and he burned his dinner. I had no reason to suspect anything, so I made my report and resumed patrol."

Dr. Paul Hoyer, an assistant medical examiner, followed Aponte to the stand. He told the jury about the human body parts that were found in the kitchen refrigerator and described how he had identified them as the remains of Sandra Lindsay by studying her left wrist. Lindsay, he said, had injured it a year before and an X-ray was on file that he was able to compare with the wrist from the freezer. "The overall shape and size matched," Dr. Hoyer said. "And the patterns matched. There is a pattern in bone," he explained, "and each pattern is unique. By comparing this we were able to say this was Sandra Lindsay."

But there was no way to determine how Lindsay had died. Nevertheless, based on the testimony of the other captives and the fact that Heidnik went to such extraordinary lengths to destroy the body, Hoyer said, the death of Sandra Lindsay was ruled a homicide.

Peruto was on his feet with an objection. He wanted the assistant medical examiner's conclusion that Lindsay's death was a homicide stricken from the record. Abraham refused. "I don't think the method of death needs to be proved to determine murder," she said. "The question is, has the Commonwealth established this was an unlawful killing?"

"The prosecution rests," Gallagher announced. Following a break for lunch Peruto would put on the defense case.

Peruto's first expert witness was Dr. Clancy McKenzie, a psychiatrist from Bala Cynwyd. He began by saying, "I'm not here to so much to defend Gary Heidnik as to explain him." He had met with Heidnik more than thirty times, spent nearly a hundred hours with him. The psychiatrist diagnosed Heidnik as a schizophrenic who didn't know right from wrong when he kidnapped the women, chained and tortured them.

After twenty years of research into schizophrenia ("my forte"), McKenzie said that schizophrenics are of two minds; they have an "infant brain" and an "adult brain."

"What caused the schizophrenia?" Peruto asked.

The disease, he said, can be traced to traumatic events in infancy, in Heidnik's case to the trauma that he experienced at age seventeen months when his mother gave birth to his brother, Terry.

He said the struggle between Heidnik's "infant brain" and "adult brain" was at the root of his schizophrenia, and that the infant side prevailed as he imprisoned the women in his basement.

McKenzie frequently lapsed into rambling, technical testimony. On more than one occasion Peruto or Judge Abraham had to rein him in. "Doc, you're killing [the jurors] with words," Abraham said at one point, but he ignored her. At another, Peruto told McKenzie, "Just answer my questions. I don't want to give the jury a medical degree."

The psychiatrist went on: Heidnik's four months of kidnapping and torture were triggered in October 1986, when Betty sent him a postcard announcing the birth of their son, Jesse. "This took him back to the point when his mother, the most important woman in his life, had abandoned him for another sibling. He decided that no woman was ever going to leave him again, that no woman was ever going to take a baby away from him again. He wanted babies. He loved children. Four times they were taken from him, and he went berserk."

Until now, Heidnik had appeared uninterested in anything having to do with the trial, but he seemed to perk up when McKenzie mentioned his mother, and appeared to pay rapt attention from then on.

"Why did he like retarded women?" Peruto asked.

"He felt rejected by society, and he knew there were other groups of people who were rejected, so he sought them out," McKenzie testified. "He knew there was great prejudice against retarded people. He knew there was great racial prejudice. He figured these people may accept him, so he sought them out."

Heidnik's "infant brain" was in full command when he dismembered Lindsay and cooked her head and froze her limbs,

McKenzie said. "He was like a two-year-old trying to hide the candy wrappers. He put body parts in a pot on the stove, in the oven, in the backyard, everywhere. The only thing he didn't do was run them up the flagpole."

"Do you know why Gary Heidnik put body parts in the freezer?" the psychiatrist asked himself. "He was planning to start the babies—once they were off the breast—on human flesh. This is infant behavior. Infants suck for six months, and then they have a wish to devour the mother's flesh." The notion that he could raise a lot of babies in his basement was that of a seventeen-month-old brain, McKenzie said.

Asked how Heidnik could starve Lindsay and hang her by one arm from a rafter, McKenzie explained that Heidnik "had no idea what was happening to that girl. He was feeding her like she was a pet. He shoved a couple of pieces of bread in her mouth."

The psychiatrist revealed that Heidnik was shocked and deeply hurt when he learned that the women were plotting to kill him. He believed that his captives understood his goal of raising a family in his basement. His captives' death plot pushed him into a psychotic state and caused him to treat the women even more harshly, McKenzie said.

He recalled Heidnik's reaction when he saw the women during the preliminary hearing: "He came to me with tears in his eyes. He was really upset. He was staring at their bellies. He said, 'There's her belly. It's flat. All that for nothing.' "

"How could he make stock investments?" Peruto wanted to know.

"At the time he became very ill he made very poor investments," the psychiatrist said, noting that Heidnik's Merrill Lynch account declined by $100,000 in a short time.

It was 4 P.M. when Peruto finished with McKenzie, so Judge Abraham recessed court for the day. Gallagher would have all evening to prepare to cross-examine the psychiatrist.

The next morning, Dr. McKenzie was back on the stand. Did he know the legal definition of insanity? the prosecutor wanted to know.

"I don't have the textbook definition," he replied.

"Did [Gary Heidnik] know what he was doing between November and April?"

"I don't agree with that statement," McKenzie answered.

"Did he know when he lured mentally deficient girls to his basement?"

"No. But which 'he' are you speaking of? His adult brain or his infant brain?"

"Did the adult brain know?"

"The adult brain was operating in greatly diminished capacity."

"Yes or no?"

"The adult brain had only partial awareness."

Gallagher pressed for a yes or no. "No, absolutely, he did not know right from wrong."

"Isn't it true that someone can fake mental illness?"

"He can't fake schizophrenia with me," McKenzie declared. A few minutes later the psychiatrist was excused.

The next expert witness for the defense was Jack Apsche, a Philadelphia psychologist who had studied Heidnik's mental records. He carried five thick notebooks to the stand and testified about Heidnik's long history of mental illness—seven of the previous twenty-six years in mental hospitals, thirteen suicide attempts since 1966.

"In your opinion, did Gary Heidnik know right from wrong?" Peruto asked.

"No," replied Apsche.

"In your opinion, did he know the nature of his acts?"

"He did not know the nature of his acts."

"Was he suffering from a mental disease?"

"Yes."

"What disease?"

"Severe schizophrenia."

Peruto's final expert was forensic psychiatrist Kenneth Kool, and his name fit him well. For the most part, he was unflappable on the stand. Heidnik, he declared, "did not have the capacity to know right from wrong."

Did it make any difference that he could drive a car? Peruto asked.

"No."

"If I told you that he placed a body in New Jersey, would that change your opinion?"

"No."

Dr. Kool said that Heidnik was delusional and psychotic.

"What is a delusion?" Peruto asked.

"A delusion is an unreality perceived by the victim of it to be a reality," the psychiatrist replied. Heidnik, he explained, believed that "God wanted him to produce a number of children, and this was essentially a pact with God." Dr. Kool added that Heidnik hid his atrocities because he believed that if he were found out he would be prevented from carrying out his pact with God. Heidnik, the psychiatrist said, "saw God's law as having supremacy over man's law."

And he agreed with McKenzie and Apsche—Gary Heidnik, he said, was insane.

On cross-examination of Kool, Gallagher managed to strike a blow at Dr. McKenzie's theory of schizophrenia. That view was held by "much, much less than five percent" of the world's mainstream psychiatrists.

Dr. Kool was the last defense witness. After a break for lunch, the prosecutor called his own mental health expert to the stand.

Dr. Robert Sadoff was a nationally known expert, and Gallagher wasted no time establishing his credentials. "I've testified in federal and state courts in twenty states," he declared as soon as he was sworn in. "I've testified before a Senate committee to discuss what should be done with people who are found guilty but mentally ill."

Dr. Sadoff admitted that he only spent twenty minutes with Heidnik, who refused to utter a single word in the psychiatrist's presence. But it didn't matter, because he was able to reach his conclusions based on medical records, police records, and the testimony of other expert witnesses.

Gallagher asked him for the legal definition of insanity. "The difference between someone who is insane and someone who is mentally ill is that the insane person doesn't know the nature and quality of his act and he doesn't know right from wrong."

"Did Gary Heidnik know what he was doing when he picked up those girls?" Gallagher asked.

"In my opinion he did."

"Did he know what he was doing when he choked and cuffed them?"

"In my opinion he did."

"Did he know it was wrong?"

"In my opinion he did know."

He called Heidnik "an incredibly bright" manipulator who'd faked insanity for more than twenty-six years. "He's manipulated the system or has exaggerated his symptoms to gain certain ends."

Finally, Gallagher wanted to know if Heidnik was responsible for his acts.

Dr. Sadoff turned to the jury and in a loud and clear voice said, "There is nothing to indicate that he did not know what he was doing was wrong at the time he was doing it."

Peruto tried hard, but he couldn't shake Sadoff. It was 3:45 on Friday afternoon when he finished his cross-examination. As he left the courtroom, the defense attorney quipped, "If he gets insanity, I'll take off all my clothes in front of the jury."

When court reconvened on Monday, Gallagher set out to further demolish Peruto's insanity defense. His first witness was Heidnik's Merrill Lynch broker, Robert Kirkpatrick. Courtroom observers noticed a remarkable transformation in the Hawaiian-shirted stock whiz when his broker took the stand. For the first time in days, Heidnik looked up. He seemed involved and interested. He hadn't paid this much attention since Dr. McKenzie testified about the roots of his schizophrenia.

Kirkpatrick recalled the day he picked up the phone at his office and the voice at the other end introduced himself as "Bishop Heidnik." That was in December 1974. On March 21, 1975, Heidnik opened an account in the name of the United Church of the Ministers of God with a check for $1,500.

Over the next twelve years they dealt mostly by phone, the broker said, and by November 28, 1986, the account was worth $545,000.

"What kind of an investor was he?" Gallagher asked.

"An astute one," Kirkpatrick answered.

Gallagher's next witness was Shirley Carter, a forty-year-old black woman who suffered from cerebral palsy. She testified that she had had a long-term sexual relationship with Heidnik that began before he went to prison in 1979 and lasted until sometime after he was released in 1983. His behavior, Carter said, was never bizarre. "He even told me how he set up a church so he wouldn't have to pay taxes."

On Tuesday, June 28, after seven days of what may have been the most gruesome testimony ever heard in a courtroom in Philadelphia, it was time for closing arguments. In a surprising departure from customary procedure, Judge Abraham ordered Peruto to go first. He didn't want to, he even objected, but Abraham overruled him. At a few minutes past eleven, Peruto began to address the jury. He paced in front of them a couple of times, then started to speak.

"The question is not whether Gary Heidnik did these heinous acts, but whether or not he was insane. We're not contesting that these women were raped, that these women were kidnapped, that these women were killed. What we're here to determine is the level of culpability of the defendant. Even though we have conceded that these acts took place, we are not conceding first-degree murder—the specific intent to kill." He asked the jurors to consider Heidnik's purpose. It was, he said, "to raise ten kids, not to kill anybody."

Heidnik, whom he called "a fruitcake," didn't set out to kill Sandra Lindsay and Deborah Dudley, Peruto said. His intent was to punish them for defying him. If he was guilty of murder, it was third degree, not first. "Third-degree murder is reckless disregard of human life."

Peruto reviewed the case. He referred to the women as Heidnik's "chosen people," the girls he wanted to reproduce with. "Is that sane? It's a case of Dr. Jekyll and Mr. Heidnik. Isn't it more likely he's insane than not?"

He finished with a flourish: "I don't want a verdict based on sympathy," he said. "Nor do I want one based on prejudice. I want you to find him not guilty based on insanity."

After a brief recess, it was Gallagher's turn. "I want you to rely upon your good old-fashioned common sense," he said in a low voice. "Rely upon your powers of observation. Go over the evidence with me."

He pointed at Heidnik; then in a voice that gradually grew louder and more indignant he said, "This man repeated sadistic and malicious acts upon his six victims. He planned. He did it, and he concealed it. Ladies and gentlemen, I submit to you, make no mistake about it, that this man committed murder in the first degree."

He told them that the murders of Lindsay and Dudley were cold-blooded and premeditated. "Just because someone does bizarre acts, the law doesn't recognize them as insane."

He called on the jurors to reject the insanity defense. "Reject the idea that this man is legally insane. Seek the truth, and I think you will find that this man, Gary M. Heidnik, is guilty beyond a reasonable doubt of the specific intent to kill two young girls." When he concluded, Judge Abraham adjourned court for the day. The jury would have the rest of the day off while she prepared her charge.

The first thing the jurors saw when they filed into Room 653 at 10:30 A.M. the next morning was a large green chalkboard behind the judge's bench. After the panel was seated, Judge Abraham rose and walked to over to it. "PRESUMPTION OF INNOCENCE," she wrote.

"The fact of Heidnik's arrest, the fact that he is on trial, doesn't mean he's guilty," she said. "He is presumed innocent."

Then she turned and wrote, "BRD." "That means beyond reasonable doubt, beyond the doubt that any reasonable person would consider." She wrote "CREDIBILITY," "DEMEANOR," and "MOTIVE," and explained each of them for the jurors.

Next she told the panel their options: guilty, not guilty, not guilty by reason of insanity, or guilty but mentally ill. And she explained the meaning of insanity: "If at the time of the crime he is, as a result of mental disease, unable to know the nature and quality of his acts or unable to distinguish right from wrong, he meets the legal test. Otherwise, he is not legally insane."

After a brief recess, Abraham discussed the degrees of murder and the other charges, then she sent the jury off to deliberate. Heidnik was led to a holding cell, where he was beaten up by two men who were in the cell with him. Heidnik was about to go down for the count when deputies intervened. He was not seriously injured.

Meanwhile the jury deliberated the rest of the day, all day Thursday, and well into Friday afternoon without reaching a verdict. Then just before 3 P.M. they sent word that they'd come to a decision. Before she ordered the bailiff to bring the panel into the courtroom, Abraham warned the spectators: "There will be no expression of pleasure or displeasure," she declared. Anyone who cheered, booed, cried, or shouted would be arrested.

None of the jurors made eye contact with Heidnik or Peruto as they filed in. When they were all seated, Abraham called for the verdict. Foreperson Betty Ann Bennett stood and read the verdicts one by one. Guilty of first-degree murder in the death of Sandra Lindsay; guilty of first-degree murder in the death of Deborah Johnson Dudley. There were eighteen guilty verdicts in all, and one acquittal, on the charge of involuntary deviate sexual intercourse.

Under Pennsylvania law, a jury that brings in a guilty verdict in a first-degree murder case is required to determine the punishment—life in prison or the death penalty. Abraham told the panel they would begin the penalty phase on the murder convictions at nine the next morning.

The heat wave that had gripped Philadelphia the week before had moved on. In its place this Saturday morning were cooler temperatures and sunny skies, perfect weather for the three-day Fourth of July weekend. Before the jurors were sent to the jury room again, there were final arguments. Gallagher went first. He reminded the panel of the gruesome deaths Sandra Lindsay and Deborah Dudley had suffered at the hands of Gary Heidnik. He reminded them that both women were beaten, raped, and tortured, that screwdrivers were driven into their ears. He urged the jury not to "rely on leniency for this man or mercy for this man." Instead, he said, "Rely upon the evidence."

The usually eloquent Peruto didn't have much to say. He began talking about intent, but Abraham cut him off. "You can't argue that at this point," she said. "That's already been disposed of." The defense attorney seemed at a loss for words and spoke for only four minutes. In the end he urged the jurors "to do the just thing" and sat down. As for Heidnik, he didn't appear to be the least bit interested. He stared at the ceiling, the walls, or the table, and rocked back and forth in his chair.

Less than two hours after they began deliberating, the jurors reached a decision.

They were somber-faced as they filed back into the courtroom. Again, Betty Ann Bennett rose to announce it: Death for the murder of Sandra Lindsay, and death for the murder of Deborah Dudley. Immediately, Abraham sentenced Heidnik to death for Lindsay's murder and announced that she would sentence him for Dudley's murder in October.

Before he was led away, Peruto promised he'd file an appeal. "Don't bother," Heidnik said. "Let's get it over with."

It wouldn't be that easy. Eleven years and five days would pass before the "House of Horrors" killer would be strapped to a gurney on July 6, 1999, and put to death by lethal injection.

He had almost gotten there once before, on April 19, 1997. In March, then Governor Tom Ridge signed his death warrant and officials at Pennsylvania's Rockview State Correctional Institution near Pittsburgh dressed him in death clothes—a white, short-sleeved shirt, beltless brown trousers, and white sneakers. Heidnik ate what he thought would be his last meal—eggs, hash browns, toast, and coffee—and read from the Bible. Then forty-one minutes before he would have been hooked up to an IV in the prison's death house, the execution of Gary Heidnik was stayed against his wishes.

Attorneys for Maxine Davidson White, the daughter he had with Anjeanette Davidson in 1978, filed a "next friend" suit in Pennsylvania's Supreme Court challenging her father's competency to be put to death.

She was nineteen years old then, a pharmacy student at Temple University in Philadelphia who had grown up in foster care. She wanted to save Heidnik's soul. "The reason she's intervening now to help her dad is she wants him to be able to go to God," said Reverend Linwood Riley, White's godfather, in a 1997 interview. "She believes that God will forgive."

She bought Heidnik two years while her suit wound its way through the courts. When the U.S. Supreme Court refused to grant an eleventh-hour stay, Heidnik was strapped to a gurney, hooked to an IV, and administered a concoction of lethal drugs. He offered no resistance and said nothing as the deadly poison made its way through the intravenous line and into his arm. At 10:29 P.M., Gary Heidnik was pronounced dead.

Among the witnesses to his execution were four sisters of Heidnik's victims. "I feel my sister can now be at peace," said Caroline Johnson, sister of Deborah Dudley.

"It's over and he's headed for the big trial," said Tracy Lomax, Sandra Lindsay's sister.

In Philadelphia, Jacquelyn Askins celebrated. She would have gone to witness the execution of her torturer, but Pennsylvania law permitted only the survivors of murder victims to witness executions. "I've been waiting on this for thirteen years," she said.

"The state has executed an extremely mentally ill and psychotic man," declared Kathy Swerdlow, a lawyer for the Philadelphia Defenders Association, which represented Heidnik's daughter.

EPILOGUE . . .

After the trial, the four women who survived Gary Heidnik's house of horrors faded from view.

- *Lisa Thomas* got her name in the papers when she sued the city of Philadelphia for negligence in the way the police handled reports of trouble at Gary Heidnik's house on Marshall Street, and again when her suit was dismissed.

- *Jacquelyn Askins* surfaced briefly when Heidnik was executed.

- *Agnes Adams's* whereabouts are unknown.

- *Josefina Rivera* was out of sight until *The Philadelphia Weekly* published an extensive interview with her in its March 13, 2002, edition, but she wouldn't allow herself to be photographed. At the time she was living and working as a waitress in Atlantic City. Her days prostituting and shooting cocaine were behind her, she said. "My story could benefit a lot of girls, the ones that see one side of prostitution. They think they can run outside, make some money and then, boom, they're on their way. They don't think anything can go wrong. Well, guess what? Something can go wrong." What went wrong was Gary Heidnik. She says she has trouble hearing "because of what he did with the screwdrivers," even though Jacquelyn Askins testified that Heidnik didn't puncture Rivera's eardrum. Instead of seeking therapy she self-medicated and went back to prostitution, figuring "this is the worst thing that could happen, so why not go back up there to make money and get more drugs?" But her friends were "dropping like flies," so she decided to get out of Philadelphia and change her life.

- *Lynn Abraham* served on the bench until 1991, when she was elected district attorney of Philadelphia. Never defeated, she remained in office until January 2010, longer than anyone in Philadelphia history. She earned the nickname "Deadliest DA" and "Queen of Death" for the number of times her prosecutors pursued the death penalty.

- *Charles Gallagher* became one of Abraham's top deputies, the head of the special investigations unit.

- *Charles Peruto Jr.* is still practicing law in Philadelphia, and is still keeping a high profile.

The IRS took the lion's share of Gary Heidnik's fortune, but the surviving women and the next of kin of the two women who died on Marshall Street each received $32,000 from his assets. Terry Heidnik, Gary's younger brother, died in Pennsylvania in 2002. As for Heidnik, after his execution, his body was claimed by his daughter and cremated, his ashes reportedly scattered over Niagara Falls.

5

NATHANIEL BAR-JONAH
The Gruesome Gourmet

He was a child molester and a sexual sadist. In 1996, cops said, Nathaniel Bar-Jonah added a new designation to his depraved resume—cannibal killer.

It was just after 7 A.M. on February 6, 1996, and Great Falls, Montana, a city of fifty-six thousand on the northwestern edge of the Great Plains, awoke to an unseasonably warm day. Just two days before, the mercury had dropped to twenty-five degrees below zero and it snowed, but for this day, a Tuesday, the weatherman promised temperatures in the midforties, a welcome relief from the bitter cold that usually grips Montana in the dead of winter.

Inside the apartment at 414 Fourth Street North, Zachary Ramsay scrambled to get ready for school. At 7:35, the fourth grader grabbed his backpack and headed out the door for his usual walk to Whittier Elementary School six blocks away.

Zach never got there.

At 10 A.M. school officials notified Rachel Howard, his mother, that her son was absent. About an hour later, she phoned police to report him missing. Zach, the oldest of her three children, would never skip school, she said, and he knew better than to go off with a stranger.

It wasn't long before search teams were going door-to-door through the Lower North Side neighborhood. They combed through trash bins and poked into nooks and crannies where a four-foot-six-inch, eighty-six-pound child could hide. Airmen from nearby Malmstrom Air Force Base joined in the search, too. Zach's father, Sergeant Franz Ramsay, was a fellow airman at Peterson Air Force Base in Colorado Springs, Colorado, and his comrades-in-arms were more than eager to pitch in. Bloodhounds, given Zach's scent from his toothbrush, sniffed along the banks of the nearby Missouri River and up and down his route to school.

The city of Great Falls is laid out in a classic grid pattern, with avenues running east to west, streets north to south. Narrow alleyways parallel many of the city's avenues. Zach's route took him down one of them, Fifth Alley North, and behind the redbrick Bitterroot Apartments. It was a walk Zach made every schoolday, and residents along the route were accustomed to seeing the curly-haired boy with the big smile.

Neighbors who saw Zach the morning he disappeared came forward with information. Carol Henry was behind the wheel of her pickup in Fifth Alley North preparing to drive her son Marvin to Great Falls High. As they pulled away, the Henrys saw Zach crossing Fifth Street North and Fifth Alley. He almost didn't make it, she said. A white four-door sedan stopped just short of hitting Zach as he made his way through the intersection. And Patrick Hall told cops that he saw Zachary cross Sixth Street

North at about 7:45. A man in a dark blue jacket was following close behind, he said, and the boy seemed to be crying. From there the trail grew as cold as a Montana winter.

In the days ahead townspeople turned out for candlelight vigils and prayer meetings. The *Great Falls Tribune* published Zach's picture every day for months, and hundreds of posters of the curly-haired boy with the big smile filled the city. They carried a description of what he'd been wearing when he disappeared: a blue coat with green sleeves, a blue football jersey with "Ramsay" in gold letters on the back, blue jeans, and black sneakers.

Meanwhile Great Falls cops were joined in the search by the FBI. The town is the kind of place where children don't vanish into thin air—not a single member of the police force had ever dealt with a missing child case that wasn't resolved happily within twenty-four hours—so they needed all the help they could get. The TV show *America's Most Wanted* featured the case, and lawmen chased down hundreds of tips that poured in after it aired.

"Every time we got any kind of lead we followed it as far as we could," said James Wilson of the FBI. The search took investigators halfway across the globe, to a military base in Italy where someone reported seeing Zach, and to other countries as well. But none of the sightings panned out, as each time lawmen were able to verify that the child was not Zachary.

The lawmen investigated Zach's parents, looking into the possibility that Zach, the only child from their union, might have been the victim of a custody dispute. While there was no love lost between Franz, who is black, and Rachel, who is white, investigators quickly eliminated Franz, who was in Colorado when his son went missing. They also ran down sightings that sent them scurrying across the state, and they fanned out to interview known sexual offenders.

One of them was Nathaniel Bar-Jonah, a bearded five-foot-eight 280-pounder with three chins who'd arrived in Great Falls from Massachusetts five years earlier. He brought with him a long history of violence and sexual sadism that could only be satisfied by brutalizing young boys.

There was snow on the ground in Great Falls the morning Zach Ramsay disappeared. Zach's route would have taken him past the Bitterroot Apartments, and a tenant there told authorities he'd seen Bar-Jonah in the alley behind the apartments at 7 A.M. McIntire, who was taking his trash out at the time, told detectives he even remembered saying hello to him.

The day Zach disappeared, a detective paid Bar-Jonah a visit. He knocked on his door but no one answered. Officers went back a second time and again no one answered. Eventually they contacted Bar-Jonah by telephone. They wanted him to come in for an interview. A meeting was set for February 26 at 1 P.M. but he never showed. There is no record that police ever followed up.

As winter turned to spring with still no trace of Zach, students at Whittier Elementary built a memorial to their missing schoolmate. They planted forget-me-nots at the front entrance, and they dedicated a plaque that read, "Lost but not forgotten. Zachary Ramsay 1996."

Principal Diane Long said she'd always remember Zach "as a special little boy with a spark in his eye and a great smile, a perky kid, a talented artist and a good citizen." He had great potential, she said. He liked science and loved to paint, draw, and doodle. Sometimes he'd entertain his classmates with his doodles.

On December 18, 2000, the day that Zach Ramsay would have turned fifteen, Cascade County Attorney Brant Light announced that he was charging Bar-Jonah with his kidnapping and murder.

The charges didn't come as a complete surprise to the citizens of Great Falls. The portly predator had been cooling his heels in the county jail for a year on charges of impersonating a police officer and five counts of kidnapping and sexual abuse, and investigators made no secret of the fact that they the considered him the chief suspect in Zach Ramsay's disappearance.

But what Light said next sent shock waves through the small city: Zachary Ramsay's body would never be found because Nathaniel Bar-Jonah had cooked, eaten, and even fed him to unsuspecting friends and neighbors in concoctions Bar-Jonah called "Roasted Child" and "Little Boy Stew."

In the days and months to come, the people of Great Falls would learn all the grisly details behind the gruesome charges.

It would leave them reeling for a long time.

Nathaniel Bar-Jonah was born David Paul Brown on February 15, 1957, in Dudley, Massachusetts. He was the youngest of Phil and Tyra Brown's three children. By all accounts, Phil was a tyrant who ruled his wife and children with an iron hand. The family struggled financially when Phil, a mechanic, was forced to stop working at age forty-nine due to a heart condition. He died in 1974.

In the late 1960s the Browns moved to a house on Elaine Street in Webster, a mill town on the south side of Lake Chargoggagoggmanchauggagoggchaubunagungamaugg, the official Indian name for what local residents simply call Webster Lake.

David—his mother called him Teddy—is remembered in his hometown as an oddball, a chubby mama's boy with one brown and one blue eye. Treated as an outcast and ridiculed by his peers, he preferred to play with much younger children.

By his own admission, Brown committed his first act of violence when he was only six or seven—he was caught in the act of trying to choke a six-year-old girl to death. Only the screams of the girl's mother stopped him.

James McDonald was one of Brown's childhood friends when they were both growing up on Elaine Street in Webster. McDonald remembers his playmate as a sullen loner whose behavior grew more and more bizarre as he got older.

Brown, he recalled, once tried to run him over with a lawn mower. "I started punching him and he tried to grab my throat, but I beat him back," McDonald said.

The Dupont family lived next to the Browns. For days someone had been scrawling mysterious messages in chalk on the sidewalk outside their home. The messages were aimed at Alan Dupont, nine, and his brother Kevin, ten. At first their mother, Dolly, thought the messages were nothing more than a childish prank, but when a sinister letter arrived in their mailbox, she changed her mind. Addressed to Alan and Kevin, the letter was made from words cut out of magazines and pasted onto a sheet of paper. It read, "Come to the cemetery at 6 o'clock and I'll give you $20 apiece but don't tell your mother and father."

Dolly didn't think it was kid stuff anymore. Her husband, Francis, called the police. At the appointed hour of six o'clock the cops were in the graveyard, where they found fifteen-year-old David Brown lying in wait behind a tombstone. After he admitted sending the letter and writing the messages, the cops asked the Duponts if they wanted to press charges. Tyra Brown pleaded with them not to.

"One mother to another, would you please give him a chance?" she begged. The Duponts agreed and nothing more came of the incident, at least not as far as the legal system was concerned, but Dupont ordered her kids to steer clear of the Brown family.

It's not known if Tyra Brown told her son to stay away from the Duponts, but the next day Dolly answered a knock on her door. It was David carrying a bouquet of flowers. He wanted to know if Kevin and Alan could spend the day at the beach with him and his family.

"Absolutely not!" Dolly exclaimed. Then Brown said something that terrified Dolly: "I have two different shades of eyes. That means I'm insane." From that point on the Browns and the Duponts were like the Hatfields and the McCoys but without the gunfire and the bloodletting.

The next known incident involving David Brown occurred in 1975, not long after he got his driver's license and just after he graduated from Bay Path Vocational Technical School where, among other things, he studied culinary arts.

He spotted eight-year-old Rick O'Connor as the boy walked alone to school one morning. Flashing a badge and identifying himself as a cop, Brown ordered the boy into his car. O'Connor recalls Brown saying, "We're looking for a boy running away from school. I'm going to take you down to the station for some questioning." O'Connor knew better than to get into a car with a stranger, but this was different. This was a cop, so he got in.

Brown drove to the police station and kept right on going. He told O'Connor, "I'm not a cop. Get down on the floor." He then drove the terrified boy to a secluded spot in the woods, where he wrapped his hands around the youngster's neck and began choking him. "Don't kill me. Don't kill me. Please, don't kill me," O'Connor recalls gasping.

"I don't know if I'm going to kill you, but I don't know if I'm going to keep you alive either," Brown said.

He squeezed so hard the blood vessels in the boy's eyes burst and the veins in the back of his neck ruptured. The more Brown squeezed the more aroused he became. Then he stopped, only to resume choking the boy again a few minutes later.

This perverted frenzy went on for four hours, then Brown ordered the boy to undress. At that point O'Connor, still in the car and certain he was going to die, released his body fluids. It saved his life.

Concerned now about soiling his mother's car, Brown lost his passion. He angrily ordered O'Connor to clean the mess with his own clothes. Then, inexplicably, he let him go, but not without a warning—he told the boy he would find him and kill him if he told anyone about what had happened.

O'Connor spent three days in the hospital recuperating from his injuries. Several weeks later he ran into Brown at McDonald's. O'Connor told his father, who called the police.

O'Connor would meet his tormentor again, this time at the police station, where he positively identified Brown as the man who had terrorized him. Brown plea-bargained to one count of assault and battery. The eighteen-year-old predator got a slap on the wrist—one year probation. But the man who would later be known as Nathaniel Bar-Jonah was just warming up. His next known assault showed that he was becoming a more sophisticated and more violent sexual predator.

On September 23, 1977, Brown, posing as an undercover state trooper, stopped Billy Benoit, thirteen, and Alan Enrickias, fourteen. The boys had just left a movie theater when Brown pulled up and ordered them to get into his car. He threatened the boys with a butcher knife, then handcuffed them and drove to a tent he had set up in the woods. After forcing the terrified boys to undress, Brown dragged Alan deeper into the woods, then wrapped his arm around his neck and began choking him from behind.

Brown squeezed as hard as he could with his arm. With his feet dangling in the air, Alan went limp, pretending to be dead. When that happened, Brown released him from the choke hold and the boy dropped to the ground. In order to be certain that the boy was dead, Brown lit a cigarette and tapped the hot ashes onto his body. Alan didn't move. Brown then kicked Alan in the ribs, sides, and legs. Once again the boy didn't flinch. Convinced he was dead, Brown went back to the tent for Benoit.

As soon as he left, Alan raced to a nearby house for help. The residents called police, who were already out searching for the two boys. They had been alerted by the boys' parents when they didn't return home from the movie theater. The cops found Billy bruised but alive inside the trunk of Brown's car. They arrested the pudgy predator after a brief chase through the woods. He confessed and gave cops a written statement. It was a chilling glimpse into the sick mind of a sexual predator.

"I was in the White City parking lot on Route 9 in Shrewsbury," he wrote. "It was probably between 9:30 and 10:00 P.M. I was going slow through the parking lot. As I was going out I saw two boys, about thirteen years old, walking up near the exit. I was driving up near them. I stopped the car and flashed a special police badge toward the passenger side of my car.

"The two boys opened the passenger door and got into the car. When the boys got into my car, one of the boys asked me to give them a ride home. I drove the car out of the parking lot and headed toward the boys' house. I drove about one or two miles, I have no idea. One of the boys pointed to a street and said you have to go down this street to go to my house. I stopped at the next street. I held up a hunting knife in front of me for a few seconds, then I put it down next to me on the seat. I said something like get down or lean over. I told them to put their hands behind their backs. They said what are you doing? They put their hands behind their backs. I cuffed them with the handcuffs. The boys were sitting right next to me.

"I went down some back roads and came out to Route 9 and then I took one of the side roads and kept driving for about two hours. When I was driving around, the boys were crying and asking questions, like where are you going? Stuff like that. I didn't give any replies. I went down some more roads and came to Route 290 and took them to Charlton.

"All three of us went to a tent I had put up three hours before. I helped them out of the car. I had the tent open and they went in. They asked me if I would take off their handcuffs and I did. I probably told one of them to sit down, the other had already sat down. One of the boys, the larger one, began asking questions: When are we going home? Why are we here? Stuff like that. I said in a little while or so. Then I stated that, not really meaning it, if you want to go home bad enough take your clothes off. They said no.

"We were in the tent about 10–15 minutes. I don't really know. They said they were cold. I said if they want to be warmer we can go in the car. They stood up and I re-handcuffed them. I escorted them to the car and they were put in the backseat. Then I put the heat on and went to Route 20 and drove to whatever road I was arrested on. I stopped the car and had the larger boy come out and the smaller boy remain. I told him to stay in the car.

"I took the larger boy into the woods. I started to strangle him. I guess mainly because he could identify me and I wanted to kill him. I started strangling the boy and after about 3 or 4 seconds he went limp. I assumed he was dead. I went back and got the smaller boy out of the car and started strangling him. I stopped strangling him because I realized the stupidness [sic] of what I was doing. I put the smaller boy back into the backseat and went to see if I could help the bigger boy but he was gone. So I started looking for him with no luck. I went back to the car and had the smaller boy get into the trunk. I told him to get into the trunk and waited until he positioned himself where the trunk lid would not hurt him when closed.

"I closed the trunk, then I continued my search for the larger boy, so that I could take them back to Shrewsbury and turn myself into [sic] the local police department. With no luck finding the larger boy I noticed a car coming down the camping area, that was shining a light. I paniced [sic] and ran to my car, started it up and left. When I was leaving I saw the blue lights coming on and I took off down the road. I ran into some shrubs and then the police car came up and stopped. I got out of the car and the police officer placed me under arrest."

The confession was signed David P. Brown, and it was dated September 24, 1977.

Brown pleaded guilty to two counts of attempted murder and two counts of kidnapping. This time there would be no slap on the wrist. He was sentenced to hard time, eighteen to twenty years in the state's toughest lockup, Walpole State Prison. After twenty-two months, Brown was transferred to the Massachusetts Treatment Center for the Sexually Dangerous in Bridgewater, after Dr. A. Nicholas Groth, a sex offender expert hired by his own attorney, turned in a devastating evaluation.

"I see [David Brown] as a lethal risk to the community," he wrote. His blistering recommendation: Brown "should be committed indefinitely to a maximum-security institution, so that if necessary he can be kept beyond his twenty-year maximum sentence."

While he was at the Bridgewater facility, staff psychiatrists noted "his violent fantasy life" and "bizarre sexual fantasies of a violent nature." Brown, they said, was "preoccupied with murder and torture" and "remained a sexually dangerous person." A caseworker at Bridgewater even remarked that Brown "expresses a curiosity about the taste of human flesh."

He was surly and combative during his first ten years at Bridgewater, a reluctant patient who was uncooperative in therapy sessions and "dangerously disturbed." But in 1990 his attitude changed. He suddenly became compliant and cooperative. He opened up to his therapists, telling them that he and a playmate had been raped and sodomized by a group of boys from his neighborhood, and that's what fueled his own sexual behavior.

Some of his therapists considered his revelation a major breakthrough, while others doubted he was telling the truth.

He joined a Christian group that was active inside the institution, and he ceased being David Brown. He was now Nathaniel Bar-Jonah. He chose a Jewish-sounding name, he said, because he wanted to know what it felt like to be discriminated against.

And he found a way to get out of Bridgewater. Inmates could petition a judge for release, which could be granted if sympathetic doctors declared them cured. According to court records, two independent doctors hired by Bar-Jonah's family evaluated Bar-Jonah. One boldly predicted that he would not reoffend, while the other concluded that Bar-Jonah's "status as a sexually dangerous person was not appropriate."

In February 1991, Suffolk Superior Court Judge Walter Steel reviewed Bar-Jonah's petition for release. The records that accompanied the petition indicated that he had completed courses in photography and the ministry, and had worked in Bridgewater's commissary. What's more, he had no record of violent or aggressive episodes, which seemed to indicate that he had learned to control his sexual impulses. The judge also had the reports of the two independent doctors, as well as the reports of the Bridgewater psychiatrists, but under Massachusetts law the burden of proof was on the state; it had to demonstrate beyond a reasonable doubt that Bar-Jonah was still dangerous and that his continued confinement was still warranted.

Despite the fact that two staff psychiatrists said that it was—one even called Bar-Jonah "a lethal danger to the community"—the judge ruled that in the absence of evidence of sexual misconduct, violence, or aggression against minors, the state had failed to prove that Bar-Jonah was still dangerous.

"Evidence in this case warrants a finding that the petitioner is a man who has resolved the underlying psychological conflict which resulted in the commission of crimes," the judge declared. "I find that the Commonwealth has not met its burden beyond a reasonable doubt that the petitioner is a sexually dangerous person."

In June 1991, Nathaniel Bar-Jonah walked out of Bridgewater a free man, but he wasn't cured. Exactly forty-three days later he was arrested again, this time for climbing into a parked car and sitting on a seven-year-old boy's lap.

On a sunny August morning, Nancy Surprise drove with her son Michael to the post office in Oxford. While Nancy ran inside to mail a letter, Michael stayed in the car. When Nancy returned, 280-pound Nathaniel Bar-Jonah was inside the car sitting on her son. As she struggled to pull the pudgy predator off her son and out of the vehicle, a passerby called police. Before help arrived, Bar-Jonah hightailed it to his home, which was nearby. He changed his clothes and at first denied what he'd done to the police officers who tracked him down. Later he explained that he really meant no harm. It was raining and he was only looking for a ride but the mother became hysterical. Despite his explanation, he was arrested and charged with breaking and entering and putting a person in fear.

Bar-Jonah did not show up with an attorney for his pretrial hearing on October 13. Instead he appeared with his mother, who suggested a deal. Tyra Brown pleaded with the judge to let her take her son to Montana. She was in the process of moving there to live near her older son, Bob. She pledged that she would see to it that Bar-Jonah would never harm anyone again.

The prosecutor agreed and the judge approved. Years later, after Bar-Jonah had become the leading suspect in the disappearance of Zach Ramsay, Worcester District Attorney John Conte tried to explain why his office agreed to the deal. The prosecutor said the best he could have hoped for at trial was six months in jail for Bar-Jonah because witness statements didn't indicate "that any of those people saw anything happen in the car."

But the prosecutor wasn't the only one who came under fire for releasing Bar-Jonah to Montana—District Court Judge Sarkis Teshoian took heat for approving the deal.

"I deemed it to be an appropriate sentence based on the information that was being made available to me," he said when he was asked about the case eleven years later. Prosecutors hadn't told him about O'Connor, Benoit, and Enrickias, nor did they tell him that Bar-Jonah had spent eleven years in a facility for sexual offenders, or that dozens of psychiatric evaluations over the years said that he was a violent sexual predator.

By September Nathaniel Bar-Jonah was living with his brother, Bob, and sister-in-law, Jill, in Great Falls. He earned money working in fast-food restaurants and selling stuffed animals, dolls, comic books, and *Star Wars* memorabilia from a booth at the

American Mall. To earn extra money he mowed lawns at the Bitterroot Apartments in summer, and kept the building's walkways clear of snow and ice in winter.

And he attended the Central Assembly of God church, where he became active in the Royal Rangers, the church's youth ministry. He asked if he could lead the group, but a police officer who was a member of the congregation alerted the pastor to Bar-Jonah's long history as a sexual offender.

"We did not give him a position with any of our children's ministries," said Pastor Alan Warneke.

Nathaniel Bar-Jonah had been a suspect from the very beginning. "The day Zach turned up missing, I went over to Nate's place, but he wasn't there," Great Falls Police Detective Bill Bellusci recalled. The next day he sent two uniformed patrol officers to the apartment at 1216 First Avenue South, where Bar-Jonah was then living with his mother. But once again no one answered the door. The cops left their calling cards but never went back.

If they had, they would have learned that Tyra Brown had been in Massachusetts since January 26, and wouldn't return until February 16. Bar-Jonah, however, had not left Great Falls, and he had access to his mother's car—a 1987 white four-door Toyota Corolla sedan.

Bellusci had first met Bar-Jonah in December 1993, when he arrested him for fondling the penis of an eight-year-old. The boy had been left in Bar-Jonah's care while his unsuspecting parents were away on an overnight trip. The family met Bar-Jonah at church and befriended him. Bar-Jonah even drove the boy to Sunday school. During questioning Bar-Jonah vehemently denied fondling the boy.

As part of his investigation, Bill Bellusci delved deeply into Bar-Jonah's past. He contacted police agencies in Massachusetts and obtained psychiatric evaluations from Bridgewater. By the time Bellusci finished his investigation, he knew everything there was to know about Bar-Jonah's sordid life prior to his arrival in Montana.

Despite his past record of sexual assaults, it would have been a difficult case to prosecute. There were no witnesses and no physical evidence to support the boy's story, so authorities hoped for a plea bargain. Bar-Jonah spent five months in the Cascade County Jail refusing to bargain with prosecutors. He was released in June 1994, when his bond was lowered from $25,000 to $10,000 with the condition that he move in with his mother and observe a 9 P.M. to 9 A.M. curfew. When three years went by without the case going to trial, Bar-Jonah's attorney filed a motion to dismiss the charges under Montana's speedy trial law. The court had no choice: Bar-Jonah was off the hook.

Although he didn't get to lock Bar-Jonah up, Bill Bellusci never forgot about the pudgy predator from Massachusetts. He stood out in his mind, the detective said, because "I knew he had been violent before and I knew he was still active."

Despite that, interest in Bar-Jonah as a possible suspect in the disappearance of Zach Ramsay waned. For the first month after Zach went missing, Bellusci worked the case around the clock, but as his backlog of other cases grew, he had less time to devote to the search. Meanwhile, other investigators zeroed in on Rachel Howard, Zach's thirty-two-year-old mother.

When children vanish, lawmen first take a close look at the immediate family. Almost from day one, they eliminated Zach's father, Franz, as a suspect because of his whereabouts (Colorado) at the time, but investigators couldn't do the same for Rachel.

For one thing, the day before Zach went missing Rachel Howard's live-in boyfriend moved out. Not long after that he shot himself. It left investigators wondering if he'd tried to commit suicide out of guilt over what he knew about Zach's disappearance, or about what he may have done.

The *Great Falls Tribune* reported that a polygraph Howard took was "inconclusive." A television interview she gave led some investigators to believe that she wasn't distraught enough. "We had a mother who was not reacting the way some people felt she should be reacting," explained Detective Tim Theisen.

"People react differently to tragedy," said Detective Bellusci. "Her reaction was to stay strong."

Lawmen staked out Howard's apartment, but they were never able to connect her to her son's disappearance. By 1998 the search for the missing boy had come to a dead end. Then on December 13, 1999, Nathaniel Bar-Jonah did something that led lawmen back to his doorstep—he went for a walk.

It was still dark in Montana at 7:43 A.M., a time when kids are heading off to school. Great Falls Police Detective Bob "Bubba" Burton was on his way to work when he spotted Nathaniel Bar-Jonah lurking near the Lincoln Elementary School. He was wearing a dark police-style jacket and a stocking cap.

The veteran investigator was very familiar with Bar-Jonah's past history as a sexual predator, and he knew that he didn't live in the vicinity of the school. What's more, he had seen Bar-Jonah walking near the school at about the same time the week before, and he remembered that witnesses reported seeing Zach Ramsay with a man in a blue police-style jacket the morning he went missing. Burton's instincts told him that Bar-Jonah was up to no good, so he picked up his portable police radio and contacted dispatch. He wanted a patrol unit to intercept Bar-Jonah and find out what he was up to.

Officer Steve Brunk was in his police cruiser when the call came over the radio. In less than a minute he had Bar-Jonah in sight. He was walking east on Fifth Avenue South. Brunk, driving west, passed Bar-Jonah, then made a U-turn and pulled up alongside him. He ordered him to step to the front of his car. In the meantime, backup arrived. Officer Michael Badgley pulled up just as Brunk was asking Bar-Jonah to remove his hands from his pockets.

"Do you have anything in your pockets I should know about?" the cop asked.

"I have a stun gun," Bar-Jonah replied.

As soon as he heard that, Brunk ordered Bar-Jonah to put his hands on top of the patrol car. While Brunk kept an eye on Bar-Jonah, Badgley came over and patted him down. In his right jacket pocket Badgley found the stun gun, but that wasn't all the pat-down produced. The cop also turned up a realistic toy revolver, a metal badge that said "Special Investigator," and two cans of pepper spray.

Despite what they found, the officers didn't think they had sufficient legal grounds to arrest Bar-Jonah, so they let him go, but they filed a report which eventually landed on Bill Bellusci's desk. He believed he had grounds for a search warrant based on Bar-Jonah's history as a sexual predator who lured young boys into his car by posing as a police officer. A judge agreed, and two days later investigators were inside Bar-Jonah's new apartment at 2527 Eleventh Avenue South.

As soon as they walked in the door, Bellusci and Sergeant John Cameron, the lead detective on the Ramsay case, were taken aback by what they saw—thousands of photographs of young children, mostly boys, were everywhere.

They were on the walls and on tables and bureaus. More were thrown into boxes, while others were neatly arranged in albums. They also saw dozens of newspaper clippings about the disappearance of Zach Ramsay and two rolls of undeveloped film, which they immediately sent to the lab for processing.

As they probed further, the detectives turned up a two-hundred-thousand-volt stun gun, stun batons, a blue police coat, a silver toy revolver, a half dozen police-style badges, a baseball cap with the logo "Security Enforcement," and a coat with a phony police badge in the pocket.

It was enough evidence for Bellusci to order the arrest of Nathaniel Bar-Jonah. He was taken into custody later that day and charged with impersonating a public servant and carrying a concealed weapon. He pleaded not guilty.

As the detectives continued their search, they became convinced that Nathaniel Bar-Jonah was responsible for the disappearance of Zach Ramsay. But the investigation would take on a whole new dimension once the film came back from the lab.

The photos depicted young boys inside Bar-Jonah's apartment. One showed a Native American boy lying on Bar-Jonah's couch with his finger in his mouth and his shirt pulled up. Another depicted a topless youngster who appeared to be asleep in Bar-Jonah's bed. There were also photos of Bar-Jonah's penis in various stages of erection. Bellusci recognized three of the boys in the photos—they had lived in the apartment directly above Bar-Jonah's. Cameron made plans to interview them and their parents.

As far as Zach Ramsay was concerned, it seemed that Bar-Jonah was obsessed with the child. He had dozens of newspaper clippings about Zach's disappearance on display in the apartment. He even had a school yearbook photo of the missing boy. What's more, the detectives noted that most of the children in the thousands of pictures in the apartment were dark skinned, as were Zach and the children who lived upstairs.

As they continued their search, the detectives unearthed still more eyebrow-raising evidence:

- A receipt from Practical Rent-A-Car showing that on January 29, 1996, Bar-Jonah paid $175 to rent a 1990 Chevrolet Celebrity station wagon. He returned the vehicle at 3:30 P.M. on February 5, the day before Zachary went missing. Over the seven days that Bar-Jonah drove the car, he managed to put 510 miles on it. Detectives were puzzled: Bank records indicated that he had little money in his checking account and had been bouncing checks at the time, yet he paid to rent a car even though he had access to his mother's Toyota. Did Bar-Jonah use the rental car to stalk Zach? Could his mother's white Toyota be the vehicle the Henrys said almost struck Zach as he walked through the alley the morning he disappeared? The detectives wondered.

- Canceled checks indicating that Bar-Jonah used taxicabs to get around town after February 6. The detectives knew that when he'd abducted young boys in the past, Bar-Jonah had used his mother's vehicle. Was Bar-Jonah afraid to drive the Toyota after February 6, because it had been used in the abduction of Zach Ramsay and he worried that it would be recognized? Or was it because it held the boy's remains? Or both? Again, the detectives wondered.

- One check in particular caught Cameron's eye—number 3686. It was made out to the Diamond Cab Company for $6.75, and it was dated February 6. Cameron subpoenaed Bar-Jonah's bank records. When he compared the microfilmed copy of the check that he obtained from the bank with the canceled check, Cameron noticed that the dates didn't match. The microfilmed copy was dated February 7. It appeared that the check had been altered after it had cleared the bank. Had Bar-Jonah altered the date in hopes of establishing an alibi?

- An ATM receipt that put Bar-Jonah at a Norwest Bank three blocks from Zach's home at 7:31 A.M. the day before the boy disappeared, while a receipt from a dry cleaner indicated that six days after Zach disappeared Bar-Jonah brought his blue police-style jacket in for cleaning and to replace a torn zipper. Was there blood on the jacket? Did the zipper tear during a struggle?

- An article entitled "The Right Ropes, The Top Knots," explaining how to tie rope knots.

- A pamphlet entitled "AutoErotic Asphyxia."

There was more. They found a calendar in the apartment that indicated that Bar-Jonah did not work at Hardee's on February 4, 5, or 6, 1996. A check with the manager verified that he had not.

The lawmen also discovered a bizarre list labeled "Lake Webster." It contained twenty-seven names including those of former Bar-Jonah victims: Rick O'Connor, Alan Enrickias, Michael Surprise, and Billy Benoit. Zachary Ramsay's name was on the list, too, only Bar-Jonah wrote "Zachery Ramsey," and the last word at the end of the entire list was "DIED."

The names were written in capital letters with no spaces between them, like this:

ZACHERYRAMSEYCHRISWESTPAHLL
MICHAELSURPRISEBILLYBENOITA
LENENRICKIASDIED

The other twenty-two names were from Bar-Jonah's hometown. For the most part, the names were arranged in chronological order with dates next to each one.

The investigators found a receipt establishing that at 2:20 P.M. on the day Zach disappeared, Bar-Jonah went to the Doctors Convenience Center, a walk-in medical clinic across the street from his apartment. Cameron subpoenaed Bar-Jonah's medical records. He learned that Bar-Jonah complained of pain in his left index finger and a sore right leg. To Cameron, the finger injury sounded similar to injuries suffered by law enforcement officials when they attempt to put handcuffs on resisting prisoners.

But the most disturbing find was a pair of encrypted lists that appeared to have been written out in Bar-Jonah's distinctive handwriting. An FBI expert decoded the writings. He told the detectives they contained what appeared to be the titles for some macabre recipes:

Little Boy Stew
Sum Yung Guy
Gay Blades Are My Favorite Food, Christmas
    dinner for two
Lunch Is Served On The Patio With Roasted Child

Barbequed Kid
Sex A La Cart
My Little Kid Desert
Hang Em High
Happy Halloween
Little Boy Pot Pies
Penises Are Yummy
French Fried Kid

The list sent chills up and down the spine of every investigator who read it. No one had to remind them that a caseworker in Massachusetts once wrote that Bar-Jonah, when he was still known as David Brown, expressed a "curiosity about the taste of human flesh." What's more, they all were familiar with an ominous psychiatric evaluation that said Bar-Jonah's bizarre sexual fantasies "outline methods for torture, extending to dissection and cannibalism."

From his cell in the Cascade County Jail, in three angry letters sent to the *Great Falls Tribune*, Bar-Jonah protested his innocence and accused police of trying to frame him.

"Let's get this perfectly clear—I did not, I repeat, I did not kill Zachary Ramsey [sic] or anyone else," he wrote, even though he had not yet been charged in the case.

In a second letter he declared, "I'm innocent pure and simple, no more no less." He wrote that he'd been attacked and beaten in his jail cell, and that he'd received dozens of death threats. Then he turned to the New Testament: "Jesus says, 'He who is without sin cast the first stone.' Well, there must be a lot of people out there who has [sic] never sinned because you are sure casting a lot of stones at me and my family."

His family, he wrote, deserved an apology from the police and the media. They "have done nothing wrong. The police and the news media OWE THEM AN APOLOGY, to say the very least. These charges may cost me my life BUT at least I know where I'll spend eternity. DO YOU?"

Bar-Jonah admitted that he was carrying a police badge, a toy pistol, pepper spray, and a stun gun when he was stopped by cops on December 13, 1999, but he said he never used any of those items on anyone. Two days later he was arrested. "It took them two days of searching the laws to find something they could arrest me on," he wrote. "I became the perfect patsy and it'll probably cost me my life."

Bar-Jonah accused Great Falls detectives Bill Bellusci, Bob Burton, and John Cameron of framing him. Bellusci, he said, had been "stalking" him since October 1996, while Burton tailed him for six months in 1999.

"They are indeed Great Falls' finest who believe they will always get their man either by hook or by crook. That if they can't prove it legally they will set them up and bully people into making a false statement. These cops remind me of the Borg on *Star Trek*, 'WE ARE THE LAW, Resistance is futile.' "

Bar-Jonah also took a shot at the *Tribune*, complaining that the paper's story about his childhood years in Massachusetts inaccurately depicted him as a loner whose only friends were much younger children. He had many friends in high school, he wrote, and the young children he played with were only a few years younger.

He denied that that he ever shoveled snow at the Bitterroot Apartments, a key to placing him near Zach the day he disappeared. "That's a lie," Bar-Jonah wrote. "I have never worked in that area."

Police, however, had canceled checks made out to Nathaniel

Bar-Jonah as payment for his labor. Jenny Brydon, the property manager, even told investigators that Bar-Jonah did shovel snow at the apartments in the days before Zach Ramsay went missing.

Finally Bar-Jonah admitted that he'd kidnapped and strangled Rick O'Connor in 1975, Alan Enrickias and Billy Benoit in 1977, and Michael Surprise in 1991, but declared that "I won't say I did something when I did not do it. I am not guilty of those charges and I did not do anything with or to Zachery Ramsey [sic] or any one else.

"So please, if you know where he is, please, call the police. Thank you!"

Lead Detective John Cameron had joined the Great Falls police force nineteen years earlier, when he was twenty years old. He'd been a detective for eight years and was considered the department's cold case expert, ever since 1997 when he solved the ten-year-old murder of a convenience store clerk. Now he wanted nothing more than to bring Zach Ramsay home and convict the person or persons responsible for his disappearance.

Cameron believed the pieces of the puzzle were finally falling into place, but he knew there was still a lot more work to do to build a solid case. For one thing, he wanted to find out if there was a connection between the encrypted list of recipes and the disappearance of Zach Ramsay in 1996, and he wanted to interview anyone and everyone who had ever rubbed elbows with Nathaniel Bar-Jonah.

Sherri Dietrich was among the first people the detectives talked to. She had arrived in Great Falls from Colorado in September of 1997, behind the wheel of a Ryder van. She had no food, no money, and no place to stay. Everything she owned was in the van.

She met Bar-Jonah at the American Mall when she went there hoping to sell some of her things. Tyra Brown had recently moved out of the apartment they'd been sharing, so he offered Dietrich a place to stay until she could get back on her feet. Dietrich stayed with him until January 1998. At first Bar-Jonah was a gracious host, but after only a week he turned surly and angry. He even warned her that he could become violent.

Dietrich told the detectives that Bar-Jonah talked to her about the missing boy. He told her that he knew Zach, that he played with him, and that he had seen him walking down the alley on his way to school the morning he disappeared.

One day, she said, Bar-Jonah told her that "whoever took Zach Ramsay was probably dressed up like a policeman."

When she asked him why he thought that, Bar-Jonah said the boy "wouldn't have gotten into a car with someone he didn't know."

Bar-Jonah explained that kids are taught from an early age to trust police officers. "If a policeman stopped by in his car and offered the boy a ride to school, the boy would probably have got into the car," he told her.

Toward the end of the interview, Dietrich told investigators that she was cleaning the apartment one day when she stumbled on a pile of children's clothing that was on the floor of a closet—a dark jacket with green sleeves and a pair of boys' black sneakers. She also found a shirt, briefs, socks, jeans, mittens, and a stocking cap in a plastic bag in the corner of the closet. When she removed the items from the bag, sand fell from them. What's more, they were "very dirty."

Later, when Bar-Jonah came home, she asked him about the clothing. She recalled him saying, "They belonged to my ex-roommate."

"Your roommate must have been awfully tiny," she replied.

The clothes Dietrich described matched the clothes Zach was wearing when he left home for school the morning he disappeared.

Detectives interviewed Teresa Sizemore-Bourisaw, a friend of Bar-Jonah's. She was a Bar-Jonah pen pal while he was in Bridge-water, and they stayed in touch by phone and through the mail after he was released. Bar-Jonah's phone records indicated that he had spoken with her the week before Zachary Ramsay disappeared. Sizemore-Bourisaw recalled that in one of their conversations Bar-Jonah told her that "Little Zach" "went to the flea market and went to Billings with me."

Cameron interviewed Keith "Doc" Bauman, who met Bar-Jonah in 1994 when both men were prisoners in the Cascade County Jail. They became fast friends, and their friendship continued after they were released.

Bauman told Cameron that he and Bar-Jonah visited each other often, and that they frequently ate lunch and dinner together at Bar-Jonah's apartment. Bauman even recalled an afternoon in August 1996 when Bar-Jonah barbecued burgers on his patio.

They weren't hamburgers, Bauman said. Bar-Jonah told him they were "deer burgers." Bauman remembered his host telling him that Hardee's was running a special that week on the burgers. After the interview Cameron checked with the manager at the Hardee's where Bar-Jonah worked. The manager told him the fast-food restaurant had never served deer meat.

Cameron talked to Pam Clark. She told the detective that she was Bar-Jonah's ex-fiancée. They met in 1995 when she was hired to work at Hardee's. In the fall of 1997 she moved in with him and Sherri Dietrich. Pam, a black woman, had known Bar-Jonah for two years prior to moving in, but after living with him for three weeks she was desperate to move out.

There was a dark side to Bar-Jonah she hadn't seen before, she said. He would lock himself in his bedroom and not come out for hours. He'd spend hours in front of the TV set watching cartoons and he acted childishly.

Pam recalled a conversation she had with Sherri Dietrich. Sherri told her that she was convinced Bar-Jonah killed Zach Ramsay.

Pam told Sergeant Cameron that Bar-Jonah had a police badge and a police ID.

She recalled that in 1996, during the time his mother was in Massachusetts, Bar-Jonah "was very angry and spent most of his time in his house, refusing to answer the door." On at least one occasion she went to visit him, but he told her he wanted to be left alone.

Pam remembered speaking to Bar-Jonah a day or two after Zach Ramsay disappeared. She told the detective that Bar-Jonah told her that Zach "was chopped up and thrown all over the forest."

Before the interview ended, Pam told the detective that Bar-Jonah's apartment always had a terrible odor. She tried hard to get rid of it, but she never could, because she was never able to figure out exactly where it was coming from.

Clark's daughter Andrea Holden corroborated everything her mother said.

During their search of Bar-Jonah's apartment, Cameron had come across a note that read, "Debbie 2109 6th Ave. No.—Mike Tyson Doll $25.00."

Cameron went to the address. Debbie's full name was Debbie Cote. She told the detective that she met Bar-Jonah in the fall of 1996. A fire had damaged her home and Bar-Jonah brought her a pie.

It was a welcome gesture at first, but afterward Bar-Jonah

frequently stopped by to see her then eleven-year-old son, Lucas. Bar-Jonah, she said, seemed "obsessed" with the boy and tried to create a situation in which he could be alone with him. But Cote, the mother of two, said she was wary of Bar-Jonah and made sure that never happened.

In the summer of 1996 she ordered a Mike Tyson doll from Bar-Jonah, who sold them at the American Mall. She recalled that when he brought it over, somehow the Zachary Ramsay case came up in their conversation. She remembered Bar-Jonah saying, "They'll never find him."

Bar-Jonah visited her again on Christmas Day, 1996. On that occasion he brought over a bowl of spaghetti with some meat. He told Cote that he "hunted, killed, butchered and wrapped the meat himself." At other times he brought over stews and chili that Bar-Jonah said were made with venison. Cote said her sons complained that "the meat tasted funny."

If Bar-Jonah had hunted and killed the meat himself, he would have taken out a hunting license. Detectives combed through all the hunting license records from 1991 through 1999. They never found one issued to Nathaniel Bar-Jonah.

While lawmen in Montana pressed on with their investigation, authorities in New England mounted one as well. They were concerned about the list of names that Great Falls detectives had found in Bar-Jonah's apartment. It seemed that half the names were from Montana, while the other half were from Massachusetts. They went looking for them.

Once the story broke, dozens of people who knew Bar-Jonah in Massachusetts called police to tell them about their experiences with him, said Webster Police Officer Michaela Kelley.

He was the misfit, the fat kid the other kids made fun of. When the other teens wore bell bottoms, Brown still wore his Levi's rolled up into cuffs. He didn't participate in sports and he kept pretty much to himself.

One woman who insisted on anonymity said she remembered him from high school and was so terrified of him she skipped her high school reunion because she feared he'd be there.

Bar-Jonah wrote her a letter while he was in Bridgewater threatening to "get even" with her—in his twisted mind he believed that she embarrassed him in high school "because we were both kind of heavy and people used to make fun of us and pair us off together."

Eventually everyone on the list was found to be alive and well, but the phone calls and visits from the police with questions about Bar-Jonah, whom they knew as David Brown, were disturbing.

"I think they were a little shaken up by it," said Officer Kelley. "It was scary for them to think he was thinking of them."

"It was a shock to me," said Wayne Belles. He had lived three doors down from Bar-Jonah in his birthplace, Dudley, Massachusetts. "I don't know why my name was down there or what purpose it served," he told a reporter for the *Boston Globe* who contacted him in January 2001, after the list was published in newspapers in southern Massachusetts.

Another name on the list was Jeffrey Jamroga of Fairfield County, Connecticut. Next to his name was the notation "1976." When he was ten years old, Jamroga attended a Royal Rangers powwow in Charlton during the summer of 1976.

The Royal Rangers are a youth group affiliated with the Assemblies of God Church. Their motto is "reaching, teaching, and keeping boys with Christ." Tyra Brown, Bar-Jonah's mother, was an active member of the Assemblies of God Church in Dudley. In 1977 she even helped found a congregation in Webster, where Bar-Jonah grew up.

Their summer powwows drew boys from all over Massachusetts, Connecticut, and Rhode Island to Charlton, to the very same site where Bar-Jonah attacked Billy Benoit and Alan Enrickias in 1977.

Bar-Jonah's connection to the Royal Rangers in Massachusetts was yet another ominous sign of his monstrosity. Zach Ramsay was a Royal Ranger, too, and investigators in Montana wondered if the boy had met him through the church group.

They couldn't be sure; no one ever recalled seeing them together at a Royal Rangers function.

By now detectives had formed a theory of the case based on Bar-Jonah's modus operandi, physical evidence, his writings, and information gleaned from friends and acquaintances, as well as eyewitness accounts of the minutes before Zach Ramsay disappeared:

Bar-Jonah, as he had done previously, posed as a policeman and either convinced or coerced Zach Ramsay to get into his mother's white Toyota sedan. He drove the boy to his apartment. At some point he handcuffed him, but Zach put up a fierce struggle during which Bar-Jonah injured his index finger and tore his blue police-style jacket. Enraged, Bar-Jonah strangled Zach and then had to figure out a way to dispose of the body. His solution was to dismember it, cook it, and feed the meat to his friends, which explains some, but not all, of the encrypted recipes:

- Lunch Is Served On The Patio With Roasted Child: Bar-Jonah served Doc Bauman deer burgers for lunch on his patio.

- Barbecued Kid: The deer burgers were barbecued.

- Gay Blades Are My Favorite Food, Christmas dinner for two: In 1996 Bar-Jonah brought Christmas dinner to Debbie Cote's family.

- Little Boy Stew: Bar-Jonah brought stew and chili to the Cote family.

- Little Boy Pot Pies: Bar-Jonah once brought the Cote family a pie.

In court they would have to prove their theory, and it would help a lot if they could prove that Zach was dead, so on April 11, detectives and FBI agents searched the apartment Bar-Jonah was living in in February 1996, 1216 First Avenue South. Investigators hadn't been there since they knocked on the door in the days after Zach Ramsay went missing. This time they didn't need to knock—they were armed with a search warrant.

They wanted to take apart the plumbing, but learned that shortly after Bar-Jonah moved out all the pipes had been changed because they had been clogging up.

They were especially interested in the garage behind the house. It was where Bar-Jonah stored the toys he sold at the American Mall. It was also where he ran weekly garage sales that attracted dozens of kids.

On April 20, a team of seventeen forensic investigators, including anthropologists from the University of Montana, began digging. They were looking for Zach Ramsay's body.

The Great Falls police and the FBI had been investigating Bar-Jonah since December "and the evidence is pointing more and more in his direction," said lead detective Sergeant John Cameron. "We're getting close. We're going to find out what happened to Zach Ramsay."

It seemed investigators were closing in when the next day they revealed they'd unearthed "possible" evidence: three small bone fragments less than six inches from the surface. A second search a few days later produced eighteen more fragments. Among the twenty-one bone fragments, investigators discovered a piece of Bar-Jonah's stationery, listing items he was selling.

The bones were sent to the state crime lab in Missoula for analysis. A few weeks later it was announced that all the fragments were from the same human, eight to thirteen years of age.

The fragments were sent to a private laboratory in Pennsylvania for DNA testing. The lab reported back in May: Four of the bones they'd tested were not the remains of Zach Ramsay. The remaining fragments were still undergoing analysis.

Investigators were undeterred. "We're working toward pressing charges, but once you do, the clock starts ticking and we want to make sure we have a thorough and complete case before we file," explained County Prosecutor Brant Light.

On June 28 lawmen in Great Falls learned the outcome of the DNA analysis of the remaining bone fragments: They were not Zach Ramsay's. Detectives had hoped the bones would tie Bar-Jonah to the missing boy; instead they were faced with a new mystery—whose bones were they?

Meanwhile, investigators never lost sight of the shocking photos they'd found in Bar-Jonah's apartment in December, especially the ones of the Native American boys who lived in the apartment directly above his. On July 5, 2000, Light filed kidnapping and sexual assault charges against Bar-Jonah, who pleaded not guilty.

BAR-JONAH ACCUSED OF FONDLING BOYS, blared the next day's *Great Falls Tribune*. "The chief suspect in the 1996 disappearance of young Zachary Ramsay was slapped with five more felony charges Wednesday in unrelated cases," read the lead paragraph.

The article then went on to detail the latest lurid charges against Bar-Jonah, who had been in the county jail on $200,000 bail since his arrest in December on charges of impersonating a police officer and carrying a concealed weapon: fondling three boys ages six, nine, and fifteen; hanging one of the boys from a hook in his kitchen ceiling, nearly choking him to death; locking another in his bedroom and forcing him to strip. The boys were the Native Americans who lived in the same building as Bar-Jonah.

The new charges—one count of kidnapping, three counts of sexual assault, and one count of assault with a weapon—were sparked by the finding of lewd photos during the search of Bar-Jonah's apartment in December.

The boys—two brothers, fifteen and six, and their nine-year-old cousin—and their parents were interviewed separately by Detectives Cameron and Theisen in 2000. The interviews were videotaped.

The detectives learned that the brothers and their mother met Bar-Jonah during the summer of 1998 after they moved into the apartment above his at 2527 Eleventh Avenue South in Great Falls. The boys were regular visitors to Bar-Jonah's apartment. He looked after them when their mother wasn't home. Several times the boys spent the night there.

Bar-Jonah treated them well at first. He took them to the movies and bought them dinners, lunches, and ice cream. And he abused them.

The fifteen-year-old—who was referred to as R.J. in court papers—told Cameron that Bar-Jonah locked him in his bedroom and refused to let him out unless he pulled down his pants. Bar-Jonah was naked at the time and forced him to touch his penis. On another occasion R.J. said Bar-Jonah handcuffed him to a pole that was outside the apartment building and left him there for half an hour.

R.J. said Bar-Jonah liked to parade around the apartment in his underwear. He had a scar on his right thigh and he would force the boy to rub it.

His six-year-old brother, referred to as S.A., said Bar-Jonah touched him in ways and places he didn't like. The boy pointed to his penis and buttocks.

The nine-year-old cousin, S.J., said he was in Bar-Jonah's kitchen one day when Bar-Jonah snuck up on him and wrapped a rope around his neck. The end of the rope was attached to a pulley. Bar-Jonah pulled the rope and the next thing the boy knew, his feet were dangling in the air and he was choking. Bar-Jonah let him dangle for about twenty seconds before lowering him to the floor. S.J. ran upstairs crying.

When asked why they never told anyone, the boys said they were afraid that Bar-Jonah would harm or kidnap them. The nine-year-old worried that Bar-Jonah would hang him again.

"That's his big thing," Brant Light told the *Tribune*. "He gets off on assaulting and choking young boys."

When five of his fellow prisoners at the Cascade County Jail got wind of the new charges, they decided to give Bar-Jonah a taste of jailhouse justice—they attacked him in his cell, stomped and punched him repeatedly before jailers could intervene. Bar-Jonah suffered only minor injuries.

After treating him for his injuries, jailers put the pudgy predator into protective custody in the jail's maximum-security section. Despite the thrashing, Bar-Jonah steadfastly refused to rat out his attackers.

He was slated to go on trial in January 2001, in Cascade

County District Court, for kidnapping and molesting the brothers and their cousins, but on November 13, 2000, Bar-Jonah's attorney, Public Defender Eric Olsen, filed a motion for a change of venue. Olsen argued that "due to the publicity which linked [Bar-Jonah] to the disappearance of Zachary Ramsay, and due to the depth of feelings in Great Falls that surrounded the emotionally charged case, he could not receive a fair trial."

For nearly a year the case had dominated the headlines in Great Falls as local media dug into every detail of Bar-Jonah's demented past and reported every detail of the ongoing investigation that was fed to them by authorities.

Judge Kenneth Neill granted the motion. He ordered a change of venue for jury selection to Butte, in Silver Bow County. Jurors would be chosen from there and then sequestered for the actual trial, which would take place in his courtroom in Cascade County.

But the media frenzy really took off after County Attorney Brant Light raised the specter of cannibalism on December 18, 2000. Two days later, the *Great Falls Tribune* ran no fewer than nine news and feature stories and one editorial related to the case:

BAR-JONAH CHARGED WITH KILLING RAMSAY

Cascade County Attorney Brant Light charged Nathaniel Bar-Jonah Tuesday with kidnapping and killing Zachary Ramsay, saying police never will find his body because Bar-Jonah ate the 10-year-old and fed him to others.

TUESDAY'S CHARGES MAY BE TIP OF ICEBERG

Charges of kidnapping and killing Zachary Ramsay could be just the beginning. "There's no signs of this case slowing," Detective Tim Theisen said. "I don't see an end to it even at the point of charges (in the Ramsay case). We still have so much left." Bill Matthews, an FBI spokesman based in Utah, said evidence has revealed possible victims in other states.

BAR-JONAH EMERGED AS SUSPECT
AFTER TORTUOUS PATH

One year ago, an off-duty police officer noticed a man dressed suspiciously like a policeman walking around Lincoln Elementary School. Former School Resource Officer Robert Burton knew Nathaniel Bar-Jonah—he and many other officers had been told about his history of using a police badge to help him kidnap and strangle young boys. What he didn't know was that his one phone call to dispatch would rekindle the cold investigation into Zachary Ramsay's disappearance.

TROUBLE STARTED EARLY,
CONTINUED IN GREAT FALLS

Nathaniel Bar-Jonah has been violent for a long time. In a psychiatric evaluation released in court documents, he recalled choking a young girl while his mother screamed at him to stop. He was 6. In the years since, Bar-Jonah, 43, preyed on young boys, often using the guise of a police officer.

EXPERTS DEBATE WHAT FORCES
CREATE A CANNIBAL

That Nathaniel Bar-Jonah may have fed human flesh to unsuspecting friends and neighbors could make this the most ghastly crime in Great Falls' history. What drives a person to cannibalism? Experts contacted by the Tribune *gave theories ranging from early childhood trauma to simple evilness.*

CONNECTING THE DOTS

Since December 1999, investigators have gathered evidence they believe proves Nathaniel Bar-Jonah, dressed as a police officer, abducted and killed 10-year-old Zachary Ramsay, who disappeared on his way to school in February 1996. Here's a look: [The article then detailed thirteen points of "evidence" from "Knew Zachary" to "Obsessed with boys," "Fixated on Zachary," "Traces of butchery," and "Untold atrocities."]

BAR-JONAH'S DEMONS

He was the odd, chubby kid who played with younger neighborhood children. He became a 43-year-old who collected Star Wars *memorabilia and prided himself on his Christian faith and his cooking.*

SCHOOL OFFICIALS PREPARED TO HELP KIDS COPE

Great Falls teachers and counselors are braced to listen to and help students upset by the news of Nathaniel Bar-Jonah's alleged killing and possible cannibalism of Zachary Ramsay. Teachers will watch for signs of distress and take cues from that, said Diane Long, principal at Whittier Elementary, the Lower North Side school attended by 10-year-old Ramsay when he disappeared Feb. 6, 1996.

A sidebar story compared Bar-Jonah to other notorious cannibal killers:

CANNIBALISM: A GALLERY OF HORROR

In the 1970s, Henry Lee Lucas met the weak-minded Otis Toole in a Florida soup kitchen. When Lucas hooked up with Toole and his 12-year-old niece, the three went on a spree of robbing, killing and raping across several states. They killed shopkeepers, women with car problems and drunks unfortunate enough to share a bottle with them.

An editorial in the newspaper, which is owned by Gannett, opined:

The filing of charges is a step toward restoring trust. We don't know what has a worse effect on a community than the unsolved disappearance of a child. For example, there may be no rhyme or reason for natural disasters, but their randomness and ubiquity make them easy to comprehend, if not to accept. Accidents and crimes that cause death or injuries are tragic, but they usually provide some resolution for survivors—blame is assessed and, when appropriate, punishment handed down.

Two days later, Public Defender Olsen blasted County Attorney Brant Light, saying "He has chosen to fan the flames of public outrage in hopes of convicting Mr. Bar-Jonah of a crime for which little, if any, meaningful evidence exists." He also blasted the media for its coverage, especially the *Great Falls Tribune*.

On the same day Olsen, citing a conflict of interest, announced that his office was withdrawing as Bar-Jonah's counsel. The day after New Year's, new counsel was appointed and the trial, which was scheduled to begin on January 16, was postponed.

On January 2, 2001, Gregory Jackson and Don Vernay, two private attorneys who specialized in death penalty cases, were assigned to represent Bar-Jonah. Both men had extensive experience defending tough cases, and the Bar-Jonah cases—impersonating a police officer, the kidnapping and sexual assault case involving the two brothers and their cousin, the kidnapping and murder of Zachary Ramsay, and a charge of witness tampering that was added on in October—would be their toughest yet.

Vernay said one of the first things he would do was speak up for Bar-Jonah. "He has been savaged in the newspaper," the attorney declared. He didn't waste any time—he came out swinging.

"Somebody in the Great Falls Police Department has a very fertile imagination," he charged in an interview with the *Boston Globe*. "There's no direct evidence linking this guy [Nathaniel Bar-Jonah] with anything. Even the circumstantial evidence is weak."

Referring to the encrypted list of recipes, Vernay said, "All I saw was a piece of paper and somebody's alleged decoding of it."

The veteran attorney said he doubted that an impartial jury could be found in Cascade County, or anywhere else in the state. Asked where an unbiased panel might be found, the lawyer quipped, "Somewhere in Newfoundland or maybe in Costa Rica."

He added, "The publicity has been shameful, it really has been. I've never seen anything like this in my twenty years, where the cops go and shoot their mouths off like this."

In February Vernay and Jackson launched a blitz of legal motions. First, they sought a gag order against the media. Judge Neill denied it. Next they filed a motion to suppress all the evidence taken from Bar-Jonah's apartment during the search of December 15, 1999. Had they prevailed, the cases against

Bar-Jonah would have collapsed for lack of evidence, but Neill denied that one, too.

They filed a motion for a change of venue, which Neill granted. The kidnapping and sexual assault case was set for trial in Butte beginning on September 10.

In August, Bar-Jonah's attorneys asked for yet another delay. Neill denied it. Later in the month they asked Neill to boot County Attorney Brant Light from the trial in the kidnapping and sexual assault case because he had been slow in turning over evidence to the defense. Judge Neill denied that, too.

With less than two weeks to trial, Vernay and Jackson went to the Montana Supreme Court with a request that it intervene and stop the trial and to hear their appeals of Judge Neill's decisions *before* rather than after the trial. The Supreme Court turned them down.

But on September 5, Judge Neill relented. He agreed to delay the trial yet again, setting it for February 12, 2002, in Butte.

On October 29, Light announced he was dropping the witness tampering charge against Bar-Jonah. The charge stemmed from a letter Bar-Jonah wrote to a former roommate allegedly asking him to lie at the pending sexual assault and kidnapping trial.

Finally, at year's end, Judge Neill set a date for the Ramsay murder trial—May 13, in Missoula, 120 miles west of Great Falls.

Butte, Montana, is a gritty mining town 150 miles south of Great Falls. It's home to the World Museum of Mining, the Dumas Brothel—the longest operating bordello in the United States (it opened in 1890 and closed in 1982)—and the Silver Bow County Courthouse.

Located at 155 West Granite Street, the courthouse is an imposing edifice. It was completed in 1913, when the city was the state's center of political and financial power. Built for $482,000, the courthouse boasts massive copper doors, elegantly painted murals in the interior, and wide front steps at the entrance. Offices and courtrooms are laid out around a rotunda that's capped by a very impressive stained glass dome.

The trial of Nathaniel Bar-Jonah, however, was held in a very unimpressive room. On February 12, 2002, more than two hundred potential jurors jammed into the tiny courtroom. They had been called in the matter of *State of Montana v. Nathaniel Bar-Jonah*. Western Montana was in the grip of a bitter Arctic cold front that had come down from Canada the day before, but that didn't stop the hardy people of Silver Bow County from answering the call to service: Virtually everyone summoned showed up. They were standing shoulder to shoulder when the bailiff called, "All rise!" Judge Neill took his seat at the bench, slammed down the gavel, and called the court to order.

Bar-Jonah was already in the courtroom. Dressed in a blue blazer and a white shirt, he sat quietly, flanked by his lawyers, Gregory Jackson and Don Vernay. Nineteen months had passed since charges of sexual assault and kidnapping had been filed against him.

Before the proceedings got under way, the lawyers and the judge met and agreed on the ground rules: There would be no reference to Zach Ramsay. No talk of cannibalism. No mention of Little Boy Stew or serving strange meals to neighbors. Those gruesome details would be left for another jury to hear in May, when Bar-Jonah would stand trial in Missoula for murdering Zachary Ramsay. Prosecutors also agreed not to bring up Bar-Jonah's previous convictions in Massachusetts, his confinement at Bridgewater, or his stated desire to taste human flesh.

It would take until Wednesday, February 20, to whittle down the jury pool to a panel of twelve citizens and two alternates.

When that was done, Light called his first witness—Sergeant John Cameron of the Great Falls Police Department. He testified about the search of Bar-Jonah's apartment on December 15, 1999, and the discovery of lewd photos of the three boys, R.J., his brother S.A., and their cousin S.J.

The next day the boys took the witness stand. The oldest, R.J., was now seventeen. He spoke softly, wept, and hid his face as he recounted how Bar-Jonah took him into his bedroom, locked the door, and commanded him to remove his pants. Bar-Jonah, he said, had his pants down, too. Then he said Bar-Jonah fondled him.

R.J.'s eleven-year-old cousin, S.J., testified that Bar-Jonah strung him up with a rope attached to a hook in his kitchen ceiling. Bar-Jonah molested him, too. "He touched me on my penis and on my buttocks," S.J. said.

When he was asked where Bar-Jonah had touched him, R.J.'s seven-year-old brother, S.A., didn't speak. Instead he pointed to his buttocks.

During their testimony, Bar-Jonah sat impassively and stared straight ahead. The job of cross-examining the boys went to Greg Jackson, who tried to gently poke holes in their stories. He couldn't.

Throughout the trial, Jackson and Vernay tried to paint Bar-Jonah as a very friendly neighbor who took the boys to the movies, bought them ice cream, and let them watch cartoons in his apartment. In his summation, Cascade County Prosecutor Light put it this way: "What they want you to believe is the defendant was just the neighborhood Mr. Rogers, the nice guy. Everybody came over to his house. Well, ladies and gentlemen, did you ever see Mr. Rogers entertaining little children with nothing on but his underwear?"

It was a powerful closing. Six hours later the jury of ten men and two women returned a verdict: guilty of aggravated kidnapping of R.J.; guilty of sexual assault of R.J.; guilty of assault with a weapon on his cousin S.J.

Bar-Jonah was acquitted of the sexual assault of S.A. On the question of Bar-Jonah's guilt on the charge of sexual assault on S.J., the jury deadlocked and Judge Neill declared a mistrial on that count only.

Bar-Jonah showed no reaction to the verdicts. After Judge Neill dismissed the jurors, he was taken to a holding cell, where he changed back into an orange prison jumpsuit and was shackled before being driven back to the Cascade County Jail.

On May 23, a sentencing hearing was held in Neill's third-floor courtroom at the Cascade County Courthouse, a structure that's every bit as impressive as the one in Butte. Completed in 1903, the French Renaissance building was constructed from gray sandstone taken from nearby quarries. Its columns are made of solid Tennessee marble. The courthouse dome is made of copper. The Statue of Justice stands on top of it. During the Second World War the dome was used around the clock to watch for enemy aircraft.

John Cameron testified that he reviewed Bar-Jonah's criminal and psychological history in Massachusetts and talked to his victims in the Bay State. He introduced a videotape of his interview with Rick O'Connor, then thirty-five and still living in Massachusetts. O'Connor recounted what Bar-Jonah did to him in 1975 when he lured him into his car and repeatedly choked him.

Tim Theisen introduced his videotaped interview with Alan Enrickias. Enrickias recounted what Bar-Jonah did to him and his friend Billy Benoit in 1977.

The court also heard from Dr. Richard Fournier, a radiologist from Pennsylvania who traveled to Great Falls at his own expense to testify at the hearing. Dr. Fournier revealed that his neighbor Bar-Jonah, then David Brown, had molested him when he was five years old and again when he was seven while living in Webster, Massachusetts. The first time he sat on him and forced him to have oral sex. The second time, Bar-Jonah exposed himself, then fondled Fournier. The doctor said he never told his parents about the incidents.

A psychologist, Dr. Paul Beljan, and a psychotherapist, Dr. John Espy, testified for the defense. They said Bar-Jonah was dangerous and "could not function as an effective member of the community . . . without posing a threat to the community at large."

Lori Kicker of the state's Board of Pardons and Parole testified that Bar-Jonah showed "no indication that he was remorseful for the hurt he had caused his victims."

When Bar-Jonah was asked if he wanted to say anything to the court, he shook his head. On May 30 he was back in court for sentencing. He listened impassively as Neill imposed sentence: ten years for aggravated kidnapping; one hundred years for sexual assault; twenty years for assault with a weapon.

"This is a total of one hundred and thirty years, said sentences to run concurrently," the judge said. Neill then ordered that Bar-Jonah never be eligible for parole.

On June 3 Bar-Jonah was taken from the Cascade County Jail to the Montana State Prison in Deer Lodge. He fully expected to return to Great Falls for the murder trial, which was originally slated to begin on May 13 but was rescheduled for October 8. It didn't happen. On October 1, Light made a stunning announcement: He decided to drop the Ramsay murder and kidnapping charges against Bar-Jonah because Rachel Howard, Zach's mother, had informed him she would testify for the defense.

The prosecutor met with her for eight minutes on September 27. She was angry and she accused police of forcing her to lie. "She indicated that she didn't believe [Bar-Jonah] did it and she was told to keep her mouth shut, and if she didn't she would be charged with a crime," the prosecutor told reporters.

Howard, Light said, claimed that she was told that if she testified that Bar-Jonah had not killed her son she would be charged with obstruction of justice.

The prosecutor said he needed Howard to tell jurors what Zach was wearing when she last saw him on the morning he went missing, and that she hadn't seen or heard from him in six years. He said he didn't believe he could win a conviction without her testimony.

Speaking to reporters, Howard revealed that she planned to testify that she'd seen her son on a videotape and was certain he was alive, even though detectives said they investigated the tape and were certain that the boy on it was not Zach Ramsay, and they denied threatening to charge her with obstruction of justice.

"From the whole beginning of this, I believed that my son was alive," Howard declared with her attorney at her side. "I did not want Bar-Jonah to be convicted of a crime that I did not believe he did."

Don Vernay was ecstatic. "We would have won in a heartbeat," he gushed. "The witnesses in this case were highly suspect. Some of them were crazy, some of them were lying. It's the flimsiest murder case I've ever seen."

The lawyer blasted the Great Falls cops, especially Cameron. "The cops, Mr. Cold Case Cameron, are incredible," he said. "They took bizarre fantasies from this kid's past and they purposely slandered him to get a conviction."

Cameron vehemently denied that anyone had coerced Howard, and he defended the investigation. Their case may have been circumstantial but it was strong, he said. A key witness placed Bar-Jonah in the alley the morning Zach Ramsay disappeared, February 6. Sherri Dietrich, his former roommate, found clothes in Bar-Jonah's closet that matched those Zach was last seen wearing. Bar-Jonah admitted to her that he knew the boy.

There was a canceled check with an altered date of February 6, 1996, the day Zach vanished. Later that afternoon Bar-Jonah went to a medical clinic seeking treatment for an injured index finger.

There was more: Encoded writings alluding to cooking young boys and strange-tasting meals served to neighbors.

And Cameron revealed that new evidence had surfaced: Notebooks in which Bar-Jonah had written "about kidnapping young boys, taking them to his basement, and holding them in a trunk."

Said Cameron, "He wrote that he was going to kill them and eat them."

EPILOGUE . . .

- *Nathaniel Bar-Jonah,* upon his arrival at the maximum security prison, requested separation from the general prison population. "Pedophiles usually do," said prison spokeswoman Linda Moodry.

  In a letter to the author, Bar-Jonah wrote: "I was convicted by the media. The cops thought if they kept charging me with something that I would get convicted on something. They fed the media with untrue statements and facts, forced people to lie, and changed people's statements to fit their agenda—to get me convicted all because I would not perform oral sex with one of Great Falls' finest."

In July 2004, Bar-Jonah's lawyers filed an appeal with the Montana Supreme Court seeking a reversal of Bar-Jonah's conviction on sexual assault and kidnapping charges. In their appeal the lawyers argued that the initial traffic stop made by police in December 1999 was improper and that evidence seized in subsequent searches of Bar-Jonah's residence should not have been allowed. They also argued that charges of cannibalism in the Zachary Ramsay case so inflamed public opinion that Bar-Jonah could not get a fair trial in the assault and kidnapping case. In December 2004, the court upheld Bar-Jonah's conviction and 130-year sentence. On Sunday, April 13, 2008, Bar-Jonah was found unconscious in his cell. He never regained consciousness. An autopsy revealed severe heart disease. His death was attributed to a heart attack.

- *Sergeant John Cameron* retired from the Great Falls Police Department in 2003.

- *Robert "Bubba" Burton,* the Great Falls cop who spotted Bar-Jonah in the vicinity of the Lincoln Elementary School on December 13, 1999, resigned from the force amid charges that he exposed himself to and sexually assaulted three women and a teenage girl while on duty. In September 2001, he pleaded guilty to official misconduct and no contest to assault charges.

- *Rachel Howard,* Zach Ramsay's mother, remained in Great Falls. There has been no trace of her son since he left for school on February 6, 1996. In January 2011, fifteen years after he disappeared, a Montana court, acting on a petition from Zach's father, Franz Ramsay, declared the curly-haired boy with the big smile legally dead. Despite the court's ruling, Rachel Howard clings to the belief that her son is alive.

6

MARC SAPPINGTON
Dahmer's Disciple, Lecter's Legacy

Marc Sappington was just following orders. Voices, he said, commanded him to drink human blood and eat human flesh.

At least that's what he told investigators who arrested him on April 12, 2001. The twenty-two-year-old high school dropout had been the object of a massive three-day police manhunt, ever since his mother followed a trail of blood on the steps leading to the basement of the house she shared with Marc.

On the basement floor were three trash bags lined up in a row. Inside were the severed body parts of Alton "Freddie" Brown, a sixteen-year-old high school student who lived with his grandmother, Theresa Loggins, less than a block from where Sappington lived at 1310 Troup Avenue in Kansas City, Kansas.

Brown frequently visited there. "The boys go down there, come home, go back, come home, but he always came home," said Loggins.

When Brown didn't come home Tuesday morning to take out the trash, she knew something was amiss.

Brown was killed by a blast from a shotgun while his back was turned. The shooter was his friend Marc Sappington. Wielding a maul—a combination axe and hammer that's used for chopping wood—Sappington severed the teen's arms at the shoulders and his legs at the knees. With a hunting knife he sliced off a chunk of Brown's right calf. He took it upstairs to the kitchen, where he fried it and ate it. The he went back to the basement and dismembered the body.

Every now and then as he chopped and carved the corpse, he'd pause to drink its blood.

When he was done, Sappington methodically and carefully placed Brown's body parts in three green trash bags—one held legs and feet, the other arms and hands, while the third held the head and torso.

Before the day was out, police would learn that Freddie Brown wasn't the only victim of the "Kansas City Vampire," just his last.

Marc Sappington doesn't look like a crazed killer. His face is pleasantly round, with high cheekbones and deep-set brown eyes. Outwardly there's nothing sinister about the five-foot-eleven 165-pounder. In fact, he looks more like the choirboy he once was than a thug, vampire, and cannibal killer. Yet in the space of four days, he butchered three of his friends, drank their blood, and ate their flesh.

The cops who questioned him on April 12 knew that Marc didn't fit the profile of a serial killer either. For the most part, serial killers tend to be older; they generally don't start their murderous ways until they are in their late twenties or early thirties, and there's also always a sexual aspect to their crimes.

For example, Chicago serial killer John Wayne Gacy raped and tortured young men during his killing spree. Many of his victims wound up under the floorboards of his house or buried in his backyard. Ted Bundy sexually assaulted his victims, all of whom were young females. Jeffrey Dahmer had sex with his male victims before and after he killed them, and then after they were dead he cannibalized them.

But with Marc Sappington, none of his killings involved sexual deviance. How, then, to explain the Kansas City Vampire?

Marc was well-known on the run-down and crime-ridden streets of northeast Kansas City, Kansas, or, as the locals refer to it, "KCK," in order to distinguish it from Kansas City, Missouri—"KCMO." On the south and east the cities are separated by the Kansas River. On the north they are on opposite banks of the Missouri River, which passes through the Kansas City metropolitan area on its way to St. Louis, where it flows into the Mississippi.

KCK is the poor sister. Its population is 147,000; KCMO's is 450,000. Where KCK's median family income is $39,000, KCMO's is $46,000. KCMO is well-known for its parkways and parks, including a world-class zoo in beautiful Swope Park. It's also the home of Major League Baseball's Kansas City Royals, the NFL's Kansas City Chiefs, the American Jazz Museum, the Airline Museum, the Negro Leagues Baseball Museum, two world-class art museums as well as the Kansas City Art Institute, and the University of Missouri–Kansas City. KCK is the home of the Kansas Speedway and an independent-league baseball team called the Kansas City T-Bones.

As settlers from Europe poured into the United States in the early 1800s, Native Americans were pushed westward. Among them was the Wyandotte tribe, which migrated to the area from

Ohio. They crossed the Missouri River in 1843 and built the first permanent settlement on what is now known as KCK. It became a jumping-off point for wagon trains heading west.

In 1868 a rail link to Topeka was completed and the growing city became a terminus for railroads bringing Western cattle to the East. It wasn't long before stockyards and slaughterhouses sprouted near the railhead. In the first year alone, the stockyards handled more than 120,000 head of cattle. Meatpacking plants sprang up along the river and provided steady employment for area residents, a number of whom were former slaves who migrated from the South in the aftermath of the Civil War. Many of them settled on the city's north side, an area bounded by the Missouri River on the east and north. Since the 1950s it's been a neighborhood plagued by crime, poverty, and drug addiction.

It's where Marc Sappington grew up, in a run-down wood-frame house at 1310 Troup Avenue. Like many kids in the hardscrabble neighborhood, he was raised by a single mother, Mary White. Marc never knew his father; he was long gone by the time Marc was born on February 9, 1979.

Mary tried with all her might to insulate her son from the mean streets of North Kansas City. She was a deeply devout woman who relied on her hellfire and brimstone religious beliefs for spiritual comfort and guidance. She worked hard, and she insisted that her son attend church with her every Sunday. She hoped Marc would grow up to be a God-fearing man.

Her efforts appeared to have been successful, at least on the surface. Marc joined the church choir, which kept him away from the gangsta wannabes who ruled the streets. But Mary had serious mental health issues of her own to deal with, and despite her best efforts, once her son became a teenager he was unable to resist the powerful lure of the streets.

For most of Marc's life Mary battled schizophrenia. The disabling brain disease had her in and out of institutions over the years. It prevented her from working, and from looking after Marc.

Although schizophrenia affects men and women with equal frequency, the disorder often appears earlier in men, usually in the late teens or early twenties, than in women, who are generally affected in the twenties to early thirties. At age sixteen Marc was showing signs of the disease, too, said his attorney, Patricia Kalb.

And by the time he entered Wyandotte High School, he was drinking heavily and getting high on "dank"—marijuana joints that are dipped in PCP (phencyclidine) and embalming fluid, then dried before they are smoked. Marc even laced tobacco cigarettes with PCP. Until he started danking, he's remembered as a bright youngster with a quick wit and an engaging personality. Although he was never a good student, he was intelligent and managed to get by with passing grades, but that all changed. He stopped going to church, and by 1996 he had stopped showing up for classes. According to school records he was dropped from Wyandotte High's roll in December 1996 for nonattendance.

Those who know Marc blame the change on his addiction to alcohol and PCP, a powerful and highly addictive hallucinogen. It was originally developed in the 1950s as an intravenous anesthesia. It was so powerful that it was taken off the market in 1965 because it often caused hallucinations.

Whether it's smoked, ingested, or inhaled, PCP can cause a severe psychotic reaction. Some users say the drug makes them feel like they are floating around; it renders them fearless and unstoppable.

The drug has also been known to cause paranoia and anxiety. Some PCP users have become very violent and delusional, and because it

```
SCD501B                    Corrections Info
C3FCTRL1                   Cell Block Depar
                  10/28/2016 CCCF Mini

Cell block: E 2      MIN
```

Time	SID#	Name	C
7:00a	14788271	MARTINEZ, VALERIE	F
7:00a	10599779	RUSSELL, KATHY	E
7:00a	10896796	TAYLOR, AMBER	E
7:00a	18622304	WHITE, KASSANDRA	E
7:00a	19788060	REEVES, AMANDA	E
7:00a	18706866	BERTASSO, TONI	E
7:00a	14222176	MELTZER, JESMINE	E
7:00a	20408547	SANDERS, KENDALL	E
7:00a	18164796	CHAVEZ, SANDENA	E
7:00a	19608544	HAWKINS, CASSANDRA	E
7:00a	21512345	QUINN, NICOLE	E
7:00a	17673095	GONZALES, JESSICA	F
7:00a	20553170	TUCKER, LILLIAN	L
7:00a	8504922	HANGLAND, CRYSTAL	
7:00a	7896890	SHOCKLEY, SHELLI	
7:00a	16025352	BOSTICK, JOELLE	
7:00a	15340637	HASSON, NICOLE	
7:00a	18236850	PYSHNY, JOSSE	
7:00a	15384793	ROTH, AMANDA	
7:00a	19119969	SMITH, TONI	
7:00a	18688638	JOHNSTON, LEAH	
7:00a	18836835	AERNI, DAPHNE	
7:00a	20618490	MERWIN, KATHERINE	
7:00a	20618490	MERWIN, KATHERINE	
7:00a	19623031	HAGEN, MELINDA	

creates an adrenaline rush, it also causes brief spurts of superstrength. Regular use, even in low doses, impairs memory and judgment.

The high can last a couple of hours or even a couple of days if it's smoked enough. What makes PCP so insidious is its low cost; it's easily manufactured in home-based laboratories and sold on the street as "angel dust," "ozone," "wack," and "rocket fuel." When it's used to lace marijuana, it's called "dank."

It took over Marc Sappington's life.

"Marc was into that heavily," said Eric Fennix, who described himself as Sappington's best friend. Sappington, he said, liked nothing better than to kick back, smoke his dank, and watch TV or a video in the basement, which was where he spent most of his time. One day he and Fennix taped a TV program about Jeffrey Dahmer. From that day on Sappington was obsessed with the Wisconsin serial killer and cannibal who in 1991 admitted killing seventeen young men and eating their body parts.

Jeffrey Dahmer was Sappington's idol, Fennix said, but he wasn't his only idol. He was also obsessed with *The Silence of the Lambs* and dreamed of becoming a legend so dangerous he'd have to be locked in a cage and guarded around the clock like the fictional Hannibal Lecter. He'd act out scenes from the movie and imagine that he was drinking human blood and biting into raw flesh.

But Sappington was no Jeffrey Dahmer. The Wisconsin cannibal preyed on young homosexual or bisexual men in gay bars. He'd offer them money to pose for photos or ask them back to his apartment to watch a video or drink beer. Dahmer's victims would fall asleep after downing a spiked drink or two and would then be either strangled or stabbed to death. Dahmer would have sex with their corpses, then dismember them with a hacksaw.

Sappington was just getting started and his modus operandi was still a work in progress, but unlike Dahmer there was no sexual aspect to his depravity. Sappington didn't go to gay bars. Three of his victims were his friends.

What Jeffrey Dahmer had that Marc Sappington wanted was fame. "He wanted to go to the pen and be executed and be a legend," Fennix said. "He wanted to be the black Jeffrey Dahmer and the black Hannibal Lecter all rolled into one." But Marc Sappington was no Hannibal Lecter either.

Lecter was brilliant; Sappington was a high school dropout. For Lecter, killing was an art, and he relished the meal he would have afterward. Sappington killed impulsively, driven by satanic voices that only he could hear.

What Lecter had that Sappington wanted so desperately was a name known the world over, but the serial killer Marc Sappington was most like was cannibal killer Richard Trenton Chase, the "Vampire of Sacramento."

Like Sappington, Chase was a schizophrenic who suffered from delusions. And like the Kansas City Vampire, Chase was a heavy dope smoker and a heavy drinker in his teen years. Both men were in their twenties and both believed they needed to drink human blood to survive.

In 1976 Chase was committed to a California mental hospital for treatment of his schizophrenia. One day he was found with his mouth covered with blood. Two dead birds, their necks broken, lay outside his window. That earned him the nickname "Dracula."

In January 1978 he went on a blood-drinking killing spree through East Sacramento, not unlike the spree Sappington would go on in Kansas City twenty-three years later. It started with the shooting death of an innocent passerby. From there the level of violence escalated quickly.

He shot Terry Walling—twenty-two and three months pregnant—to death in her home and dismembered her with a kitchen knife. Before leaving, he filled an empty yogurt container with her blood and drank from it. Less than a week later, Chase butchered thirty-eight-year-old Evelyn Miroth, her six-year-old son, Jason, and her twenty-two-month-old nephew, David Ferriera.

The three victims were shot to death; two were dismembered. A single bullet to the head killed Miroth. Chase then cut open her abdomen and removed her intestines. He collected her blood in a container and drank it. After shooting Jason in the head at close range, Chase left the house with David's corpse, leaving behind a bullet hole in a pillow that had been in the toddler's crib.

Crime scene investigators determined that David's body had been mutilated in the bathroom, where Chase cracked open the toddler's skull and ate portions of his brain. Chase then took the toddler's body back to his apartment, where he dismembered it and ate more organs.

In all, six people died before police ended Chase's bloody rampage. As police hunted for him, they drew up a profile. They said he was a disorganized killer with a history of mental illness and/or drug use. They also said he'd be an unemployed white male. With the exception of race, the profile fit Marc Sappington, too.

Ironically, like Sappington, Chase's rampage was driven by hero worship also, only his hero was the Hillside Strangler, the media's name for cousins Kenneth Bianchi and Angelo Buono, who kidnapped, raped, and murdered girls and women in Los Angeles in 1977 and 1978.

Aside from race, there was another element behind Sappington's rampage that was different. Besides his addiction to dope and alcohol, he was obsessed with snuff movies—a genre of film that purports to depict the real-life murder of one or more of the actors, often in combination with bizarre sexual scenarios. One of his favorites was *Faces of Death*, a series of seven films produced between 1978 and 1996 that show people and animals dying horrible deaths.

The macabre series opens in a hospital operating room with a close-up of an open chest cavity and a beating heart. In another scene, the camera records an autopsy. The chest and abdominal cavities are slit open, as is the skull, so that the brain can be removed.

There are scenes of dead dogs and barbecued monkeys, baby seal clubbings, car wrecks, tiger attacks, an actual political assassination, the execution of a prisoner in a gas chamber, plus scenes of cannibalism and satanic orgies with and without corpses.

Most of the scenes were either faked or cut from stock footage, but they were gruesome and stomach-turning nevertheless. Sappington just loved watching them over and over again on his VCR. And he loved gangsta rap, the more violent the lyrics the better. Among his favorites were rappers Eazy-E, Ice Cube, Dr. Dre, MC Ren, and DJ Yella.

When news of Sappington's arrest hit the newspapers and TV and radio stations in the Kansas City area, the men and women who had been his teachers at Wyandotte High reminisced about their former student, trying to find an explanation for the inexplicable. Some recalled him as "nice and quiet," while others said he was a malicious troublemaker who influenced other kids to act out in school.

Neighbors told a similar story. They said Sappington had been friendly and easygoing, but that a change had come over him. They knew of his drug use, but hardly anyone knew of the demons that were inside his head.

Eric Fennix knew. He had an explanation. "Satan was talking to him," he said. "Satan was telling him the world was coming to an end."

Neighbor Juan Smith had a hard time reconciling the easygoing Marc Sappington he knew with the one he'd seen on TV and read about in the newspapers. "It's like he turned his face all of sudden, kind of like a coin where you see one side but you don't see the other side until you flip it."

Other neighbors recalled that just the summer before, Sappington had been preaching about God and talking about the Bible.

"Marc rode his bike up to our house and said he had come to talk to us about the Bible," recalled Quameeka Saunders, Freddie Brown's sister. "He preached the Bible to us and handed out Bible Scriptures."

For the most part, however, residents of the gritty north side weren't all that shocked to learn that their friend and neighbor had been dubbed the "Kansas City Vampire."

David Mashak was the first to die by the hand of Marc Sappington. On Friday, March 16, 2001, Sappington and a friend from the neighborhood, Armando Gaitan, managed to get their hands on an assault rifle. It was a beautiful weapon, the kind that can transform a wannabe gangsta into a real-life one. So Sappington and Gaitan, sixteen, went looking to pull off an armed robbery. The weekend was coming and they needed money for dank and for booze.

What Gaitan had in mind seemed simple enough: They'd find someone to rob, show the gun, demand that their prey give up his cash and jewelry, and flee. All Sappington had to do was demonstrate that they meant business by brandishing the assault rifle.

Mashak was chosen at random. The newly married businessman was alone at his auto detailing shop on State Avenue about four miles from Sappington's home on Troup Avenue. It was still winter in the Midwest and the auto detailing business had been slow all week. The weatherman predicted snow for the weekend—a forecast that didn't bring customers.

As Mashak busied himself with paperwork, Gaitan and Sappington brazenly entered through the front door and announced a holdup. Even though Mashak offered no resistance, Sappington couldn't keep from squeezing the trigger. He opened fire and the young businessman went down in a hail of bullets. Gaitan and Sappington ran away without taking anything. A witness who saw them flee was able to provide cops with a sketch description of the two robbers. Sappington went home and smoked his dank, while Gaitan hightailed it out of town.

Detectives, however, were able to identify the teen through a pager he left behind at the shop. They tracked him to Texas. Within two weeks he was back in KCK, but he steadfastly refused to tell detectives the name of his partner in crime.

While Gaitan sat in the Wyandotte County Juvenile Detention Center, the gunning down of Mashak had only whetted Sappington's appetite for murder. It gave him a sense of power that he'd never had before. He couldn't wait to kill again, but it would be three weeks before he could find a suitable victim.

Spring came early to the Midwest in 2001. As soon as April arrived, temperatures began to climb. By the middle of the first week of the month, the Kansas City metropolitan area was enjoying summerlike weather with temperatures in the eighties, but by Friday, April 6, the weatherman was predicting that a cold front would move in, bringing rain, colder temperatures, and severe thunderstorms, with the possibility of tornadoes.

Terry Green had planned to go fishing on Friday. He got his gear ready and borrowed his sister's car, but when he heard the weekend weather report, he changed his mind. The twenty-five-year-old father of two decided to hang out with his longtime friend Marc Sappington instead. He drove over in his sister's car, a burgundy Mercury Sable, which he parked outside Sappington's house, but if he was expecting to spend a pleasant evening with his pal, he would be in for a rude awakening: As soon as he entered the basement, Sappington turned on him. When Green wasn't looking, he picked up a hunting knife he had hidden in a corner of the basement and plunged it into his pal's stomach again and again.

"It was him and me, so I stabbed him," Sappington later explained nonchalantly. He chose Green because "he just happened to come over." Green didn't go down easily. He fought hard to stay alive, but the first wound was deep and he was unable to overcome Sappington's furious attack.

Green's blood splashed all over the walls and furniture. There were puddles of it on the basement floor. Sappington got down on all fours and started to lap up his dead pal's blood, but paranoia set in and the vampire began fearing that neighbors might have heard the ruckus, so he dragged the body out of the basement, wrapped it in a blue tarp, and loaded it into the Mercury. Then he drove four miles to the River Market Antique Mall in KCMO, where he left the car in the parking lot and walked away.

He returned home and for the next two days got high on dank and watched *Faces of Death* and thought about his next kill. By Monday morning the dope-smoking Sappington was in a bloodthirsty frenzy.

Meanwhile, the burgundy Mercury sat in the parking lot for three days, until mall employees noticed a horrible stench coming from the car. They called police, who found Green's body under a blue tarp on the backseat.

As far as the police in KCK were concerned, Terry Green's murder was a Missouri crime. They had heard about the gruesome discovery in KCMO, but were relieved that they didn't have yet another murder on their hands. In the first three months of 2001 alone, the city had recorded twenty-three homicides, which put it on a pace to break its record of seventy-one murders, which was set in 1995.

Three days after he murdered Green, Sappington killed again. His victim this time was Michael Weaver, a twenty-two-year-old dry cleaning store worker. He was also Eric Fennix's stepbrother.

On the morning of April 10, Weaver left his home on Garfield Avenue to go to work. Sappington happened to be outside. He had been wandering around the neighborhood looking for someone to kill when the two men crossed paths. Sappington decided his best friend's stepbrother would be his next victim.

After the two young men exchanged greetings, Weaver turned and headed for his car. As he climbed into his Oldsmobile, Sappington attacked him from behind, stabbing him in the back with a hunting knife.

Although he was mortally wounded, Weaver was able to pull the car away from the curb, but he didn't get very far. As he turned a corner, he lost control of the vehicle and crashed into a pole.

Sappington ran to the car and climbed in. He managed to push Weaver over to the passenger side. He drove the car a block and pulled into an alley, where he left Weaver to bleed to death. But before fleeing the scene, Sappington once again wielded his knife; only this time he used it to cut away Weaver's bloody T-shirt. Raising the tattered shirt over his head, Sappington twisted and squeezed it in order to wring blood from it. As the red liquid began dripping from the shirt, Sappington opened his mouth and let it trickle in.

Weaver's body would go undiscovered until nine the next morning. In the meantime, the bloodthirsty killer, now a full-fledged serial killer, was determined to murder again; only this time he would add a new dimension to his killing spree—the eating of flesh.

After fleeing the alley, Sappington raced for home. A few hours later he spotted Alton "Freddie" Brown walking down the street. According to investigators, the sixteen-year-old Brown looked up to Sappington. He saw him as a big brother. Sappington invited him to hang out with him. When the teen turned his back, Sappington raised his loaded twelve-gauge shotgun and pulled the trigger.

No one heard the blast, or if they did they didn't pay any attention to it. The houses along Troup Avenue and the streets that surround it are spaced far apart from one another. They are mostly one- and two-story structures on large lots surrounded by trees and vegetation and set back from the road.

Sappington spent the next few hours carving up Brown's body and lapping up his blood. He sliced off a large chunk of the teen's right leg and carried it upstairs to the kitchen, where he placed it in a frying pan. A few minutes later he ate it.

When Mary White returned home hours later Marc was nowhere to be found, but she did notice a trail of blood leading to the basement. Although she hardly ever went down there—it was considered her son's exclusive domain—she followed the trail. What she saw horrified her and sent her running for help.

"In my twelve years as a homicide investigator, I'd never seen anything as horrible as this," said Lieutenant Vince Davenport, commander of the KCK Police Department's Homicide Division. Neither had Officer Elaine Moore, one of the first officers who responded to Mary White's 911 call.

Blood was everywhere. So, too, were chunks of flesh. They were stuck to the walls, on the floor, and on the furniture. But it was the contents of three green trash bags that sickened investigators the most. They held the severed body parts of Freddie Brown. In one bag were his legs and feet. Another contained his arms and hands. A third held his torso and head.

By 11 P.M. that night, a massive manhunt was under way for Marc Sappington. By morning every cop on the 130-man KCK force had his photo. Detectives who were off duty were called in to work the case. Neighboring police departments were notified, as was the KBI, the Kansas Bureau of Investigation.

The search for Marc Sappington took on even greater urgency after detectives tied him to the attempted kidnapping of thirty-six-year-old Anita Washington. Less than a half hour before Brown's body was found, Sappington tried to carjack her at gunpoint at the corner of Ninth Street and Walker Avenue as she drove home with a car full of groceries. Sappington ordered her to drive toward Missouri. Luckily, she was able to open the car door and run. She escaped unharmed while still in Kansas. The description she gave to police of the man who abducted her matched Sappington perfectly.

The manhunt ended on the evening of April 12, when cops spotted Sappington on foot at Seventeenth Street and New Jersey Avenue, less than one mile from his home. He was armed with a handgun but offered no resistance when officers took him into custody at gunpoint. They read him his rights and took him to police headquarters on Minnesota Avenue.

For nearly two hours he sat in the interrogation room and said nothing as Lieutenant Davenport and other detectives tried to question him. They played good cop, bad cop. They cajoled, threatened, yelled, and chatted. They were about to give up and take their young prisoner to a holding cell when suddenly he opened up and started confessing.

He began by talking about voices and vampirism and cannibalism. The voices started, he said, in December, when he was drinking and smoking marijuana and PCP.

"They were telling me different things," he declared as investigators turned on their video camera.

"What do you mean?" a detective asked.

"They were telling me I had to eat flesh and blood to live. If I didn't, I would die," he replied.

By midnight of April 6, the voices were speaking to him all the time. The night Green came over they were louder and more persistent than ever. He said he decided to kill his friend for no reason other than the fact that he happened to be there. Then he tried to drink some of Green's blood. He told investigators that he panicked and decided to dispose of Green's body.

"I took him to Missouri and left him in a parking lot," he said.

After that, voices gave him deadlines. "I set my watch so I'd know when to eat before the time ran out," he said.

After a couple of days the voices told him that he had to eat flesh and drink blood within seven hours, so he roamed the streets hunting for another victim. He said he walked around looking at people and asking the voices, "What about him? What about her?" But the voices never answered.

"I couldn't get near anyone, and when I did I couldn't get the courage," he said. So he went to Weaver's house and sat outside, frustrated that he couldn't find someone to eat—until Michael Weaver opened the door and walked outside. To Sappington that was an omen. "It convinced me it was meant to happen," he said.

He recounted how he snuck up behind Weaver and stabbed him in the back. He described how the wounded man tumbled out of the car, got back in, and drove off, but crashed into a pole about a block away. He told the cops that he ran to the car and drove it to an alley, where he left Weaver to die, and that before he fled he tried to wring the blood from the dying man's T-shirt. But he never got to eat his best friend's stepbrother, and he failed to wring out enough blood to satisfy the voices.

"I felt like my head was in a clamp. I felt that I had to eat or I would be the one the voices would attack," Sappington recalled. Then he told them about Freddie Brown.

He was outside his house a few hours later when he saw the teen walking toward him and invited him in. They hung out for a while; then Sappington shot him in the back with his shotgun. He sliced off a piece of Brown's leg, fried it, and ate it. Then he went back to the basement and dismembered the body.

When one of the detectives asked why, Sappington said he planned to freeze the remains. "I wanted to preserve the body so I would not have to hurt anyone else," he explained.

Detectives are trained in logic and the art of deduction. They didn't buy Sappington's story. It sounded to them like he was making it up as he went along. While on the surface it seemed that the voices were in control, telling Sappington when to kill and what to do afterward, the voices never chose his victims—by his own admission, those decisions were his alone, and his methodology, according to his story, was nothing more than chance.

"The really scary thing is that the victims could have been anybody," Lieutenant Davenport said. "He talked to me about going out on the street and looking at people, asking the voices in his head 'What about him? What about her?' These people never knew that it could have been them, they could have been killed and eaten."

It took Sappington about an hour to confess his crimes. The entire time he was in a very lighthearted mood, smiling and laughing, even cracking jokes about cannibalism and the grisly deaths of his friends. He never showed remorse for what he had done. At one point during the interrogation he reached out and grabbed the back of an investigator's thigh and asked, "Can I have some of that?"

The lawmen didn't laugh.

When the questioning was over, Sappington agreed to go for a ride with detectives. They wanted him to show them exactly where he was when he spotted Green, Weaver, and Brown, as well as locations where he dumped evidence.

Detective Kern Young was one of the investigators in the car with Sappington. As they drove to Troup Avenue, Young noticed that the confessed cannibal killer was staring at him. "He began talking about being hungry and staring my way," Young remembered. "Then he started laughing."

Later, as he was being booked into the Wyandotte County Jail on charges related to the abduction of Anita Washington, Sappington slapped his hands down on the booking desk and said, "I'm here, I'm hungry, where's my roommate?" Then he laughed.

Again, the lawmen weren't amused.

The next day prosecutors filed murder charges against Sappington—three counts of premeditated first-degree murder, punishable by death or life in prison with no chance of parole for fifty years on each count.

Meanwhile, tight-lipped cops released few details about the gruesome killings, or about the man they had charged with the grisly slayings.

"The only comment I want to make is about the motive," Lieutenant Davenport told reporters. "We believe Mr. Sappington was motivated by deviant cannibalistic tendencies."

It was a carefully crafted statement, and puzzled reporters pressed him for an explanation, but the head of the homicide unit would not reveal more. For one thing, he didn't want to jeopardize the case against Marc Sappington, and for another the investigation was far from over.

But just the mere mention of the word "cannibal" was enough to ignite a media frenzy. News crews descended on the Wyandotte County Courthouse. The gruesome story made headlines around the world. Marc Sappington had gotten his wish—he was famous, at least for a little while.

Meanwhile detectives still hadn't closed their files on the Mashak murder. They were convinced, however, that Sappington was the triggerman, so they went back to Armando Gaitan, who was still in the juvenile detention center. When they told the gangsta wannabe how Green, Weaver, and Brown died, he quickly realized that he wasn't protecting a fellow thug, but a psycho. He named Sappington as the shooter.

On Sunday, Sappington's heartbroken family released a written statement to reporters. "The family of Marc Sappington would like to express our heartfelt prayers and deepest sympathy to the bereaved families. We were totally shocked to hear the current allegations and feel they are out of Marc's character. There is nothing we can say or do to take away the hurt and pain of the families. We can only express our sorrow and pray that God will strengthen us all."

It was signed, "From Marc Sappington's mother, uncles, aunts, cousins and other family members."

On Monday Judge Robert Serra's courtroom was packed with reporters and relatives of the three victims. They were there for Sappington's arraignment on three murder charges. Just moments before deputies brought him in, prosecutors handed the judge a fourth charge, this one for the murder of David Mashak. Sappington pleaded innocent in all four cases. His bail was set at $3 million.

At the hearing, Lieutenant Davenport was more forthcoming than he had been announcing Sappington's arrest: "I can say that of the three victims, one was mutilated, and there was evidence of cannibalism. And that the core motivation for all three killings, of the recent killings, was cannibalism."

As for Mashak, Davenport said there was no evidence that his murder was anything other than a robbery that went bad.

"I'm happy he's behind bars. That's where he belongs," said Valerie Mashak, the slain businessman's wife. Ironically she and Sappington were classmates at Wyandotte High.

"I didn't think it was going to be him, with these murders happening back-to-back. It was shocking."

As the grieving families buried their sons, Marc Sappington sat in the Wyandotte County Jail. He had few visitors, and jailers said he seemed unremorseful, but they noticed that he did have a hearty appetite.

The lead prosecutor for the case of *Kansas v. Marc Sappington* was Wyandotte County Assistant District Attorney Jerry Gorman. He announced that he intended to seek the death penalty for the premeditated murders of Terry Green, Michael Weaver, and Alton Brown. At a probable cause hearing in January 2002, Sappington's attorney, Patricia Aylward Kalb, entered a plea of not guilty by reason of insanity.

Three and a half years would pass before the case would come to trial. By then prosecutors had dropped the death penalty. If he was found guilty, Sappington faced a sentence of life in prison. If he was found not guilty by reason of disease or mental defect, he would be remanded to a state hospital for the criminally insane. In order for that to happen Kalb would have to demonstrate to a jury that Sappington was unaware that what he did was wrong, or that he was unable to stop himself.

She had a tough row to hoe. The first question that had to be decided was whether or not the cannibal killer was competent to stand trial and assist in his defense.

Initially Wyandotte County District Court Judge J. Dexter Burdette said he was, but in September 2002, when the trial was first scheduled to get under way, the judge, at the request of Sappington's attorney, granted a second competency evaluation. The trial was postponed until January 2003. Then with jury selection about to start, Kalb requested another postponement. Sappington, she said, "was having some problems."

Judge Burdette asked the prosecution's psychiatrist, Dr. William Logan, to evaluate the accused. Logan reported that, in his opinion, Sappington was indeed suffering delusions and would be unable to assist in his defense. Burdette had no choice but to rule that Sappington was incompetent to stand trial.

He postponed the proceeding indefinitely and ordered Sappington to Larned State Hospital for further evaluation and treatment. Four months later hospital staff reported that Sappington was fit to stand trial, which prompted Burdette to set a new date. Then in July Sappington was delusional again.

Doctors finally determined that Sappington wasn't taking the antipsychotic medication that had been prescribed for him. At a hearing, Defense Attorney Kalb admitted that her client refused his medication at least eleven times so far in the month of July. Kalb explained that Sappington refused to take his medicine because it wasn't the proper dosage and it left him confused and lethargic.

That brought Assistant DA Jerry Gorman to his feet. It seemed that Sappington had learned how to manipulate the system: By not taking his meds in the weeks before the trial he would become delusional and the trial would be postponed.

"This has happened twice as we are set to go to trial," Gorman fumed. "I want an order to force him to take his medication."

Judge Burdette agreed. In June, the U.S. Supreme Court had ruled that authorities can not forcibly medicate a defendant solely to make him competent to stand trial. They could, however, order forced medicating when the defendant was deemed dangerous to himself or to others.

Dr. Logan testified that without his antipsychotic medication, Sappington was a threat and, given the right dosage, he would be competent to stand trial. Based on the psychiatrist's testimony, Judge Burdette ordered the Wyandotte County Sheriff's Department to forcibly medicate Sappington.

"This is solely an issue of dangerousness," the judge declared. From then on the Kansas City Vampire never missed his daily dose of antipsychotic medication.

July 19, 2004, was a brutally hot Monday in Kansas City, and Marc Sappington's trial was at last under way. He would finally stand trial for murdering Terry Green, Michael Weaver, and Alton "Freddie" Brown, as well as for kidnapping and aggravated burglary stemming from his carjacking of Anita Washington. He would go on trial for murdering David Mashak at a later date.

It didn't take long to seat a jury of twelve and one alternate from the pool of eighty potential jurors who reported for jury duty that day. In the afternoon Jerry Gorman, the assistant district attorney prosecuting the case, gave his opening statement.

The prosecutor charged that Sappington's PCP use and not his mental illness caused him to hear voices. Gorman told the jurors that police found trash bags that contained the dismembered body of Alton "Freddie" Brown inside the house on Troup Avenue that Marc Sappington shared with his mother. He also told jurors that Sappington confessed to the murders of Michael Weaver and Terry Green. The motive, he said, was cannibalism: He killed Green and Weaver to drink their blood. He killed Brown to drink his blood and eat his flesh.

As Gorman spoke, Brown's distraught mother, Tammy Saunders, couldn't bear to listen. She ran from the courtroom in tears.

"I thought I was ready for this day. I'm glad to see it come, but I'm not saying it will give me peace of mind," she said later. "I know you are not to have outbursts in court, but I couldn't listen to what he had done to my baby."

Saunders vowed that despite the gruesomeness of what she was hearing, she would be in the courtroom daily until the trial was over. "I just want him to see us every day and see how serious this is and what he's done, what he's taken from us," she said. "There will be times when I will leave the courtroom, I know this. But I'll come back in. I'll be here."

When it was her turn to deliver an opening statement for the defense, Kalb announced that she would defer it until later in the trial.

Gorman opened the proceeding with the videotaped interview Sappington had given to detectives the night he was arrested. Kalb objected, but Judge Burdette overruled her.

As the video started, Sappington, who had been sitting at the defense table with his shoulders slumped, perked up. When he saw himself on TV, he smiled.

The jurors watched intently as Sappington answered his interrogators' questions about eating his victims' flesh and drinking their blood. They heard him say that voices commanded him to do it, and that if he didn't do as they said, he would die.

They listened as he described in ghastly detail the murders of Terry Green, Michael Weaver, and Alton "Freddie" Brown, and how he made the decision as to who would live and who would die. They sat dumbfounded as Sappington admitted that he drank blood and ate flesh, and that he put the body parts in trash bags so that he could eat them later.

The panel heard him talk about his troubled life and addiction to PCP, and they heard him joke with the detectives. He seemed to be enjoying himself.

The point of the video was to demonstrate that Marc Sappington was in control of his actions; he knew what he did was wrong, and therefore he was guilty.

Over the objections of Kalb, the jurors got to see another videotape, this one shot by crime scene investigators at Marc Sappington's house the day Freddie Brown was murdered.

"The court is including the videotape because not only does it show the scene of the crime, but as gruesome as it is, it reflects the true crime scene that investigators found in the defendant's basement," Judge Burdette explained.

Among other items entered into evidence were the maul Sappington used to dismember Brown's body, the twelve-gauge shotgun Sappington used to gun him down, and the knife he used to butcher Michael Weaver.

ADA Gorman called Sappington relative Frank White, a distant cousin, to the stand on the third day of the proceeding. White recalled that he was walking home at about 1 A.M. on the morning of April 7 when he ran into Marc, who was standing next to a car that had been backed into an alley next to Sappington's house.

He motioned for White to walk toward him, and when he did, Sappington led him into the alley and showed him a body covered by a blue tarp that was lying in the backyard.

"You've got to help me. Would you please help me?" White recalled Sappington asking.

"What did you tell him?" prosecutor Gorman asked.

"I said, 'I can't,' and I just walked away." White said he didn't know whose body was under the tarp.

As he turned to leave the alley, Sappington yelled to him, "Blood is thicker than water." White didn't say anything about what he'd seen that night until he was questioned by police. His testimony demonstrated consciousness of guilt and bolstered the prosecution's contention that Sappington knew what he was doing.

On day four, KCK Detective Kern Young testified about the ride he took with Sappington after his interrogation, and how the confessed cannibal killer kept looking over in his direction.

"He began talking about being hungry and staring over my way. Then he started laughing," the detective recalled.

The only one in the courtroom who was even remotely amused was Marc Sappington.

On Friday, the fifth and last day of testimony, defense attorney Patricia Aylward Kalb delivered her delayed opening remarks. She told the jury that because of his mental disorder, Marc Sappington should not be held responsible for the crimes he was charged with. Sappington, she said, had been schizophrenic since he was sixteen, which was when he began hearing voices in his head. It was the schizophrenia and not the PCP that caused them.

"He was in a constant struggle from a very early age between good and evil," she said. "He thought [the murders] were something he was commanded to do . . . and that God and the devil were in a constant battle for his soul."

Kalb called Dr. William Logan to the stand, even though he'd originally entered the case as a prosecution witness. The psychiatrist confirmed that Sappington suffered from schizophrenia. On cross-examination, the doctor said that there was no way to determine whether he was suffering from schizophrenia when he committed the murders.

Rufus White, Marc's uncle, testified that Mary White, his sister and Marc's mother, was schizophrenic, too, and that the illness ran in the family. He said that not long after his nephew was arrested, his sister entered a long-term care facility, which explained why she was not at the trial.

After the defense rested, Gorman and Kalb summed up their cases, after which Judge Burdette charged the jury. A little more than an hour later the panel announced that they had reached a verdict: Marc Sappington was guilty of all three counts of premeditated murder, and he was guilty of kidnapping and aggravated burglary.

Sappington said nothing and showed no emotion as the verdicts were announced. When the proceeding was over, he stood up, put his hands behind his back so that a deputy sheriff could handcuff him, and was led out of the courtroom.

Asked for his reaction, Assistant District Attorney Jerry Gorman declared, "I think the most important thing is that Mr. Sappington never will walk the streets of Kansas City, Kansas, again."

The prosecutor said he would push for consecutive "hard fifty" life sentences, which would mean the convicted cannibal killer would have to serve at least fifty years in prison on each count before being eligible for parole. The goal, said Gorman, would be to keep Marc Sappington behind bars until he died.

"When the jury came back so quick, I thought it wasn't good," said Tammy Saunders, Freddie Brown's mother, tears rolling down her cheeks. "I have a lot of anger and hatred," she added.

Michael Weaver's stepbrother Eric Fennix said that despite what Marc Sappington had done to his family, "He will always be a friend. I can't hate him for killing my little brother. I hope Marc gets better."

On September 3 Marc Sappington was back in court, this time for sentencing. Before passing sentence, Judge Burdette allowed the relatives of his victims to address the court. They had all come with photos of their murdered loved ones.

Tammy Saunders stood up with a framed picture of her son, Freddie Brown. "Marc Sappington," she said, "didn't have any mercy, and I ask you not to show any mercy on him."

Relatives of Terry Green and Michael Weaver echoed her sentiments. When his turn to speak came, Sappington apologized for his crimes. He told the judge they were motivated by a "will to live." He added, "Just because I don't display feelings don't mean I don't have them."

Then it was Judge Burdette's turn. He looked directly at Sappington and said, "You are the closest thing to a homicide time bomb. There is no way I am going to endanger the community again."

With that, the judge passed sentence: three life terms for the murders, with no chance of parole for seventy-five years; six and a half years for kidnapping; and two and a half years for aggravated burglary. All the sentences were to run consecutively.

EPILOGUE . . .

On September 27, 2004, Marc Sappington went on trial for the murder of David Mashak. Despite Sappington's claim that Gaitan was the triggerman in the botched armed robbery, after deliberating for three and a half hours the jury found Sappington guilty. Judge Burdette tacked on another life sentence. Sappington was remanded to the custody of the Kansas Department of Corrections. He is currently incarcerated at the Lansing Correctional Facility in Lansing, Kansas.